T0155871

Lecture Notes in Computer Science   12647

More information about this subseries at http://www.palgrave.com/gp/series/7409

Yan Jia · Zhaoquan Gu ·
Aiping Li (Eds.)

MDATA:
A New Knowledge
Representation Model

Theory, Methods and Applications

 Springer

Editors
Yan Jia
Harbin Institute of Technology, Shenzhen
Shenzhen, China

Zhaoquan Gu (ID)
Guangzhou University
Guangzhou, China

Aiping Li
National University of Defense Technology
Changsha, China

ISSN 0302-9743 ISSN 1611-3349 (electronic)
Lecture Notes in Computer Science
ISBN 978-3-030-71589-2 ISBN 978-3-030-71590-8 (eBook)
https://doi.org/10.1007/978-3-030-71590-8

LNCS Sublibrary: SL3 – Information Systems and Applications, incl. Internet/Web, and HCI

This Springer imprint is published by the registered company Springer Nature Switzerland AG
The registered company address is: Gewerbestrasse 11, 6330 Cham, Switzerland

Preface

With the fast development of information technologies, many researchers are dedicated to knowledge representation, a high-level understanding and abstraction of massive data. Although many knowledge representation models have been proposed, such as symbolic logic models, semantic networks, expert systems, semantic webs, and knowledge graphs, these models cannot represent procedural knowledge, i.e. dynamic knowledge that changes with temporal and spatial factors.

In this edited book, we introduce a new knowledge representation model called MDATA (Multi-dimensional Data Association and in Telligent Analysis). After investigating a large number of related works in knowledge representation and cognitive models, we propose the MDATA model on the basis of the widely adopted knowledge graphs. By modifying the representation of relations and properties in knowledge graphs, dynamic knowledge can be efficiently described with temporal and spatial characteristics. The MDATA model can be regarded as a high-level temporal and spatial knowledge graph model which has strong capabilities for knowledge representation.

Similar as knowledge graphs, there are many key technologies in the MDATA model, such as entity recognition, relation extraction, property extraction, etc. The MDATA model pays particular attention to temporal and spatial characteristics, and the recognition of such temporal and spatial characteristics is important. These characteristics could be time period, location, or even IP address. In order to improve the knowledge graph, knowledge reasoning and completion are necessary, such as entity reasoning and relation completion. In the MDATA model, the dynamic knowledge should also be updated by reasoning, which combines the temporal and spatial factors. As many existing technologies have been proposed in constructing knowledge graphs, we need to extend them to the MDATA model.

The MDATA model can represent knowledge from different dimensions and it can be applied in many critical applications. The outbreak of the coronavirus pandemic has caused serious consequences. By representing personal knowledge such as dynamic travel information by the MDATA model, we can identify close contacts of infected persons in an efficient way. Considering network attacks that might happen every day around the world, the MDATA model can combine the analysis of massive data from log or network traffic to detect attack events. For social network analysis, in which information updates quickly and people's opinion might change, the MDATA model can represent such dynamic knowledge for better analysis, such as computing individual influence, community detection and sentiment analysis.

To promote the MDATA model, we have brought together research teams from many universities, research institutes, and companies, such as the Harbin Institute of Technology, Shenzhen (China), Guangzhou University (China), National University of Defense Technology (China), Zhejiang University of Technology (China), Hangzhou Dianzi University (China), The University of Queensland (Australia), The University of New South Wales (Australia), etc. We have applied the MDATA model in many practical applications: for example, we have developed a cyberspace security situation awareness system that can detect various network attacks in a timely way. We have also organized many seminars and workshops to exchange the latest research, such as the MDATA workshop in the IEEE International Conference on Data Science in Cyberspace. We hope the MDATA model will be widely adopted in various areas and can promote the study of knowledge representation significantly.

The edited book is broken into 14 chapters. The first two chapters introduce the background and the representation method of the MDATA model. Some key technologies are then introduced from Chapter 3 to Chapter 9, including entity recognition, entity alignment, knowledge reasoning, etc. In the remaining five chapters, we introduce applications of the MDATA model, including network attack detection, social network analysis, etc.

This book can be treated as a handbook of knowledge representation models. This book introduces some key technologies in the MDATA model and it also covers applications in which the MDATA model has a valuable role to play. These applications are just a small sample of many potential applications that can benefit from the model. This book offers in particular an in-depth introduction of the model and the related technologies. The MDATA model should be of interest to readers from other research fields such as databases, cyberspace security, and social networks as the need for knowledge representation arises naturally in many practical scenarios.

Should you have any questions or suggestions, please contact the editors via e-mail to jiayanjy@vip.sina.com, zqgu@gzhu.edu.cn, or liaiping@nudt.edu.cn.

January 2021

Yan Jia
Zhaoquan Gu
Aiping Li

Organization

Editorial Team

Yan Jia	Harbin Institute of Technology, Shenzhen, China
Zhaoquan Gu	Guangzhou University, China
Aiping Li	National University of Defense Technology, China

Program Committee

Zhihong Tian	Guangzhou University, China
Bin Zhou	National University of Defense Technology, China
Qi Xuan	Zhejiang University of Technology, China
Yizhi Ren	Hangzhou Dianzi University, China
Weihong Han	Guangzhou University, China
Le Wang	Guangzhou University, China
Ye Wang	National University of Defense Technology, China
Mohan Li	Guangzhou University, China
Shanqing Yu	Zhejiang University of Technology, China
Jinyin Chen	Zhejiang University of Technology, China
Hongkui Tu	National University of Defense Technology, China
Rong Jiang	National University of Defense Technology, China
Xiang Wang	National University of Defense Technology, China
Qingpeng Zhang	City University of Hong Kong, Hong Kong, China

Contents

Introduction to the MDATA Model

Yan Jia[1], Zhaoquan Gu[2(⊠)], Aiping Li[3], and Weihong Han[2]

[1] Harbin Institute of Technology, Shenzhen, Shenzhen 518055, China
jiayanjy@vip.sina.com
[2] Guangzhou University, Guangzhou 510066, China
{zqgu,hanweihong}@gzhu.edu.cn
[3] National University of Defense Technology, Changsha 410073, China
liaiping@nudt.edu.cn

Abstract. Knowledge is human's high-level understanding and summary of massive data. Intelligence is based on knowledge, and many works aim at representing knowledge and understanding intelligence. Although many models could represent static knowledge efficiently, it is still difficult to represent dynamic knowledge, especially which changes with time and space factors. In this chapter, we introduce a new knowledge representation model, Multi-dimensional Data Association and inTelligent Analysis (MDATA for short). We introduce three main parts in the MDATA model, knowledge representation, knowledge acquisition, and knowledge usage. We also discuss some potential applications that MDATA could be adopted and works greatly to improve the efficiency by the stronger ability of representing knowledge.

Keywords: MDATA · Knowledge representation · Cognitive model

1 Background

Knowledge represents human's high-level understanding of the world. However, knowledge is difficult to formalize, systematize or accurately describe in general. Some works assume knowledge represents the basic facts that are well-known by people, and some works assume knowledge is obtained through long-term studies or experience. As knowledge represents highly condensed information from massive data, it is important to understand how knowledge could be represented and how to understand the knowledge by humans.

Static knowledge implies some existing facts that would not change easily. For example, the Pythagorean Theorem can compute the length of the hypotenuse side of a right-angled triangle according to the other two sides. This kind of knowledge is well known and widely accepted by people. However, **dynamic knowledge** would change by temporal or spatial characters. For example, "apple" means a kind of fruit before the Apple company was founded. After then, "apple" can also mean the company or even a specific type of mobile phones.

Knowledge can be also classified into declarative knowledge and procedural knowledge. **Declarative knowledge** represents the facts that can be easily

© Springer Nature Switzerland AG 2021
Y. Jia et al. (Eds.): MDATA: A New Knowledge Representation Model, LNCS 12647, pp. 1–18, 2021.
https://doi.org/10.1007/978-3-030-71590-8_1

described in the forms of words or symbols by people, such as a personal history, different names of fruits, and mathematic theorems. In addition, declarative knowledge could be recorded in the memory of humans or any other intelligent systems. This kind of knowledge could be used to answer many questions, such as "what day is it today", "what is the color of an apple", etc. Different from declarative knowledge, **procedural knowledge** represents the method or the procedure of doing something. For example, how to drive a car and how to cook eggs. Such knowledge demonstrates the procedure of doing or achieving something, and it cannot be easily described only by words or symbols. These terms are widely used in different areas, such as in cognitive psychology.

Artificial intelligence tries to understand and learn how human intelligence is gained; the critical and fundamental step is to represent knowledge of different forms. A naive method is to use symbols to represent different knowledge. For example, we use "apple" to denote a kind of fruit, and use "dog" to represent a kind of animal. These symbols help humans memorize and describe objects. Knowledge could be summarized by experience or learned by extant knowledge, for example, we need to turn on the tap to get water. How to generate new knowledge by the extant knowledge (symbols) becomes a vital challenge. Many elegant works are proposed in representing knowledge. The classic ones are symbolic logic, semantic networks, expert systems, semantic web, and knowledge graphs. These representation methods could solve the problem of understanding knowledge to some extent, and the knowledge graphs are still widely adopted in various areas nowadays.

However, the existing representation methods could not describe the procedural knowledge and dynamic knowledge properly. For example, the symbolic logic method could generate new knowledge by logical language or programs, but the generated ones are also static knowledge. The semantic networks could link different types of symbols; they could be used to represent declarative knowledge or static knowledge clearly, but they are difficult to represent procedural knowledge or dynamic knowledge. The most widely adopted knowledge graphs could infer new knowledge or connections between the entities, but they can only represent the declarative knowledge and the meta knowledge for knowledge inference. Some works also modify knowledge graphs with temporal characteristics or events, but there still lacks a systematic representation method.

In this chapter, we introduce a new knowledge representation model called Multi-dimensional Data Association and inTelligent Analysis (MDATA for short). We assume knowledge could varied according to temporal or spatial characteristics. For example, the president of a country in different years might be different, we need to update the president knowledge by time; people from different regions or countries may speak different languages, we need to record the language knowledge for different spatial positions. Hence, we modify the knowledge graph representation model with both temporal and spatial characteristics: an entity in the knowledge graph has both temporal property and spatial property, while the relation, linking two entities in the knowledge graph, is also expressed with temporal property and spatial property. Once some specific knowledge is updated according to temporal or spatial factors, the MDATA model could add the corresponding information easily. The MDATA modle could be regarded as a high-level temporal and spatial knowledge graph model, which could systematically represent the dynamic knowledge.

In this chapter, we will introduce some classic knowledge representation models in the next section. In order to understand how humans generate intelligence, we introduce several cognitive models in Sect. 3. In Sect. 4, we introduce the MDATA model, including the main idea and three parts of the model. Some typical applications are introduced briefly in Sect. 5. Finally, we summarize the chapter in Sect. 6.

2   Knowledge Representation Models

Many works are dedicated to representing knowledge in a well-defined way. In this section, we will introduce some typical representation models, including symbolic logic model, semantic network, expert system, semantic web, and knowledge graph.

2.1   Symbolic Logic Model

Humans usually use different symbols to represent different objects in the world, such as people's names, company names, etc. Symbolic logic model can represent logical expressions by using symbols or variables, which are easier to compute than natural languages. Logical expressions not only have meanings with related facts or knowledge, but also could compute the truth table of each expression under all possible situations.

There are mainly three levels: propositional logic, first-order logic, and higher-order logic. *Propositional logic* is a branch of mathematical logic which studies the logical relationships between propositions and derives properties from them. Atom proposition defines variables with two different values (true or false), and complex proposition is composed of atom propositions and basic logical connectives (negation, and, or, imply, if and only if). For example, $P \wedge Q$ is a complex proposition where P and Q are two well-defined atom propositions.

First-order logic introduces predicates to represent richer knowledge compared with propositional logic. There are two common used qualifiers: universal quantifier and existential quantifier. For example, we can represent the sentence "every man is mortal" as the first-order logical expression:

$$\forall x, man(x) \rightarrow mortal(x). \tag{1}$$

High-order logic introduces qualifiers that could be added to the predicates, which improves the representation ability of logical expressions. The high-order logic can also be expressed by a set of first-order logic.

The symbolic logic model could be utilized for automatic reasoning. The typical application is the general solving program [1], which was the first useful intelligent program solving lots of problems by reasoning mechanism. There are also some other famous automatic reasoning results, such as Robinsons Resolution Principle [2], theorem proving and deduction by question-answering systems [3,4].

2.2 Semantic Network

Semantic network, also known as frame network, is also a knowledge representation model which describes semantic relations between concepts in a network [5,6]. The network consists of vertices and edges, where the vertices represent different concepts and the edges represent semantic relations between concepts. Generally speaking, semantic network could be expressed by multiple semantic triples, which later improved to different versions: knowledge graph [7,8], semantic link network [9], and semantic similarity network [10].

Semantic network is implemented by graph structures. The nodes represent entities such as concept, state, etc.; while the edges represent the relation between nodes. Each semantic triple can be expressed as $(Node_1, Edge, Node_2)$ or $(Entity_{head}, Relation, Entity_{tail})$. $Node_1$ or the head entity $Entity_{head}$ can be regarded as the subject, while $Node_2$ or the tail entity $Entity_{tail}$ denotes the object of the sentence. When many semantic triples exist in the network, they consist a semantic network.

A typical example of semantic network is WordNet [11], a large lexical database of English. WordNet groups similar nouns, verbs, adjectives and adverbs to sets of cognitive synonyms and it resembles a thesaurus. WordNet not only groups words by their meanings, but also labels the semantic relations among the words. Such semantic network has good properties such as it is well-structured and it can be applied in other areas easily. However, it lacks systematic grammar and method for inferring new knowledge.

2.3 Expert System

To represent knowledge, a trivial idea is to build a knowledge-based system. However, building the system that contains all knowledge is very difficult. Expert system is then proposed, which denotes the programs that could code the expert's knowledge in a particular domain, containing a lot of knowledge and experience of experts in a certain field [12]. The first expert system was developed in the late sixties and it had become very popular in the seventies. There are some typical expert systems as follows: $DENDRAL$ was the first expert system for chemical field, $MYCIN$ was built to identify bacteria causing severe infections, $XCON$ was designed for computer system configuration, etc.

Expert system can be regarded as an intelligence program that simulates human experts to solve problems in some specific areas. It usually contains several main parts. Knowledge base collects domain knowledge that are needed for problem solving, including basic facts and rules. Inference engine is the core executive mechanism to solve the problems, which aims to interpreting and inferring knowledge; inference engine and knowledge base are separated. Knowledge acquisition part could obtain, modify and expand knowledge base; such knowledge can be obtained manually, semi-automatically or automatically. Interactive interface enables humans solve problems; by inputting basic information and answering related questions raised by the system, the system could output reasoning results about the problem through the interactive interface.

Although expert system had drawn much attention, it is costly to build and maintain since the knowledge are mainly input by experts from a specific field. Knowledge acquisition has become a bottleneck in building the expert system.

2.4 Semantic Web

Semantic web builds on the semantic network, which describes the relations between resources and data on the web. Semantic web could enable people to create data stores on the Web, build vocabularies, and write rules for handling data.

The semantic web is a web of data that could be connected. World wide web is widely used nowadays; however, the content of the network was only human readable at the beginning. For example, when we browse a web page, we can easily understand the contents on it, such as the texts or the images; while the computers only know that it is a web page. In order to make computers understand the web data, Resource Description Framework (RDF) is proposed as a standard language, which could make the data on the network also readable by machines. The main idea is also to represent knowledge by triple $(subject, predicate, object)$, where each item has a uniform resource identifier (URI) for data linking. More standard languages are proposed for more flexible presentation, such as RDF schema (RDFS for short), ontology web language (OWL for short), etc.

Semantic web greatly promotes knowledge representation methods. By generating and linking data by the standard languages (such as RDF), many knowledge graphs are then constructed, such as some famous ones including DBpedia [13], Yago [14], Freebase [15], etc.

2.5 Knowledge Graph

Knowledge graph is widely applied in many fields and it has become one of the most popular information technologies in recent years. Knowledge graph depicts knowledge in terms of entities and their relations, which can be considered as a type of ontology. Knowledge graph has drawn much attention in both academical and industrial areas since Google proposed the concept and adopted it in the search service, which is proved to largely improve searching quality and user's experience.

Constructing a large-scale knowledge graph needs to integrate many advanced technologies in machine learning, database, natural language processing, etc. There are several key steps in constructing a knowledge graph.

Knowledge extraction contains many detailed tasks, such as concept extraction, entity recognition, relation extraction, etc. Traditional expert systems rely heavily on manual input by experts, but many knowledge extraction methods could extract knowledge from structured and unstructured data, greatly improved knowledge acquisition efficiency. *Knowledge fusion* removes ambiguity between entities and relations in different knowledge graphs and a larger graph was obtained through this step. *Knowledge reasoning and completion* discover explicit knowledge on the basis of the existing knowledge, which could largely enrich and expand the knowledge graph. *Distributed knowledge representation* transforms entities and relations to numerical vectors, which makes knowledge reasoning much easier. Many elegant methods in the above fields were proposed to improve the knowledge graph.

Knowledge graph can be widely adopted in many practical scenarios. Google firstly applied it in the search engine; after understanding user's query requirements, the search engine not only find out the key words suiting the query, but also returns a complete information about the related knowledge. Knowledge graph can also be adopted in intelligent question answering system. For example, Siri could provide rich answers, which is the result of introducing knowledge graph. Knowledge graph was also utilized in social network, which could help users find information that are most relevant. For example, knowledge graph is used in Facebook's graph search product to improve the experience. In addition, knowledge graph can be adopted in many specific areas, such as finance, medical treatment, e-commerce, transportation, etc.

Although there are many knowledge representation models, these models cannot represent dynamic knowledge efficiently. Some works also proposed temporal knowledge graph [16] to improve the representation ability, they split knowledge graph into different time stamps or modified distributed representation methods [17–19], there still lacks a systematical representation model about such dynamic knowledge.

3   Cognitive Models

Many works try to understand how human intelligence is formalized and there are some classic cognitive models such as ACT-R (adaptive control of thought" Crational) model, IBLT (instance-based learning theory) model, and SOAR (state operator and result) model. In this section, we introduce these cognitive models briefly.

3.1   ACT-R Model

The ACT-R cognitive model [20,21] was proposed by Anderson, a famous psychologist in cognitive science. The fundamental theory of the model is based on the mechanism and structure of human brain for cognition, which tries to understand how human beings acquire knowledge, organize knowledge and generate intellectual activities.

The pioneering work was the ACT (Adaptive Control of Thought) model, proposed in 1976, which emphasizes the control process of human's advanced thinking. The theory was developed by many researchers and these results were elaborated in the book "The Architecture of Cognition" [22], which addresses the basic theories from all aspects of psychological processing activities. At the same time, Anderson et al. combined the theory of HAM (Human Associative Memory) model with the ACT model to create a new theoretical model, which mainly involves the representation of declarative knowledge, and analyzes how these representations affect human behaviors. However, it only focuses on declarative knowledge, and does not discuss procedural knowledge.

After that, Anderson et al. introduced the difference between declarative knowledge and procedural knowledge. Regarding that procedural knowledge is mainly realized by production rules, they proposed the production system model ACT-E, which can reflect the combination of procedural and declarative knowledge. These works established a set of ACT* theory [23].

Generally speaking, an ACT production system consists of three parts: working memory, declarative memory and productive memory. Working memory mainly includes the information extracted from declarative memory, the coding of information imported from the external world and the information executed by various productive activities. The difference between working memory and declarative memory is that working memory mainly stores temporary knowledge. For example, the information of the external world will be temporarily stored in working memory after information coding, while the long-term information formed by the external world's information will be stored in declarative memory. Generative memory is to match the materials in working memory according to the conditions or rules of production, and send the execution actions after successful matching to the working memory.

The ACT cognitive system lasted for 10 years, until Anderson et al. proposed the new model ACT-R. This model was developed as a computational simulation system to reflect the development of ACT* cognitive theory in the past ten years. The ACT-R system can be regarded as a programming language platform, which could show many psychological research results about human cognitive behaviors. The latest ACT-R 6.0 version can support different system platforms and 7.0 version has improved many functions of the original system [24].

3.2   IBLT Model

The IBLT (instance-based learning theory) model was proposed in [25, 26], which assumes human intelligence comes from historical instances, i.e. people learns from instances and would take effective countermeasures when he/she faces similar situations.

Specifically, the IBLT model assumes the main knowledge element is an *instance*, which is defined as a triplet with the form of Situation, Decision, and Utility (SDU) slots. The *situation* part is described as a set of environmental cues or conditions; the *decision* part represents the set of actions applicable to a situation, and the *utility* part means the evaluation of the decision in that particular situation. Knowledge is gained during the process by observing the current situation, recording the adopted decision and the obtained utility. When similar situations appear later, people could select the most appropriate decision from the stored SDU slots in memory.

The IBLT model provides a generalized solution for future decision-making, which is quite similar with the intuitive idea of reinforcement learning: observing the current environment, making different actions and recording the corresponding effects, feeding back to the current environment, and then constantly updating. The IBLT model provides more intuitive explanation for decision-making schemes.

The IBLT model is more complicated than accumulation of instances, and there are five learning mechanisms during the process of dynamic decision-making in the IBLT model:

- Instance-based knowledge. This mechanism implies the accumulation of knowledge in the form of SDU slots;
- Recognition-based retrieval. People will retrieve the SDU slots according to the similarity between the situation being evaluated and the situation stored in the instances;
- Adaptive strategies. This mechanism means people could select appropriate strategies according to the varying situation in the dynamic task;
- Necessity. This is to control the continuation of alternative search;
- Feedback updates. This mechanism is to update the utility of the SDU slots according to the latest evaluation.

With these above mechanisms, people could learn and improve the instances in dynamic environment. Specifically, when people interacts with the dynamic task, he/she will retrieve knowledge that is similar with the environment by adaptive strategies. When the actual actions achieve good results, feedback mechanism would update and improve the accumulated knowledge. The IBLT model is also realized on the ACT-R system and the results showed that the performance of the model were highly close to the practical results of humans through a series of experiments.

3.3 SOAR Model

The SOAR (State Operator And Result) model is proposed to represent the general intelligence of humans [27], which focuses on knowledge, thinking, intelligence, memory, etc. There are three important parts in the model:

- *State* implies the current situation, which is similar to the situation part in the IBLT model;
- *Operator* means different functions on the state and various operators could generate knowledge in different areas;
- *Result* also records the evaluation, similar to the utility part in the IBLT model.

The SOAR model assumes states could be changed by different operators and different results are produced. The SOAR model is a kind of general problem solving program, which stores knowledge on the basis of block theory, uses rule-based memory to search appropriate knowledge, and output corresponding operations. The process can be regarded as inputting current state, state description, proposing candidate operators, comparing candidate operators, selection of the most appropriate operator, and output.

The model assumes human knowledge is composed of concepts, facts and rules, and the knowledge is preserved in the brain. Therefore, human brain can be regarded as the "knowledge base", which stores knowledge of different forms. Human's memory is complicated: short-term memory provides temporary storage space for language understanding, learning and reasoning, while long-term memory provides the information needed for information processing on the basis stored knowledge.

The original SOAR model only considers long-term memory and working memory, in which long-term memory is the information encoded as production rules, while the working memory is information encoded as graphs of symbols. The symbol based working memory stores people's evaluation of the current state. People could utilize the long-term memory to retrieve relevant knowledge, and update the results by selecting different operators.

The SOAR model shares similar idea with the IBLT model, and it has been widely adopted with many related applications. Many works extend the SOAR model with more modules, such as emotion module, operator selection by reinforcement learning, episodic memory models, etc.

4   What is the MDATA Model

Although there are many knowledge representation models and cognitive models, they cannot represent dynamic knowledge efficiently, especially these knowledge changing by temporal and spatial characteristics. In this section, we introduce the proposed MDATA model, which aims to represent dynamic temporal and spatial knowledge in a systematic way.

4.1   Overview of the Model

The MDATA model is composed of three main parts:

- **Knowledge Representation** means the representation method of knowledge;
- **Knowledge Acquisition** means the methods to acquire, generate and infer knowledge;
- **Knowledge Usage** means the methods to apply the existing knowledge.

We introduce these three parts in the following parts.

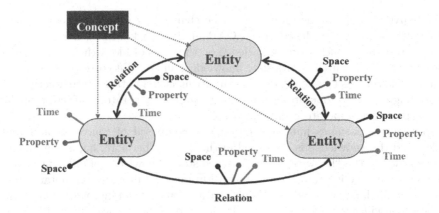

Fig. 1. An illustrative graph representation example of the MDATA model.

4.2 Knowledge Representation

The intuitive idea of representing the MDATA model is to add temporal and spatial characteristics to both relations and entities. Building on traditional knowledge graph, we represent the MDATA knowledge as follows:

$$MDATA - Representation = <Concept, Entity, Relation, Property>. \quad (2)$$

In the representation, concept also means a set of abstract concepts, i.e.

$$Concept = \{concept_i \mid i = 1, 2, \ldots, N\}. \quad (3)$$

Entity is also a set of existing entities, where each entity is a specific example of some concept, i.e.

$$Entity = \{entity_i \mid i = 1, 2, \ldots, n\}. \quad (4)$$

Different from traditional knowledge graph, relation is represented with temporal and spatial characteristics as the following equation:

$$Relation = \{R_{ij}, [TimeZone], [Location] \mid R_{ij} = <entity_i, entity_j>\}, \quad (5)$$

where relation R_{ij} represents the relation between two entities, $[TimeZone]$ implies the temporal characteristics, and $[Loc]$ denotes the spatial characteristics. Relation in the MDATA model has rich information such as when the relation appears or disappears, and where the relation exists.

Similarly, property also has temporal and spatial characteristics and it can be formulated as the following equation:

$$Property = \{property_i, [TimeZone], [Location] \mid property_i \vdash entity_j\}. \quad (6)$$

This means $property_i$ belongs to some entity $entity_j$ and the property is also influenced by temporal and spatial characteristics.

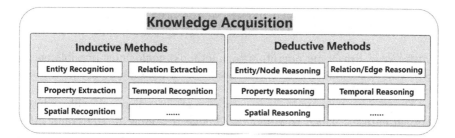

Fig. 2. Different methods of knowledge acquisition.

Knowledge can also be represented by graphs. As shown in Fig. 1, spatial and temporal characteristics are added to both relations and entities to represent richer information. In the next chapter, we will introduce more details about this representation method.

4.3 Knowledge Acquisition

There are many methods to acquire knowledge from massive data. The existing works extract entities or relations from texts, and we call these methods of acquiring explicit knowledge as *inductive methods*. Some knowledge is not known beforehand and the methods acquiring implicit knowledge are referred to as *deductive methods*.

As shown in Fig. 2, we divide knowledge acquisition methods into two categories. The inductive methods or operators to obtain main components of the MDATA model, including:

- *Entity Recognition* operators (or methods) could recognize entities from massive data, such as name, country, etc.
- *Relation Extraction* operators (or methods) extract relation between different entities, such as friend relation between people.
- *Property Extraction* operators (or methods) extract property information of entities, such as nationality of people, hobbies, etc.
- *Temporal Characteristic Recognition* operators (or methods) recognize temporal characteristics of relations or entities. Such temporal characteristics include exact time, time interval, or sequential characteristics.
- *Spatial Characteristic Recognition* operators (or methods) recognize spatial characteristics of relations or entities. The spatial characteristics include location, place, etc.

Some methods are also widely studied in constructing knowledge graphs, such as entity recognition and relation extraction. In the proposed MDATA model, the challenges are to recognize temporal and spatial characteristics for relations and entities, which could benefit represent dynamic knowledge.

Similar as constructing knowledge graphs, knowledge could be inferred from existing facts. For example, we can infer someone's hobby according his/her friends' hobbies. In the MDATA model, we also need to deduce some implicit knowledge and we define the following deductive operators or methods:

- *Entity/Node Reasoning* operators (or methods) could infer possible entities according to the existing MDATA knowledge. It corresponds to node reasoning in the graph.
- *Relation/Edge Reasoning* operators (or methods) infer possible relations between entities, which corresponds to edge reasoning in the graph. Many existing works, such as probabilistic reasoning, embedding based reasoning, are widely adopted.
- *Property Reasoning* operators (or methods) infer entities' properties according to the existing knowledge.
- *Temporal Characteristic Reasoning* operators (or methods) infer temporal characteristics of relations and entities. For example, the operator can infer when the relation begins or disappears, during when some property exists.
- *Spatial Characteristic Reasoning* operators (or methods) infer spatial characteristics of relations and entities, such as the location of some people's university.

Different from inductive methods, deductive methods need to infer implicit knowledge, especially temporal and spatial characteristics of the existing knowledge in the MDATA model.

4.4   Knowledge Usage

The third part of the MDATA model is knowledge usage, which includes the operators and methods to use the knowledge. As shown in Fig. 3, many operators could be defined in the MDATA model.

There are some common operators of knowledge usage:

- *Entity Query* operators (or methods) could output entities that satisfy query conditions.
- *Relation Query* operators (or methods) could output relation knowledge that satisfies query conditions.
- *Property Query* operators (or methods) could output property knowledge that satisfies query conditions.

The MDATA model could be regarded as a high-level temporal and spatial knowledge graph, there are two another query operators:

- *Temporal Characteristics Query* operators (or methods) could output exact time, time intervals, or sequential characteristics that satisfy query conditions.
- *Spatial Characteristics Query* operators (or methods) could output location or space information that satisfies query conditions.

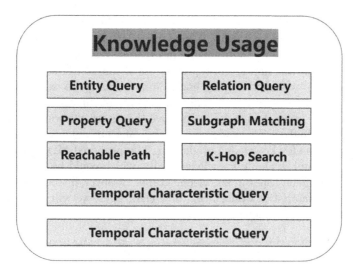

Fig. 3. Different methods of knowledge usage.

In order to achieve high query efficiency, the MDATA model construct temporal index and spatial index, which make difference with knowledge graphs. These indexes could also improve query efficiency of entity, relation, and property.

The MDATA model could be utilized to integrate knowledge from multiple domains and be adopted in various applications. We introduce some typical customized operators:

- *Subgraph Matching* operator could identify a subgraph from a large MDATA graph.
- *Reachable Path* operator could compute whether there exists paths between two entities.
- *K-Hop Search* operator could find out the related entities within k-hop of a given entity.

The introduced operates could be adopted in many applications, such as deciding whether two people know each other, finding out possible network attacks, item recommendation, etc. Different applications may need different operators, please refer to graph computing for more relevant operators.

4.5   Comparison with Other Models

The MDATA model could represent static knowledge and dynamic knowledge. Compared with other knowledge representation models, the MDATA model has stronger ability to represent knowledge. Specifically, symbolic logic model can only represent some deterministic knowledge, deduced by logic rules, while it cannot represent dynamic knowledge as the logic rules would change dynamically. The semantic network, expert system, semantic web ic capable of representing static knowledge, but they are difficult to infer implicit knowledge. For example, expert systems need customized rules to represent knowledge in a certain area, implicit knowledge is unobtainable in practice. Knowledge graph is widely adopted in many areas, and it can represent static knowledge and infer implicit knowledge as well by embedding methods. Some works try to extend the knowledge graph model to represent dynamic knowledge by slicing knowledge graph according to time index, which might improve the representation capability, but it intuitively limited to the predefined setting of time index and hardly scalable to future time for knowledge prediction. The proposed MDATA model can represent static and dynamic knowledge easily, which could be considered as a high-level temporal and spatial knowledge graph. However, introducing temporal and spatial characteristics would bring new challenges, we will introduce these challengesshoud in the following chapters.

5   Typical Applications of the MDATA Model

The MDATA model has strong ability in representing dynamic knowledge. In this section, we will briefly introduce how the model could be applied in different applications.

5.1   Network Attack Detection

Cyberspace has been regarded as the fifth battlefield among all governments and the security problem has drawn much attention from all the world nowadays [28]. As more and more cyber-attacks emerge, which causing severe consequences, detecting networks attacks has become one of the most important tasks in cyberspace.

Many methods detect network attacks by analyzing the log data or the network traffic data. A normally adopted way is to design detection rules for each attack. For example, SQL (Structured Query Language) injection attack could inject attack data into database's query command through external interface; one main rule to detection such attack is to decide whether there exists duplicate parameters in the traffic network. The defined rules could help detect possible network attacks. However, with the development of information technologies, network attack methods have also been greatly improved. Many attacks cannot be easily detected by some simple rules. For example, the APT (Advanced Persistent Threat) attacks adopt multiple attack tools and are usually fulfilled in multiple steps; traditional rule-based detection methods cannot work well. Although some works use deep neural networks to learn the features of these attacks, they still cannot achieve good performance since they might detect many false attacks.

The challenges of detecting network attacks, especially complicated attacks such as APT, lie in:

- The network security states would change according to many related procedures. For example, a vulnerability exists on a computer, but it is fixed if the corresponding patch is packed. Hence, we need to update the network state timely;

– Many complicated attacks usually fulfill an attack by multiple sequential steps and the detection method needs to utilize the temporal characteristic (sequential order) to analyze the attack;
– Many complicated attacks might fulfill an attack from multiple attacker hosts and the detection method needs to utilize the spatial characteristic (the IP address of these hosts) to associate possible attack events.

The MDATA model could be utilized to detect network attacks more efficiently. In handling the first challenge, the MDATA model could update network state knowledge by inferring possible relations. For example, a vulnerability of a computer disappears when the patch is packed; the time intervals could represent when the vulnerability exist. The MDATA model could record the exact time of each attack step; combining these steps could analyze the complicated attack, which addresses the second challenge. Similarly, the MDATA model, recording the IP address of attacker hosts, could associate attack events whose IP address belongs to the same network segment.

Since knowledge graph cannot represent dynamic knowledge efficiently, it is difficult to adopt it for detecting network attacks. However, the proposed MDATA has good properties, we could apply the MDATA model to detecting network attacks and this could greatly improve detection accuracy and efficiency.

5.2   Social Network Analysis

With the widespread usage of social media, we are now in a small social network where people are connected by expressing opinion, sharing information, etc. The consisted network connects every one in the world, shortening the distance between each other. Analyzing the social network has many applications in both research areas and in practical scenarios. For example, a film company could analyze the social network to find out potential audience who would like to watch the movie and to predict the sales. By collecting tweets on the social network and analyzing the interactions between people, we can detect hot events and judge public opinion towards the events.

There are many tasks in social network analysis and we introduce some tasks as follows:

– The analysis of individual influence could assign an influence value to each person, which implies the impact factor of the person to others.
– Community detection could identify a group of people who share the same opinion or have similar interest in the social network.
– Sentiment analysis of the network could find out people's sentiment towards some public event.
– Influence maximization aims to maximize the influence by selecting a number of people who broadcast the message.

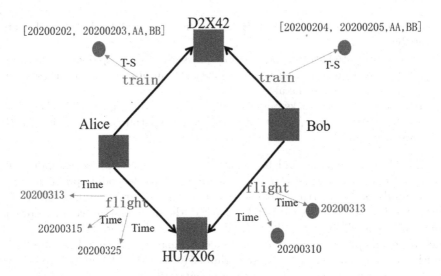

Fig. 4. Representation of epidemic association analysis.

Traditional methods are applicable in analyzing static social networks, but the networks could vary dynamically. For example, the network topology varies when a new person joins the network, a same person might express two different opinions at different times, and a community might change according to different spatial characteristics. It is urgent to analyze dynamic social networks efficiently.

In this book, we propose the MDATA model to represent dynamic knowledge, which could be directly adopted in analyzing dynamic social networks. Each person could be an entity in the MDATA model and their connections are the relations that they share the same opinion, work at the same place, etc. When the social networks vary dynamically, the MDATA model could also update the knowledge by modifying the temporal and spatial characteristics. For example, a new person joins the network, we construct a corresponding entity and the temporal characteristics would record the joining time or interval; when a same person express different opinions, these opinions would be assigned with different time intervals for temporal analysis; a community changes and the spatial characteristics also update the information to record the changing process of the community. The proposed MDATA model could be adopted in social network analysis and the model might promote and improve the analyzing methods.

5.3   Personnel Association Analysis Against Epidemic

The outbreak of the coronavirus (COVID-19) pandemic has caused very serious consequences in almost every country. It has become a very serious problem to fight the epidemic. Many governments have issued mandatory policies to fight the epidemic, such as the quarantine and isolation guidelines, which have shown great success in fighting the epidemic. However, it is still an important and urgent problem to provide information technologies based analysis against the epidemic.

There are many kinds of epidemic data, such as personnel flight data, communication data with others, travel data, etc. In order to judge whether some people has the risk of getting infected, it is needed to combine data of different areas for associate analysis. For example, we represent two person's knowledge as Fig. 4. Alice and Bob travelled by trains and planes; the entities include Alice, Bob, a specific train number, and a specific flight number. The MDATA model adds temporal and spatial characteristics to the relations as follows.

- We add the temporal-spatial characteristic to the *train* relation, including when people took the train, where they got on and off;
- We add the temporal characteristic to the *flight* relation, including when people took flights.

Traditional knowledge representation methods might only conclude that both Alice and Bob took a same train or a same flight, but it is incorrect since they might took the train or flight at different time. Hence, the MDATA model could overcome the problem; the temporal and spatial information confirm that Alice and Bob took the same flight on 20200313. If one of them was injected, the association analysis could find out close contacts during the epidemic efficiently.

6 Chapter Summary

In this chapter, we introduce the MDATA model, a cognitive model that could represent dynamic knowledge efficiently. Although many representation models were proposed, such as symbolic logic model, semantic network, expert system, semantic web, and knowledge graph. However, these models cannot represent dynamic knowledge efficiently. We propose the MDATA model on the basis of knowledge graph, which introduces temporal and spatial characteristics to relations and entities; the MDATA model greatly improves the ability to represent knowledge. We also introduce some typical application of the MDATA model and we wish this model could be widely adopted in various areas.

References

1. Ernst, G., Newell, A.: GPS: A Case Study in Generality and Problem Solving. Academic Press, New York (1969)
2. Robinson, J.A.: A machine-oriented logic based on the resolution principle. J. ACM **12**(1), 23–41 (1965)
3. Green, C.C., Raphael, B.: The use of theorem-proving techniques in question-answering systems. In: Proceedings of the 23rd ACM National Conference, Washington, DC (1968)
4. Ramakrishnan, R., Ullman, J.D.: A survey of deductive database systems. J. Logic Program. **23**(2) (1995)

5. Richens, R.H.: Preprogramming for mechanical translation. Mech. Translation **3**(1) (1956)
6. Sowa, J.F.: Semantic networks. In: Encyclopedia of the Sciences of Learning (1987)
7. Kejriwal, M., Knoblock, C.A., Szekely, P.: Knowledge Graph. The MIT Press, Cambridge (2021)
8. Noy, N., Gao, Y., Jain, A., Narayanan, A., Patterson, A., Taylor, J.: Industry-scale knowledge graphs: lessons and challenges. In: Queue (2019)
9. Carley, K.M., Kaufer, K.S.: Semantic connectivity: an approach for analyzing symbols in semantic networks. Commun. Theory (1993)
10. Jiang, J.J., Conrath, D.W.: Semantic similarity based on corpus statistics and lexical taxonomy. In: ROCLING (1997)
11. WordNet. https://wordnet.princeton.edu/
12. Puppe, F.: Knowledge representations and problem-solving methods. Systematic Introduction to Expert Systems. Springer-Verlag, Berlin Heidelberg (1993). https://doi.org/10.1007/978-3-642-77971-8
13. Depedia. https://wiki.dbpedia.org/
14. Yago. https://yago-knowledge.org/
15. Freebase. http://www.freebase.be/
16. Leblay, J., Chekol, M.W.: Deriving validity time in knowledge graph. In: WWW (2018)
17. Dasgupta, S.S., Ray, S.N., Talukdar, P.: Hyte: hyperplane-based temporally aware knowledge graph embedding. In: EMNLP (2018)
18. Ma, Y., Tresp, V., Daxberger, E.A.: Embedding models for episodic knowledge graphs. J. Web Semantics **59**, 100490 (2019)
19. Garcia-Duran, A., Dumancic, S., Niepert, M.: Learning sequence encoders for temporal knowledge graph completion. In: EMNLP (2018)
20. Anderson, J.R., Libiere, C.: The Atomic Components of Thought. Lawrence Erlbaum Associates Publishers, Hillsdale (1998)
21. Ball, J., Rodgers, S., Gluck, K.: Integrating ACT-R and Cyc in a large-scale model of language comprehension for use in intelligent agents. In: AAAI (2004)
22. Anderson, J.R.: The Architecture of Cognition. Psychology Press, Boca Raton (1995)
23. Heise, E., Westermann, R.: Andersons theory of cognitive architecture (ACT*). In: Westmeyer, H. (ed.) Psychological Theories from a Structuralist Point of View. PSYCHOLOGY. Springer, Berlin, Heidelberg (1989). https://doi.org/10.1007/978-3-642-84015-9_5
24. ACT-R website. http://act-r.psy.cmu.edu/software/
25. Gonzalez, C., Lerch, J.F., Lebiere, C.: Instance-based learning in dynamic decision making. Cogn. Sci. **27**(4), 591–635 (2003)
26. Gonzalez, C.: The boundaries of instance-based leraning theorey for explaining decisions from experience. Pammi VS **202**, 73–98 (2013)
27. Newell, A., Rosenbloom, P.S., Laird, J.E.: SOAR: an architecture for general intelligence. Artif. Intell. **198733**(1), 1–64
28. Chen, R.-D., Zhang, X.-S., Niu, W., Lan, H.-Y.: A research on architecture of APT attack detection and countering technology. J. Univ. Electron. Sci. Technol. China (2019)

The Framework of the MDATA Computing Model

Yan Jia[1], Aiping Li[2(✉)], Zhaoquan Gu[3], Bin Zhou[2], Ye Wang[2], Xiang Wang[2], and Hongkui Tu[2]

[1] Harbin Institute of Technology, Shenzhen 518055, China
jiayanjy@vip.sina.com
[2] National University of Defense Technology, Changsha 410073, China
{liaiping,binzhou,ye.wang,xiangwangcn}@nudt.edu.cn,
tuhkjet@foxmail.com
[3] Guangzhou University, Guangzhou 510006, China
zqgu@gzhu.edu.cn

Abstract. The cyberspace has expanded from traditional internet to ubiquitous cyberspace which interconnects human, machines, things, services, and applications. The computing paradigm is also shifting from centralized computing in the cloud to collaborative computing in the front end, middle layer, and cloud. Therefore, traditional computing paradigms such as cloud computing and edge computing can no longer satisfy the evolving computing needs of big data in ubiquitous cyberspace. This chapter proposes a computing architecture named Fog-cloud Computing for big data in ubiquitous cyberspace. Collaborative computing by multiple knowledge actors in the fog, middle layer, and cloud is realized based on the collaborative computing language and models, thereby providing a solution for big data computing in ubiquitous cyberspace.

Keywords: MDATA · Fog-cloud computing · Collaborative computing

1 Introduction

Information technology is a catalyst promoting the development of various industries. As cyberspace expands from the information-oriented Internet to the ubiquitous cyberspace interconnected by human, machines, things, services, and applications, traditional computing models such as high-performance computing [1], cloud computing [2], fog computing [3], edge computing [4], and multi-agent systems [5,6] can no longer meet the needs of big data analysis and processing in cyberspace. In this chapter, we introduce a new framework for the MDATA computing, which benefits various applications that need the analysis of multi-dimensional data.

Y. Jia et al. (Eds.): MDATA: A New Knowledge Representation Model, LNCS 12647, pp. 19–31, 2021.
https://doi.org/10.1007/978-3-030-71590-8_2

1.1   The Development of Cyberspace

The rapid development of the Internet, mobile Internet, Internet of Things, and social networks has made cyberspace increasingly prosperous and promoted the development of cyberspace from a single Internet to ubiquitous cyberspace. Ubiquitous cyberspace is a self-adaptive intelligent network based on the Internet. It integrates various wired and wireless networks with the Internet of Things, the Internet, and sensor networks. It comprehensively utilizes a large number of sensors and intelligent processing terminals and the software, services and applications running on these terminals to realize the safe and effective connection of human, machines, objects and information at any time and any place. The expansion of cyberspace has made the traditional "back-end processing as the center" cloud computing model unable to meet the ubiquitous cyberspace computing needs brought by "Internet + Internet of Things + mobile Internet". We come across an inevitable revolutionary that changing the "back-end processing as the center" computing to the "combining the background with the edge and the middle layer" computing.

1.2   The Requirements for the Characteristics of Big Data

Big data [7] refers to a collection of data that is difficult to effectively collect, manage, and analyze with existing data processing technologies within a certain time range. We will analyze the challenges faced by big data in cyberspace from the following 5V characteristics.

1. Volume: The amount of data has grown from terabyte (TB) level to petabyte (PB) level or even zettabyte (ZB) level. It is difficult for a single application or a data center to quickly process such a large amount of data. There is an urgent need for the applications and data centers to cooperate as multi-intellectual agents like humans.
2. Variety: There are various types of information, such as text, video, audio, picture, specific types, and even the cross-fusion of these types. It is difficult for a single individual, company or research institution to analyze and process different types of data at the same time. It is urgent to create a computing framework that collaborates and protects their own intellectual property rights and data ownership.
3. Velocity: Due to the high-speed data generation, it is necessity to have the capability of real-time processing at the source of the data and at the edge or middle layer that not far from the source while knowledge and information interact constantly between them and the cloud layer.
4. Veracity: Data and its sources are uncertain and unreliable so that reliable calculation and cross-validation of data from different sources are indispensable.
5. Value: There is extremely valuable information in a large amount of data. However, the value of valuable information is basically domain-specific. Therefore, cooperation amongst experts from related domains are needed to optimize the value of big data.

As a result, big data in ubiquitous cyberspace urgently needs a large number of individuals, research institutions, and companies to cooperate to conduct computing collaboratively based on protecting their intellectual property rights, data privacy, and ownership. This is the reason why the current computing model hardly meet these requirements.

1.3 "Information Island" and Protection of Intellectual Property Rights

Big data in cyberspace, especially data of Internet of Things, data of sensors and data of mobile applications, are mostly owned by different individuals, organizations or institutions. Due to issues of privacy protection, ownership protection, and confidentiality agreements, the current "information islands" phenomenon of big data is prevalent [8]. It is difficult to centralize data and knowledge to one data center for unified storage, search, analysis and exploring. In terms of data mining, experts scattered in various research institutions and organizations around the world have achieved fruitful results in their respective industries and research fields, but it is also difficult for a single organization or institution to solve the problems that current systems faced in the ubiquitous cyberspace. Therefore, we urgently need wide cooperation using existing state-of-the-art techniques on the basis of protecting respective intellectual property rights to meet the computation requirement of the ubiquitous cyberspace.

In order to solve the above problems, we propose a general architecture of intelligent "Fog-cloud Computing" for big data in ubiquitous cyberspace. With this architecture, knowledge actors in the front end (fog end), the middle layer, and the cloud can collaborate with each others to fulfill the real-time and fusion analysis processing requirements on the basis of the protecting intellectual property rights.

A knowledge actor is an autonomous and intelligent software with its own domain, goals and functions logically, and its own knowledge base, learner, reasoner, executor and coordinator physically. A knowledge actor can not only inference knowledge according to the goal of a task and provide functions according to the needs of the task, but also can cooperate with each other to complete a certain task. The Fog-cloud computing architecture can be applied to ubiquitous network big data computing scenarios such as the Internet of Things, smart homes, and question answering robots. Among them, big search [9] in network space is a typical application of Fog-cloud computing. Currently, smart voice assistants (such as Siri [10] and HiVoice [11]) perform collaborative computing with users' personal privacy data on the local mobile phone and Internet data on the cloud. These products reflects the basic idea of "Fog-cloud computing" in the ubiquitous cyberspace.

In this chapter, we first introduce the definition of the Fog-cloud computing in the next Section. The architecture is described in Sect. 3, which consists of different types of knowledge actors. We then introduce the method to build the MDATA model on the Fog-cloud computing framework in Sect. 4 and we introduce some typical applications based on the framework in Sect. 5. Finally, we summarize the chapter in Sect. 6.

2   Definition of Fog-Cloud Computing

To satisfy users' computing goals, Fog-cloud computing is a cooperative process of knowledge actors consisting of knowledge actors from the fog-end that extract knowledge from the immense data ocean, the middle layer that fuse and integrate different types of knowledge, and the cloud where deploy intelligent computing operations. As shown in Eq. 1, Fog-cloud computing is composed of three parts: the knowledge actor, the relationship between the knowledge actors, and the collaborative operation between the knowledge actors.

$$Fog - cloudComputing = \{KnowledgeActor, R, Operation\} \tag{1}$$

where $KnowledgeActor = \{KnowledgeActor_1, ..., KnowledgeActor_n\}$ represents the whole set of n knowledge actors and R is the whole set of types of relations. $R_{jk} \subseteq R$ represents the relation between $KnowledgeActor_j$ and $KnowledgeActor_k$ where $j, k = 1, ..., n$. $Operation$ is the cooperative activities and computations among the knowledge actors related to a certain task, $Task_m$ for example.

The knowledge actor is a smart software component, which can be a simple target-oriented knowledge extraction software component in the fog end or a large-scale knowledge actor in the cloud (such as a health knowledge actor, a weather forecast knowledge actor, and a common sense knowledge actor). The knowledge actor has the characteristics of self-learning, self-evolution, description, management, flexible online assembly, and distributed deployment. The coordination problem can be solved among the knowledge actors. A knowledge actor $KnowledgeActor_i = \{ID, O, A\}$ has three components, namely the identifier (ID), the object (O), and the internal architecture (A). The object can be represented as follows:

$$O = \{CollectData, KnowledgeAcquisition, Inference, \\ Computing, Merging, ...\} \tag{2}$$

The architecture of a knowledge actor has several components including the Task Executor, the Knowledge Base, the Inference Engine, the Learning Unit, the Task Planning and Decision Maker (TPDK), the Cooperator, the Knowledge input and output interface (KInterface), the Cooperative Interface (CInterface), the data interface (DInterface), and the task input interface (TInterface), etc. Figure 1 gives an intuitive structure of the knowledge actor. The architecture A can also be formalized by the following equation:

$$A = \{TaskExecutor, KnowledgeBase, InferEngine, LearnUnit, TPDK, \\ Cooperator, KInterface, CInterface, DInterface, TInterface\} \tag{3}$$

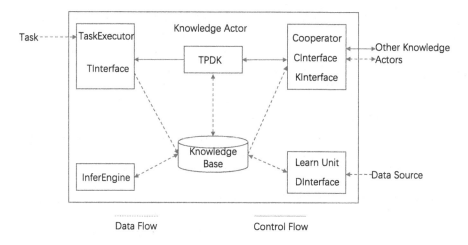

Fig. 1. The architecture of the knowledge actor

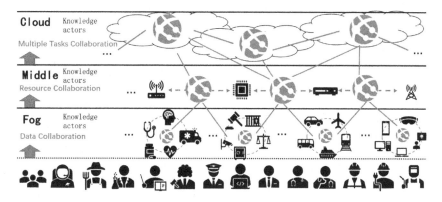

Fig. 2. The architecture of Fog-cloud computing

3   The Architecture of Fog-Cloud Computing

The "Fog-cloud computing" architecture for ubiquitous cyberspace big data is shown in Fig. 2. It consists of front-end computing at the fog end, fusion computing at the middle layer, and back-end cloud computing on the basis of multiple knowledge actors and their collaborative reasoning. Each level is running on different platforms. The main difference between Fog-cloud computing and others (such as edge computing and cloud computing) is the ability to support highly collaborative computing.

3.1   Cloud Knowledge Actors

The cloud knowledge actor is usually the remote background processing center. It is the gathering place of edge IoT nodes, web applications, mobile apps, and

Internet intermediate nodes scattered around the world. It is also the distribution center of content in the massive fog end and middle layer knowledge actors. The cloud knowledge actor is sensitive to the context, time, and location of the fog end and middle layer knowledge actors. It is the global center of Fog-cloud computing. Cloud knowledge actors usually store non-private global and contextual data and conduct global reasoning of knowledge.

The cloud knowledge actor has the following characteristics:

- It has strong computing and storage performance and a stable network environment;
- Usually, it needs to analyze and calculate the data of the middle layer and the fog-end knowledge actors;
- The obtained knowledge is distributed in a wide range and usually requires a large scale time and location analysis and calculation;
- It is necessary to carry out collaborative inference calculation with the middle layer and the fog end knowledge actors;
- Due to the huge amount of data and complex calculations, offline analysis and calculation are usually conducted.

The cloud knowledge actor usually runs on the following computing clusters and platforms.

1. Distributed Storage Cluster: The Fog-cloud computing platform is oriented to big data computing tasks in ubiquitous cyberspace. It obtains information from massive data sources all over the Internet and the Internet of Things, and extracts, processes and integrates various functional knowledge actors to form knowledge based on specific tasks. As an operating platform with a large number of intelligent knowledge actors, it will inevitably store a large amount of structured, semi-structured and unstructured data, including files, web pages, knowledge maps, audios and videos, etc. The distributed storage cluster is composed of a number of storage servers and index servers. It is constructed with a dedicated data storage management system such as a distributed file system or a graph database.
2. AI Computing Cluster: The AI computing cluster is used for high-density computing tasks such as images, audios, and videos training. The AI computing cluster adopts a central processing unit + graphics processing unit (CPU+GPU) architecture, and consists of several high-density computing server nodes through high-speed interconnection.
3. Streaming Data Processing Cluster: The streaming data processing cluster is used for real-time processing of massive data streams obtained from data sources and fog end knowledge actors. These data streams may come from sensors, mobile terminals, and remotely deployed intelligent crawlers. Mass stream data needs to be cleaned, filtered and calculated in real time, and then stored in a distributed storage cluster as the material for knowledge discovery.
4. High-speed Cache Cluster: The high-speed cache cluster is used to store data that needs to be fast accessed, such as indexes and hot data. In order to response in real-time, the high-speed cache cluster mainly adopt memory to provide services.

5. Message Exchange Cluster: The message exchange cluster provides the under-lying communication infrastructure for collaborative computing between a large number of knowledge actors. The server nodes in the cluster are config-ured with high-speed network interface bandwidth.

3.2   Middle Layer Knowledge Actors

The middle layer knowledge actor is located between the fog end and the cloud. It is usually deployed on servers that close to edge nodes. Sometimes it is also deployed on convergent nodes such as gateways, routers, and communication base stations. The middle layer knowledge actor usually runs on servers with strong computing and storage capabilities. Compared with cloud nodes, it is closer to the edge nodes and data sources of the fog end. It is the local center. The middle layer knowledge actor plays a core role in Fog-cloud computing. On one hand, the middle layer knowledge actor can access massive amounts of data on the Internet and perform collaborative computing with the cloud knowledge actors. On the other hand, the middle layer knowledge actor can access data in the local edge nodes, and can conduct collaborative calculation based on the geographical distribution of edge nodes. The middle layer knowledge actor plays an important role for the combination of global cyberspace computing and local data. It is the core component of Fog-cloud computing.

The middle layer knowledge actor has the following characteristics: (i) It has strong computing and storage performance and is capable of more complex calculation and analysis. However, the network is relatively stable; (ii) It is close to the data source and can conduct spatial-temporal analysis and calculation; (iii) It can realize the collaborative inference calculation based on the data on multiple edge nodes; (iv) The data and knowledge of the connected fog terminal edge nodes are heterogeneous; (v) Near real-time analysis and calculation and feedback are usually performed.

3.3   Fog End Knowledge Actors

There is a huge number of fog end edge nodes, including devices in the smart Internet of things, sensors in sensor networks, applications in the mobile Internet, smart home devices, and vehicles (cars, drones, etc.) that install smart devices. They are the source of big data. Many of these edge nodes also have certain computing capabilities, which can be used to deploy local real-time computing and data acquisition knowledge actors. The fog end knowledge actor has the following characteristics: (i) The computing and storage capacity is weak, and the network is not stable enough; (ii) It is the direct source of data; (iii) It has time and location information; (iv) It can move in a larger range; (v) The Knowledge actor can conduct real-time calculation and feedback.

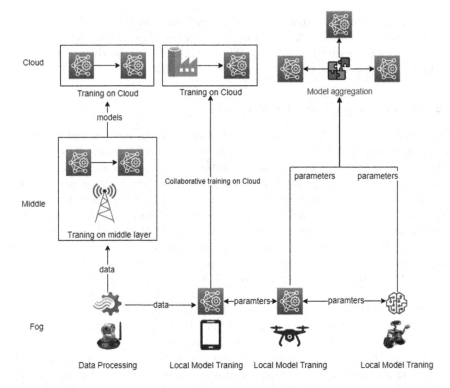

Fig. 3. An example of Multi-knowledge-actor Collaborative Computing

3.4   Multi-knowledge-actor Collaborative Computing

Multi-knowledge actors distributed in the fog end, middle layer, and cloud perform collaborative computing and task scheduling with the support of collaborative computing language. The language defines a series of objects, such as Domain, KnowledgeActor, Action, Problem, and Goal. A multi-objective optimization oriented task planner schedules tasks of multiple knowledge actors. After the knowledge actor has been created and assembled, the task planner generates specific collaboration strategies. The multi-objective optimizer solve the optimization problem of task scheduling in the space of tasks for the collaborative computing of multiple knowledge actors. The knowledge actors are assembled online according to the specific collaboration strategy and deployed to demanded computational nodes The collaboration operations among knowledge actors develop both in the inter-layer collaboration (e.g. bottom up knowledge aggregation from fog to cloud) and intra-layer collaboration (e.g. data and knowledge sharing and joint learning based model training in a same layer). An example is shown in Fig. 3. During the execution of the task, the knowledge actors can dynamically join or exit the task according to the load of the system.

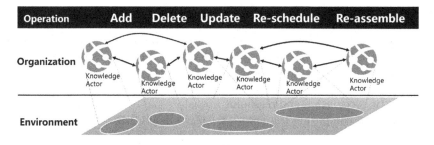

Fig. 4. Managing multiple knowledge actors in Fog-cloud computing

4 Building MDATA Model on Fog-Cloud Computing Framework

Fog-cloud computing framework provides a distributed environment for multiple knowledge actors, in which the Multi-dimensional Data Association and inTelligent Analysis (MDATA) model can be decently deployed with multiple knowledge actors assembled in different layers. Both vertical and horizontal managements of multiple knowledge actors also help MDATA represent, acquire and use dynamic knowledge by implementing operations including *Add*, *Delete*, *Update*, *Re-Schedule* and *Re-assemble* (shown in Fig. 4). Next, we introduce the mechanism from the three main parts of MDATA model.

4.1 Distributed Knowledge Representation of MDATA

As mentioned in Sect. 1, adding temporal and spatial characteristics to both relations and entities making MDATA be intrinsically different from normal graph representing models. As real world changes dynamically, temporal and spatial characteristics evolves all the time with little regulation for most things. These dynamical changes not only exist on evolving entities and relations (e.g. *Marriage* and *Partnership*), but also on affiliated properties (e.g. *Education* and *Affiliation*). As a result, there is a big increase in demand for gathering, storage, processing, computing and communicating abilities. Furthermore, privacy protection requirement also arises. In other words, Knowledge representation of MDATA will not be fulfilled locally with single knowledge actor.

Fog-cloud computing framework allows a uniform MDATA-representation of general interface to form:

$$MDATA - Representation = <Concept, Entity, Relation, Property>. \quad (4)$$

Where, entity is a set of existing entities referring to a specific example of some concept. As mentioned before, relation is represented with temporal and spatial characteristics. With collaborative computing among multiple knowledge actors, MDATA model could partially represent and update a subgraph at specific time or location requirement for the specific task without involving the immense $[TimeZone]$ and $[Location]$.

4.2 Distributed Knowledge Acquisition of MDATA

Distributed knowledge acquisition of Fog-cloud computing framework allows inter-layer and intra-layer collaborative knowledge acquisition. Inductive methods and deductive methods are easily shifted as needed. Upon basic entity/relation/ property extraction and Reasoning operations, temporal/spatial characteristic recognition and reasoning operators can be assembled in any layer of the fog-cloud computing framework to infer missing facts.

4.3 Distributed Knowledge Usage of MDATA

Distributed knowledge usage of Fog-cloud computing framework significantly improve the knowledge efficiency and reduce the cost of data usage. Various query operators of MDATA will be carried out in applications in fog layer which avoids high computational workloads and cost of communication. In the other hands, more collaborative computing will be conducted for distributed knowledge acquisition and graph updating computation.

5 Typical Applications

In this section, we show how the Fog-cloud framework can be applied in some typical applications. Considering the typical applications that benefit from the MDATA model, we introduce network attack detection and epidemic analysis as the examples.

5.1 Network Attack Detection

In order to detect network attacks efficiently, we need a lot of cyberspace security knowledge. Since network attacks vary dynamically, such as different attacks are conducted through different IP addresses, traditional knowledge graph cannot satisfying the dynamics of the network attacks. The MDATA model could represent dynamic knowledge with good spatial and temporal characteristics, it thus can be applied in detecting network attacks.

However, there is a lot of cyberspace security knowledge which cannot be efficiently represented. The proposed Fog-cloud framework can be applied to detect network attacks timely. According to the framework, we introduce how the knowledge actors perform.

The fog end knowledge actor monitors the events that happen on a computer or a server. The fog end knowledge actor could detect some simple attacks according to pre-defined rules or some easy features. For example, the rule of detecting SQL (structured query language) injection event could be easily designed from previous attacks. Once some events trigger these rules, the simple attack event could be identified. As the assets are distributed in different computers or servers, the fog end knowledge actor can be deployed on each single computer or server; then the actor can monitor the attack events. Furthermore, the actor also records the security information, such as the vulnerability information of the asset and the features of some simple attack events.

The middle layer knowledge actor could combine the analysis of various fog end knowledge actors. For example, a local area network consists of multiple computers within a small area. Similarly, the middle layer knowledge actors connect multiple fog end knowledge actors for a comprehensive analysis. Although fog end knowledge actor can find out some simple attack events, the limited computation capability and limited information make it difficult to analyze a complicated attack event. Some attacks are conducted on different IP addresses, the middle layer knowledge actor could combine related attack events to find out such complicated ones. Introducing these actors could help find out some complicated attacks.

The cloud knowledge actor can be regarded as the central unit for knowledge fusion, which is similar as cloud computing. The cloud knowledge actor stores a relative complete information about cyberspace security knowledge, such as the knowledge about APT attacks. Be collecting the information from the middle layer knowledge actors, the cloud knowledge actor can identify the complicated attacks efficiently, by comparing with the existing security knowledge.

In order to guarantee network attack detection efficiency, the middle layer knowledge actors play an important role. Traditional cloud computing would collect all data from edge devices, it is costly to handle all these data. In the fog-cloud framework, the middle layer knowledge actors only collect related data, which reduces a lot of irrelevant data; then the cloud knowledge actor only need to handle the related data and this could reduce large time in detecting complicated network attacks.

5.2   Epidemic Analysis

The coronavirus (COVID-19) pandemic is still a vital problem in almost every country. In order to analyze the epidemic situation, we apply the fog-cloud framework to compute the MDATA knowledge.

The epidemic analysis is highly related to multi-dimensional data. For example, the personnel flight data records a person's travel information, which can be utilized to decide whether some people travel together. As there is a lot of epidemic data, traditional frameworks or knowledge representation methods cannot satisfy the requirements of real time computing. The fog-cloud computing framework could solve the problem with high efficiency and accuracy.

The fog end knowledge actor analyzes the epidemic information from a single dimension. For example, the actor judges whether one person has close contact with an infected person according to the flight data, or it judges whether two persons have been together from the communication information. Each fog end knowledge actor is responsible for analyzing the relationship between different persons in a specific domain, which could provide accurate analysis result.

The middle layer knowledge actor combine the information from multiple fog end knowledge actors. Similar as network attack detection, the actors only utilize some related information for a comprehensive analysis. For example, a middle layer knowledge actor analyzes some specific person by combining his/her related information in the fog end knowledge actors. By removing irrelevant information, these actors could improve the analysis efficiency and accuracy.

In order to compute the epidemic situation from a global perspective, the cloud knowledge actor could combine the information from the middle layer knowledge actors, which act as the central unit for epidemic analysis.

The MDATA model could associate multi-dimensional information for a comprehensive analysis, but traditional computation models, such as the cloud computing, cannot satisfy the requirements of the MDATA model. The proposed fog-cloud computing framework can be easily applied and two typical applications are described.

6 Chapter Summary

This chapter presents a software architecture named Fog-cloud computing for big data in ubiquitous cyberspace. The architecture includes three components, namely the cloud, middle layer, and fog end. We describe the basic concept of Fog-cloud computing and clarify the relationship between the three components. The key technologies of Fog-cloud computing include multi-level, multi-granularity and multi-modal data representation, multi-knowledge-actor collaborative reasoning, time and location fusion analysis, trusted search and privacy protection, etc.

The Fog-cloud Computing architecture is suitable for typical ubiquitous cyberspace big data computing applications. It provides a solution for collaborative computing in the ubiquitous cyberspace front end, middle layer, and cloud. Fog-cloud computing can be applied to ubiquitous network big data computing scenarios such as the Internet of Things, smart homes, and question answering robots. Among them, cyberspace big search is also a typical case of Fog-cloud computing, which is oriented to people, objects, information and services in the ubiquitous cyberspace. It can provide intelligent answers to users after correct understanding of users' intent and knowledge acquired big data of cyberspace.

References

1. Gibson, G.A., Schroeder, B.: A large-scale study of failures in high-performance computing systems. IEEE Trans. Dependable Secur. Comput. **7**(4), 337–351 (2010)
2. Song, A., Dong, F., Luo, Z., Jin, J.: Cloud computing: architecture and key technologies. J. Commun. **7**, 3–21 (2011)
3. Zhu, J., Addepalli, S., Bonomi, F., Milito, R.: Fog computing and its role in the Internet of Things. In: Gerla, M., Huang, D. (eds.) Proceedings of the First Edition of the MCC Workshop on Mobile Cloud Computing, MCC@SIGCOMM 2012, Helsinki, Finland, 17 August 2012, pp. 13–16. ACM (2012)
4. Zhang, Q., Li, Y., Xu, L., Shi, W., Cao, J.: Edge computing: vision and challenges. IEEE Internet Things J. **3**(5), 637–646 (2016)
5. Chen, J., Liu, D., Yang, K.: Agents: present status and trends. J. Softw. **11**(3), 315–321 (2011)

6. Murray, R.M., Olfati-Saber, R., Fax, J.A.: Consensus and cooperation in networked multi-agent systems. Proc. IEEE **95**(1), 215–233 (2007)
7. Cukier, K., Mayer-Schönberger, V.: Big Data: A Revolution That Will Transform How We Live, Work, and Think. Houghton Mifflin Harcourt, Boston (2013)
8. Grieco, L.A., Coen-Porisini, A., Sicari, S., Rizzardi, A.: Security, privacy and trust in Internet of Things: the road ahead. Comput. Netw. **76**, 146–164 (2015)
9. Li, X., Li, A., Wu, X., Fang, B., Jia, Y.: Big search in cyberspace. IEEE Trans. Knowl. Data Eng. **29**(9), 1793–1805 (2017)
10. López, G., Quesada, L., Guerrero, L.A.: Alexa vs. Siri vs. Cortana vs. Google assistant: a comparison of speech-based natural user interfaces. In: Nunes, I. (ed.) AHFE 2017. AISC, vol. 592, pp. 241–250. Springer, Cham (2017). https://doi.org/10.1007/978-3-319-60366-7_23
11. Baker, M.: Real, unreal, and hacked. IEEE Pervasive Comput. **17**(1), 104–112 (2018)

Spatiotemporal Data Cleaning and Knowledge Fusion

Huchen Zhou, Mohan Li$^{(\boxtimes)}$, Zhaoquan Gu, and Zhihong Tian

Cyberspace Institute of Advance Technology, Guangzhou University,
Guangzhou 510006, China
zhouhuchen@e.gzhu.edu.cn, {limohan,zqgu,tianzhihong}@gzhu.edu.cn

Abstract. Knowledge fusion aims to establish the relation-ship between
heterogeneous ontology or heterogeneous instances. Data cleaning is one
of the underlying key technologies supporting knowledge fusion. In this
chapter, we give a brief overview of some important technologies of
knowledge fusion and data cleaning. We first briefly introduce the motivation and background of knowledge fusion and data cleaning. Then,
we discuss some of the recent methods for knowledge fusion and spatiotemporal data cleaning. Finally, we outline some future directions of
knowledge fusion and data cleaning.

Keywords: MDATA · Spatiotemporal data · Data cleaning ·
Knowledge fusion

1 Introduction

Knowledge Graph (KG) uses graph-structured data to express the correlation
between different knowledge [1]. In KG, nodes represent specific objects, concepts, information resources or data about them, and edges represent semantic
relationships between nodes. In order to improve the retrieval efficiency of users
and allow computers to understand massive amounts of information like humans,
the research and applications of KG have attracted widespread attention from
the academia and industry. A KG may involve many heterogeneous knowledge
and data from different sources. How to integrate these heterogeneous knowledge
and data while ensuring the quality of knowledge and data is a very important
issue. Therefore, when building and using KG, we must consider how to filter
out those "dirty data" and useless information.

Knowledge fusion is to integrate different knowledge into a unified form. On
the one hand, knowledge fusion can complement incomplete knowledge and help
people and computers better understand the meaning of information. On the
other hand, it can combine small knowledge graphs to obtain larger knowledge
graphs, thereby expanding the boundaries of knowledge.

Knowledge fusion and data cleaning are inseparable. Data cleaning is one of
the underlying key technologies supporting knowledge fusion. Through knowledge fusion and data cleaning, structural heterogeneity and semantic hetero-

© Springer Nature Switzerland AG 2021
Y. Jia et al. (Eds.): MDATA: A New Knowledge Representation Model, LNCS 12647, pp. 32–50, 2021.
https://doi.org/10.1007/978-3-030-71590-8_3

geneity in KG can be solved, and inaccurate "dirty data" can be identified and cleaned up.

In the data preprocessing stage of knowledge fusion, data cleaning is paramount. The quality of the original data will affect the final knowledge fusion result. Data quality refers to the degree of compliance with the following four indicators in knowledge dissemination, namely accuracy, completeness, consistency and currency. Recent evidence shows that it is not enough to only consider the accuracy of data and knowledge in a certain scenario.

Spatiotemporal correlation plays a vital role in the process of knowledge fusion and data cleaning. Data currency data currency corresponds to the time relevance. It is to ensure that data keeps pace with the times and will not be eliminated. The main purpose of data currency research is to determine whether a given data item is the latest [5]. In the real world, there are many physical sensor devices that have interference problems. Therefore, the data is usually stale or erroneous. In many specific scenarios, such as stocks, futures markets and temperature detection scenarios, there is a great demand for data currency.

A previous research report stated that using two real data sets containing readings from IoT smart city sensors [6] and retail transactions [7], the data are 20% and 16% outdated, respectively. When updates are missing or incorrect, changes made to real-world entities will not be reflected in databases. This will further lead to data obsolescence. There is not much research on the spatial correlation characteristics of data. However, it is very necessary to study spatial correlation. For example, it makes sense to link "No. 230 Waihuan West Road" (the address of Guangzhou University) to the entity Guangzhou University. In addition, linking cyber attacks with IP addresses is also a useful spatial correlation. In summary, these cases support the view that the temporal and spatial characteristics of knowledge and data are crucial.

Regarding knowledge fusion, it is an effective way to solve the problem of knowledge graph and knowledge base heterogeneity. There is an ocean of knowledge and data resources on the Web, and these resources play a key role in big data society. The core problem of knowledge fusion is how to find the specific objects of fusion and establish the mapping between the objects to solve the heterogeneous problem. In knowledge fusion, how to ensure the quality of knowledge, disambiguate knowledge, find the true value of knowledge, and update the correct knowledge to the knowledge base has received considerable attention. Knowledge fusion have been studied on many knowledge bases, for example, Wikipedia [2], Freebase [3], Schema.org, YAGO [4], OpenKG.CN, etc. Among them, the development of Wikipedia is surprising. The update speed and scale is very pleasurable. Many existing studies are based on Wikipedia. One of the key issues to be solved in knowledge fusion is entity linking, which is also called entity alignment, entity matching or record matching.

Recently, a lot of work on the subject of knowledge fusion and data cleaning has emerged. Most of the existing work focuses on specific core issues in knowledge fusion and data cleaning. In the field of knowledge fusion, current research involves core issues such as entity linking, knowledge base construction, and entity matching. In the field of data cleaning, current research involves data detection, data restoration, etc. Knowledge fusion and data cleaning are closely related, but each has its own focus. Therefore, from the perspective of knowledge fusion and data cleaning, this chapter attempts to summarize some recent related technologies.

The rest of this chapter can be summarized as follows. Section 2 discusses data cleaning research on spatiotemporal dimensions. In Sect. 3, we introduce the basic process of knowledge fusion for knowledge graphs, and discuss several typical methods in details. We conclude this chapter in Sect. 4 and look forward to the shortcomings in the existing research on knowledge fusion and data cleaning. Some future research directions are also proposed.

2   Spatiotemporal Data Cleaning

2.1   Background

Knowledge fusion first preprocesses data, and it only makes sense to fuse the correct data. Along with this growth in knowledge fusion, however, there is increasing concern over data cleaning. Dirty and erroneous data is a growing public challenge concern in data analysis. Much of the ambiguity and conflict in knowledge fusion comes from the evolution of data. Since the data in the real world will change with the change of time and space, this will lead to conflict of knowledge. For example, the semantics of "Apple" has gradually evolved from "a fruit" to "Apple Inc", "iPhone" and other new semantics in recent years. Therefore, if you want to construct a highly accurate knowledge graph, an angle that cannot be ignored is that you need to correlate knowledge with its spatial and temporal dimensions for analysis. In order to achieve this goal, the quality management of the space-time dimension of the data used to extract knowledge is also very important. Therefore, this section will introduce some data cleaning methods related to the spatial and temporal dimensions. These methods may provide some ideas for the upper level knowledge fusion. Data cleaning research involves many aspects. This chapter focuses on several methods related to the spatial and temporal dimensions. The general data quality and data cleaning process is shown in Fig. 1.

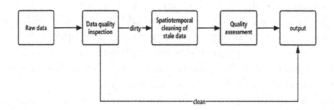

Fig. 1. Spatiotemporal data cleaning. Spatiotemporal data cleaning.

2.2   Problem Definition

Data cleaning mainly includes error detection and data repair stages, and also includes the judgment of temporal and spatial attributes.

A relation R with attributes $A_1, ..., A_n$ is an finite set of nary tuples $r_1, ..., r_m$. A database D is a finite set of relations $R_1, ..., R_m$. Cell $r[A_i]$ is the i-th position in tuple in D, and v_c as the value in cell c. Given a database D and a query history $H = <q_1, q_2, ..., q_{|H|}>$, each query is a that updates the value of $r[A]$ from a to b at time t. Assume that the query history H is correct, and only one cell is updated every time t. We assume that $q_c^*.t$ is ground true, if $q_c.t = q_c^*.t$, then it is current. Otherwise it is stale. Our purpose is to make the cells of database D have currency. The H and $q_c^*.t$ maybe not ture. So given the D and H, the error detection problem is to find a set ε of stale cells in D with $p < \beta$, β is a currency threshold. Assuming that v_t^* is the true value of cell c and v_t' is the estimated value of the true value, the purpose of data restoration is to estimate all v_t' in set ϵ, and finally generate a clean database D. We think the sign of successful repair is $v_t' == v_t^*$.

2.3   Related Methods

Stream Data Cleaning Based on Constraints. Streaming data is often "dirty" due to unreliable readings obtained by sensors [18] or errors in stock price extraction. Even the stocks and flight records that we usually think are very reliable, many inconsistent data are observed [19]. This section discusses related examine starting from SCREEN [21], a stream data cleaning method based on constraints. The SCREEN method completes the task of stream data cleaning in three steps: The first and foremost, Determine the repair problem under the constraint of speed, find the repair sequence with the smallest difference from the input, meet the principle of minimum repair [20], and model the problem as a linear programming problem. There is one more step, design an online cleaning algorithm. When calculating streaming data online, decompose the global optimal into the optimal of each data point, and design a median rule to get as close as possible to each point, and then calculate the local optimal to clean up. The last but not the least, based on an adaptive window (the window is used to compare two data points), the data points are modeled as random samples, and the distributed approximation is used to adjust the size of the window. Use the window to make a constraint on the speed and fix the detected data error points in the window.

In addition, Existing data cleaning algorithms for time series data include stream data cleaning based on linear regression [50]. Holistic Data Cleaning [38] is also constraint-based data repair. Unfortunately, it is only for general data and does not support online cleaning of streaming data.

Stream data cleaning methods based on speed constraints can handle stream data well, and control the time in linear time while following the principle of minimum repair [20], there are many minimum repair principles [55]. The method based on speed constraint can solve some shortcomings of smooth cleaning, and can also deal with out-of-order data points and error data with large spikes. On the contrary, the disadvantage is that when the time series shifts from abnormal to normal, the SCREEN method cannot handle it well, and it cannot handle continuous "dirty values", and it is not very satisfactory in terms of overall accuracy. In the next section we will talk about the latest cleaning method based on time series.

Time Series Cleaning. Data errors are very common in time series. The approach used in this section is similar to that used by other researchers in Sect. 3.1. Existing methods are more focused on anomaly detection [23,24]. Repairing the "dirty value" can improve the clustering of spatial data. For these time series data, the wrong data cannot be simply discarded, and it must be repaired based on the facts. This subsection starts from the time series-based cleaning method iterative minimum repairing (IMR) [37] and discusses related study. The main idea of IMR is to combine the advantages of natural tenses captured in anomaly detection with minimal changes. By performing a minimum repair in each iteration of the error prediction, the error value is gradually repaired. This method designs a pruning and incremental calculation algorithm to reduce the parameter estimation from linear time to constant time. The IMR algorithm combines the detection technology of the ARX model [25] to repair the data. In the first place, calculate the $ARX(p)$ model, $ARX(p)$:

$$y'_t = x_t + \sum_{i=1}^{p} \phi_i(y_{t-i} - x_{t-i}) + \epsilon_t \tag{1}$$

$p$is the order of model. Calculate the parameter ϕ_k and the current $y^{(k)}$ of k iterations according to $ARX(p)$. Then calculate the possible repair value $\hat{y}^{(k)}$ according to the parameter x, $y^{(k)}$,$\phi^{(k)}$ of $ARX(p)$. Considering the minimum principle of data restoration [27], the restoration with the smallest difference from the original input is selected with higher confidence. The last but not the least, use incremental calculations, only the changing values are considered to increase the calculation parameters. The study offers some important insights that time performance can be significantly improved through pruning and incremental calculations, higher repair accuracy can be achieved through lower time performance.

Data cleaning based on time series is generally divided into related research in the following three directions:

Anomaly Detection Method on Time Series, ARX is used for anomaly detection in many fields of economy and society [25].

Smooth-Based Data Cleaning,there are simple moving average (SMA) [24], exponentially weighted moving average (EWMA) [51], Savitzky Golay Filter [36].

Constraint-based Data Cleaning,the method introduced in Sect. 3.1 [21], the speed-based constraints and the work in this section have their own advantages and disadvantages, and can handle different situations. Taken together, the algorithm in this section can model the difference between the error and the true value, rather than the original value. Performs better when repairing consecutive "dirty" points. We have noticed that the research in this section can solve a problem that cannot be solved by the study in Sect. 3.1. That is, when the time series shifts from abnormal to normal, the time series-based cleaning (IMR) can perform normally, but the IMR method cannot handle giant Spike error.

Spatiotemporal Cleaning of Stale Data. Data currency has a pivotal role in the field of traditional business intelligence applications and accurate data analysis. The criteria for judging old data cannot depend solely on the attribute of time. Each entity has its own update patterns in time and space. This section starts with the CurrentClean model [22] and discusses related studies. Current-Clean believes that it should consider the spatial update of adjacent cells in the tuple. This method defines the parameters as follows: H is a sequence of labeled real update value, which represents the update history of values in a cell from a to b at time t. H is an external information, which can be obtained from database transaction logs, database flashback recovery features, or by computing the difference between successive data snapshots over a time period. β is currency threshold, $current(c) < \beta$ means cell c is stale. This chapter proposes a probabilistic system called CurrentClean. There are three modules in the system,

1) Spatiotemporal inference: the model extends a class of graphical models to capture the space-time correlation between update times. It instantiate Spatiotemporal Probability Model (STPM) modeling the update on the cell and defining a set of inference rules to model the spatiotemporal update pattern. The model is called **Umodel**;
2) Current Estimation: A Umodel is set to learn the update patterns in H, and gives the joint probability distribution of update events on all units on D in the time specified by H. Given the update history of cell c, the model can calculate the update probability without H, which gives the possibility that c is the latest;
3) Data Repair: CurrentClean builds a probabilistic repair model, called **Rmodel**. Rmodel is a dynamic probabilistic relationship model that captures the spatial and temporal distribution of the values in database D. Rmodel performs statistical learning and inference on the joint distribution, and uses the maximum posterior distribution inference to calculate values on stale data units.

By the way, the latest related research has explored the methods mentioned in the previous two sections for data cleaning of time series data based on the rate of change of a single cell [21,23], with time validity determination research on methods [5]. A probabilistic model has also been proposed. It learns from the clean distribution in the data to minimize dirty values [28].

Overall cleaning framework: HoloClean [52] is a widely used and holistic data cleansing framework that provides overall data repair by combining multiple inputs (integrity constraints, external dictionaries, and statistical documents), and uses probabilistic inference (DeepDive) to infer the current data. ERACER [53] uses a probabilistic graphical model to model the correlation of attributes. But neither of these two methods can identify the update pattern across database units, and the performance of the recall for identifying stale values is poor. The ActiveClean framework [54] built a modern machine learning data cleaning framework, and also designed a visual interface. Such a cleaning framework helped data analysts a lot. This is a cleaning framework for real world scenarios.

From the current point of view, CurrentClean is a relatively good data cleaning method with good performances on Recall and F1-score; but the time complexity of the method is very high and the algorithm needs to be improved. Notably, now there is such a research point in the field of data quality, that is, this data cleaning system does not yet have an online mode.

2.4 Discussions on Spatiotemporal Data Cleaning for MDATA

A major feature of MDATA is the integration of time and space dimensions. Therefore, the data cleaning method considering the space and time dimensions is very inspiring for the cleaning of MDATA. The spatio-temporal data cleaning involved in MDATA mainly includes two aspects:

- Some spatiotemporal attributes of MDATA, such as period, activity range, etc., may need to be analyzed and refined on raw spatiotemporal data. If raw spatiotemporal data is dirty, then MDATA knowledge representation will also have problems. Therefore, spatiotemporal data cleaning is the cornerstone of the accurate construction of MDATA knowledge representation.
- After the spatiotemporal attributes are generated, they may still have knowledge conflicts for some reasons. The cleaning technology of spatiotemporal data is also instructive for the verification and disambiguation of these knowledge.

In addition, the classic data cleaning method is also very useful for the cleaning of MDATA, but since it does not specifically involve the spatiotemporal characteristics that MDATA specifically emphasizes, it will not be repeated here.

The current data cleaning technology still cannot completely solve all the problems related to data quality. In particular, it is difficult to eliminate as many data errors as possible without destroying any useful information. For the English environment, there has been a lot of related work in the current data cleaning research field, but multilingual data cleaning has not attracted widespread attention. Multilingual data cleaning is still at a relatively early stage, and current algorithms are basically designed for specific fields. Therefore, multilingual data cleaning still needs to be further studied.

3   Knowledge Fusion

3.1   Background

Over the past decade there has been a rapid development of knowledge fusion in natural language processing and artificial intelligence. The knowledge fusion can be roughly divided into two major categories: Open network knowledge fusion and knowledge fusion of multi-source knowledge base. Open network knowledge fusion is mainly through the fusion of the knowledge acquired from the Internet and the knowledge existing in the knowledge base. Multi-source knowledge base is the fusion of overlapping or complementary knowledge in different knowledge bases. Open network knowledge fusion has received substantial interest. This section will elaborate on its related methods. The steps of knowledge fusion are shown in Fig. 2.

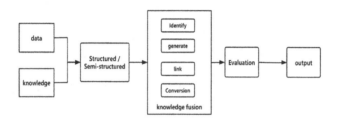

Fig. 2. Knowledge fusion.

The purpose of knowledge fusion is to preprocess knowledge and perform fusion operation on the processed knowledge followed by evaluating the knowledge and updating the evaluated knowledge to the knowledge graph or knowledge base in the end. Several typical methods currently exist for the knowledge fusion, including entity linking, attribute graph matching and constructing high-precision knowledge base.

3.2   Problem Definition

The knowledge graph contains an ontology layer that describes abstract knowledge and an instance layer that describes facts. The ontology layer is used to describe abstract concepts, axioms, and attributes in a specific field. The instance layer is used to describe specific entity objects, the relationships between entities, and contains a lot of facts and data. A Knowledge Graph G is consists of a combination of entities and relationship triples in the form of $< h, r, t >$, where r is a relationship between two entities h (subject) and t (object). Given two KGs G_1 and G_2, the task of knowledge fusion is to find all pair $< h_1, h_2 >$ where $h_1 \in G_1, h_2 \in G_2$, and entity h_1 and h_2 represent the same real-world entity. In general, it is to fuse the knowledge graphs of two into one target knowledge graph.

3.3   Related Methods

Entity Linking. Entity linking is to map the mention in the text to the entity in the given knowledge base or knowledge graph. The meaning of mentions is usually ambiguous, different named entities may have the same representation, and the same entity may have multiple aliases. So, entity linking remains a major challenge in text understanding. There are many existing methods for entity links, such as the end-to-end neural entity linking model [8] and the multi-relation neural model modeling potential relationships between mentions to strengthen entity linking [9].

We will now demonstrate a new method on this problem. The basic idea of the method used in this section [10] is as follows: In this chapter, global entity linking are defined as sequence decision problems, and deep reinforcement learning is used to solve sequence decision problems. The model of this method has three modules, namely (1) local encoder (2) global encoder (3) entity selector.

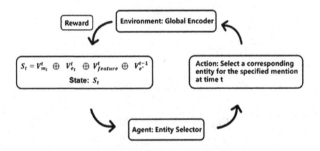

Fig. 3. The basic idea of deep reinforcement learning based entity linking.

Modules (2) and (3) are defined as deep reinforcement learning environment. The functions of each module are described as follows.

(1) Local Encoder: Embed the reference context word [11] sequence into the Long Short-Term Memory (LSTM) to encode it into a fixed size vector representation V_{m_t}, then, the candidate entity pretrained embedding and the candidate entity context word description encoded by the LSTM neural network are concatenate together. The result is a vector representation $V_{e_t^i}$. At Last, V_{m_t} and $V_{e_t^i}$ are concatenate into a vector representation, which is used as the input of the entity selector, and this representation is input into a multilayer perceptron (MLP) to calculate the local similarity. Figure 3 is the basic idea of deep reinforcement learning based entity linking.

(2) Global Encoder: First break the text into certain paragraphs. Then, according to the calculation result of the local similarity, the disambiguation mentions orders are sorted. After performing all actions in the sequence, the agent will get a delay reward. Notably, the last output of the global encoder is also the current input of the entity selector.

(3) Entity Selector: As shown in Fig. 3, in the deep reinforcement learning model, the entity selector is considered as an agent, which is actually a strategy network. State is the concatenate result of the output of the local encoder and the feature vector of the candidate entity and the output vector of the global encoder at time $t-1$. Action is defined as selecting a corresponding candidate entity for the specified mention at time t. The reward is a delayed reward. The entity selector selects the candidate entity for the mention which is the result of the entity linking.

There are two main techniques for entity linking, that is, mention identification and entity disambiguation. Entity linking model can be roughly divided into local model and global model. The local model only considers how the entity linking task is completed for a single entity, while the global model optimizes the result of entity linking from the perspective of the entire entity set. In the early stage, the disambiguation of the mention was carried out separately through the local model. The methods proposed by [30–33] use the similar ideas which rank mention according to the difficulty of mention disambiguation when performing entity linking. However, these methods do not take into account the impact of previous disambiguation mention on subsequent disambiguation. In other words, they have insufficient consideration at the global model level. Since the results of entity linking may affect each other for different entities, it is necessary to consider the issue of entity linking from the global view. An end-to-end model for entity linking is proposed by [8]. The main idea is to connect the mention recognition process and the entity disambiguation process to obtain the embedding of the mention, and then perform the entity disambiguation according to the similarity in both local and global view. In the Disambiguation-Only model, there are entity disambiguation methods that consider local and global influences and relationships between entities [9].

Reinforcement learning (RL) is good at solving sequential decision problems, so local and global models can be introduced naturally based on RL. RL is more and more widely used in Natural Language Processing (NLP). But the effectiveness of the method based on reinforcement learning needs to be improved. There is a way to use reinforcement learning to do relational classification tasks [34] to filter out noisy data and redundant structure in sentences. Another work proposes an actor-critic method to do sequence prediction for machine translation [35]. Futhermore, there is a work using reinforcement learning to solve the problem of dialogue generation. However, how to define the reward value in natural language processing is still an open problem. The method provided in [35] gives a good example of defining reward. The reward is computed from the text classifier's prediction based on the structured representation, and the structured representation is determined by a sequence of actions which delete or retain a word.

All in all, the entity linking methods based on deep reinforcement learning can solve the shortcomings of existing methods very well. They regard the global entity linking as a sequence decision problem and reduce the introduction of noisy data. This is the first time that deep reinforcement learning combine with entity linking to take advantage of each other. The good combination of global model and local model achieves good results on the existing well-known datasets. However, One of the main obstacles is RL is difficult to apply well in natural language processing. Many NLP studies are based on datasets for learning; however, the vitality of reinforcement learning is that it needs continuous feedback with the environment while the environment needs infinite labeled samples. Based on the current situation, the NLP environment cannot give reinforcement learning such an environment, and the feedback may not be necessarily of high quality. Although there are some challenges in the application of RL method in the field of NLP, there are still many methods trying to use RL to solve the NLP problem involved in Entity Linking in recent years. This is mainly because Entity Linking often involves sequential decision-making, and RL usually models the problem as a Markov decision process, so it is suitable for dealing with sequential decision-making problems in many scenarios. However, for NLP problems, a large amount of labeled corpus is still needed in many applications, so it is more common to use supervised learning. Using RL to solve NLP problems requires more careful and natural modeling of the environment, actions, and rewards. How to better complete the modeling still needs further research.

Entity Matching. Entity matching (also known as duplicate identification, record linking or entity resolution) is a key task of data integration and data cleaning. Its purpose is to identify entities that refer to the same entity in the real world [39]. Entity matching can either perform on a data set of text type, or perform on a data set of graph structure. Graphs keys (GKs) aim to uniquely identify entities represented by vertices in a graph. Therefore, we can try to solve the Entity Matching problem in the knowledge graph based on GKs. GKs have been researched and applied in emerging knowledge fusion technology [12] and fact verification [13]. The method to be described in this section [14] proposes a class of Ontological Graph Keys (OGKs). OGK is a variant of the graph key, which relaxes the constraints and adds ontology matching in the conventional graph keys. The entity matching algorithm (OGK-EM) in this chapter first uses "top-down" fashion to decompose each OGK into a set of entity keys with a tree pattern, and conduct early verification. For the purpose of refining, "Bottom-up" synthesis by merging two similar matches from the dependency graph. As a result of limited resources, proposed a budget-based method of OGK-EM called BOGK-EM. The BOGK-EM algorithm is matched based on limited costs.

The state-of-the-art research on entity matching is Magellan entity matching management system [26]. it is an easy access to an interactive script environment. Other examination is active learning method based on random sampling [40], exploring advantages and limitations of deep learning in entity matching [41]. For text and dirty data, complex deep learning methods have advantages over existing methods but require longer time. It should be pointed out that introducing domain-specific knowledge into deep learning models is a good research direction. The method in this section is based on ontology-based entity matching, which solves the previous problem of too strict graph keys, and solves the nodes and structures that cannot be described with different syntax but have the same semantics. However, the time complexity of calculation still needs to be strengthened. The calculations involved in graph-based calculations are very large. Out of consideration, a set of cost-based algorithms with pruning are designed to optimize the calculation time. In the future, the graph embedding can be compared with the method in this section, and there may be new discoveries. Deep learning is also a very hot technique using in NLP, and the methods of entity matching are flourishing. Enterprises also have great demand for this. For example, some huge demand for consumer behavior prediction requires entity matching. Therefore, entity matching is a promising and valuable research direction.

Entity Alignment. Another task in knowledge fusion is entity alignment. The task of aligning entities across knowledge graphs is to find the real entities of the same world from two different knowledge graphs. The issue of entity alignment is very similar to Entity matching. The reason why we discuss it separately here is because when we talk about "entity alignment", we more often refer to entities in the knowledge base. However, the entities involved in Entity Matching may refer to entities in a broader sense, such as records in a relational database, or an element in an XML document.

There are currently many solutions to this task. The three most common methods are string-similarity-based methods, embedding-based methods, and graph-neural-network-based methods. String-similarity-based methods determine the alignment relationship between entities by calculating the similarity between texts [56,57]. Embedding-based methods embed the entities, relationships, and attributes in the knowledge graph into a low-dimensional dense vector space [58–60]. These methods use vectors to reflect the characteristics and relationships of each element, and then compare the vector similarity to determine the alignment of entities. The method in [60] is based on embedding to complete the entity alignment task. Its advantage is that by embedding attributes, this method almost avoids the seed entities needed in most other entity alignment methods. The method is mainly composed of the following three parts, (1) predicate alignment, (2) embedding learning, (3) entity alignment. It consists of three parts: 1. The predicate alignment part corresponds to the two KG predicates and rewrites them into a unified name. Because there are certain rules for naming different predicates, such as *rdfs:label*, *geo:wgs84pos#lat*, and *geo:wgs84pos#long*, etc. There are also some predicates that are locally identical, for example, *dbp:diedIn* vs. *yago:diedIn*, and *dbp:bornIn* vs. *yago:wasBornIn*. Therefore, this method unifies the expression of the predicate, thus establishing the predicate alignment between the graphs. 2. Embedding learning, Through predicate alignment, the triples of the two knowledge graphs share a unified predicate space. In the same space, it can learn the structure embedding and the embedding of attribute characters, and finally generate a unified entity vector space. First, it uses TransE [61] to learn structure embedding, and pay more attention to the learning of triples of alignment predicates. Then, it learns attribute embedding, structure embedding and character embedding learned to generate embedding. 3.It puts the previously obtained embedding into the entity alignment equation to calculate the correct entity pair.

$$h_{map} = \arg\max_{h_2 \in G_2} \cos(h_1, h_2) \tag{2}$$

The overall flow chart of this method is shown in Fig. 4.

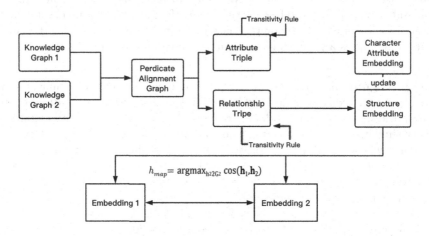

Fig. 4. Entity alignment.

With the rise of graph neural network technology (GNN), graph-neural-network-based entity alignment methods have also benn studied [62–65]. These methods are based on GNN learning the node representation in the graph, obtain the representation vector of the entity in the knowledge graph, and further complete the entity alignment task in the knowledge graph by comparing the similarity of the vectors. However, most of the existing GNNs learn node representations for relatively simple graphs, and knowledge graphs are a kind of complex graphs, so how to make GNN-based methods work better on entity alignment tasks requires further research.

Construction of High-Precision Knowledge Base. Knowledge Base (KB) is the foundation of knowledge fusion and many popular applications. Maintaining high accuracy of knowledge is essential for KB. However, knowledge base that stores the subjective or factual attributes of an entity cannot simply estimate the accuracy of knowledge. The method proposed by [15] proposes a high-precision knowledge base method for establishing location and its subjective and factual attributes. The purpose is to build a knowledge base that roughly refers to each (location-attribute) pair, and records whether this location has that attribute. It is mainly for modeling the data in google map. It is necessary here to clarify exactly what is meant by Yes Rate. Yes Rate is defined as the proportion of users who agree that the entity has this attribute and is modeled as a random variable with beta distribution. In order to tackle the cold start, this method uses a preset yes rate value. To get better performance, they further observe the votes of other (position-attribute) pairs and modify the parameters in the model. The method in this section consists of three parts with three learning models: The first part is a multi-task baseline. Location embedding e_l obtained from the input location information x_l can be used as the input of the multi-task learning neural network to estimate the probability that the l-th location entity has each attribute. The second part is the Alien Vote architecture which is built on the basis of multi-task learning. Based on Alien Vote, a vector is generated for each pair (l, a). More precisely, V_{la} is a vector for each location l and attribute a, the content of which is the yes rate of the attribute different from a contained in location l. That is,

$$V_{l\bar{a}} = \{(l', a') : l' = l, a' \neq a\} \tag{3}$$

Use e_l and V_{la} embedded links as neural network input, we finally get the probability of each attribute that the l-th position entity has. The third part is the Independent Alien Votearchitecture, the model is to establish a neural network for each attribute, and generate a probability that a position l has the attribute a by inputting alien voting vector and auxiliary information vector. Since a part of the knowledge base is subjective knowledge (that is, knowledge based on human opinions), it is very difficult to verify this part of knowledge without manpower. Therefore, this method uses crowdsourcing to complete knowledge verification, and then build a high-precision knowledge base. The knowledge base constructed by the crowdsourcing method has high accuracy and we will be further discussed below.

The Method Based on Crowdsourcing: Crowdsourcing based Methods building a knowledge base can reduce the gap between existing objective knowledge and subjective queries [42]. There are also many methods [43,44] model users' expertise and task difficulty, and the trained model can infer the true label of the task. However, crowdsourcing methods suffer from the high cost issue, so there are some crowdsourcing cost optimization works [16,17]. The alien vote method in this section is similar to the Co-Factor model method based on word embedding [45]. The completeness of the knowledge base (i.e., the proportion of real facts covered in the knowledge base) is also very important, and there are works detecting the completeness of the knowledge base [46].

The Method Based on Sememe: In linguistics, Sememe is defined as the smallest semantic unit of human language. Recently, a considerable literature has grown up around the theme of sememe. There is a multilingual encyclopedia that uses Babel Net, a multilingual encyclopedia, to construct a multilingual sememe knowledge base. It is a method to mark meanings for words in many different languages [47]. There is also a method for modeling semantic assemblage using sememe [48], and a work to evaluate the semantic rationality of sentences [49].

3.4 Discussions on Knowledge Fusion for MDATA

Since the knowledge representation of MDATA is more complex than the classical knowledge representation, involving major entities, secondary entities, and spatiotemporal attributes, the problem of knowledge fusion is also more complicated to solve. On the one hand, the relationship between different entities is more volatile; on the other hand, the result of knowledge fusion may also change with the temporal and spatial changes of the real world.

- When doing entity linking, entity matching, and entity alignment, we first need to distinguish relations between primary entities and secondary entities. Generally speaking, a primary entity is more (but not absolute) "important" than a secondary entity. Therefore, it is necessary to match primary entities first. After the fusion of primary entities are completed, the results of the primary entity can be used as a reference to match the secondary entities. However, since a secondary entity may be related to multiple primary entities, the selection of the reference entities is also a problem worthy of further discussion.
- In addition, since many entities or relationships in MDATA have clear spatio-temporal characteristics, some fusion results may only be correct when certain spatiotemporal conditions are met. Therefore, as time goes by or spatial conditions change, the results of knowledge fusion may also change. How to determine the temporal and spatial conditions of the fusion and how to perceive the changes in the fusion results in time are very challenging issues.

4 Chapter Summary

In the information age, knowledge graph and knowledge base heterogeneous problems are widespread, and knowledge fusion technology is urgently needed to break this heterogeneous barrier. Data quality and data cleaning is the first step in knowledge fusion. If there is no guarantee of correct data, the fusion of knowledge is useless. The principal theoretical implication of this study is that we describe several methods of knowledge fusion, considering spatiotemporal data quality and data cleaning, including entity linking, ontology-based attribute graph matching, knowledge base construction, and data detection and data repair. The advantages and disadvantages of current technology are introduced respectively.

Open network knowledge fusion in knowledge fusion is now a hot research topic. With the increasing scale of data and knowledge bases in the network, the technical requirements for knowledge fusion are becoming higher and higher. Not only better knowledge fusion technology is needed, but also higher quality knowledge fusion technology is needed. A major technical hotspot in knowledge fusion is entity linking. At present, the research field of entity linking includes short text and entity linking research lacking contextual language environment, and research of building end-to-end entity linking. How to better integrate prior knowledge is also a research point. The research hotspot in the field of data quality and data cleaning is to establish an overall cleaning framework. Existing research on data quality and data cleaning in English has been relatively mature. However, there are many differences between Chinese and English data cleaning. At present, the methods of data quality and data cleaning in Chinese are only for specific fields, and lack of mature general framework. In addition, the time complexities of the data cleaning and knowledge fusion methods are relatively high, so that a lightweight framework is required.

All in all, looking at the areas of knowledge integration, data quality and data cleansing, there is still much work to be done. If the representation of MDATA is introduced, many (maybe inherently difficult) problems may face greater challenges. Through the above analysis and discussion, we hope to provide some help and inspiration for knowledge fusion and data quality research.

References

1. Singhal, A.: Introducing the knowledge graph: things, not strings. J. Google (2012)
2. Hachey, B., Radford, W., Nothman, J., Honnibal, M., Curran, J.R.: Evaluating entity linking with wikipedia. Artif. Intell. **194**, 130–150 (2013)
3. Bollacker, K., Evans, C., Paritosh, P., Sturge, T., Taylor, J.: Freebase: a collaboratively created graph database for structuring human knowledge. In: Proceedings of the: ACM SIGMOD International Conference on Management of Data (SIGMOD 2008), pp. 1247–1250. Association for Computing Machinery, New York, NY, USA (2008)
4. Suchanek, F.M., Kasneci, G., Weikum, G.: YAGO: a core of semantic knowledge. In: Proceedings of the 16th International Conference on World Wide Web (WWW 2007). Association for Computing Machinery, New York, NY, USA, pp. 697–706 (2007)
5. Li, M., Li, J., Cheng, S., Sun, Y.: Uncertain rule based method for determining data currency. IEICE Trans. Inf. Syst. **101**(10), 2447–2457 (2018)
6. Australian Government, "Smart city sensor data" (2017). https://data.gov.au
7. Chen, D.: Online retail data set (2015). https://archive.ics.uci.edu/ml/
8. Kolitsas, N., Ganea, O.E., Hofmann, T.: End-to-end neural entity linking. arXiv preprint arXiv:1808.07699 (2018)
9. Le, P., Titov, I.: Improving entity linking by modeling latent relations between mentions. In: Proceedings of the 56th Annual Meeting of the Association for Computational Linguistics, pp. 1595–1604 (2018)
10. Fang, Z., Cao, Y., Li, Q., et al.: Joint entity linking with deep reinforcement learning. In: The World Wide Web Conference, pp. 438–447 (2019)
11. Mikolov, T.,Chen, K., Corrado, G., Dean, J.: Efficient estimation of word representations in vector space. CoRR abs/1301.3781. arXiv:1301.3781 (2013)
12. Dong, X.L., Gabrilovich, E., Heitz, G., Horn, W., Murphy, K., Sun, S., Zhang, W.: From data fusion to knowledge fusion. VLDB **7**(10), 881–892 (2014)
13. Lin, P., Song, Q., Shen, J., Wu, Y.: Discovering graph patterns for fact checking in knowledge graphs. In: DASFAA, pp. 783–801 (2018)
14. Ma, H., Alipourlangouri, M., Wu, Y., et al.: Ontology-based entity matching in attributed graphs. Proc. VLDB Endowment **12**(10), 1195–1207 (2019)

15. Kobren, A., Barrio, P., Yakhnenko, O., et al.: Constructing high precision knowledge bases with subjective and factual attributes. In: Proceedings of the 25th ACM SIGKDD International Conference on Knowledge Discovery & Data Mining, pp. 2050–2058 (2019)
16. Chen, X., Lin, Q., Zhou, D.: Optimistic knowledge gradient policy for optimal budget allocation in crowdsourcing. In: International Conference on Machine Learning, pp. 64–72 (2013)
17. Karger, D.R., Oh, S., Shah, D.: Budget-optimal task allocation for reliable crowdsourcing systems. Oper. Res. **62**(1), 1–24 (2014)
18. Jeffery, S.R., Garofalakis, M., Franklin, M.J.: Adaptive cleaning for RFID data streams. VLDB **6**, 163–174 (2006)
19. Li, X., Dong, X.L., Lyons, K., et al.: Truth finding on the deep web: is the problem solved?. arXiv preprint arXiv:1503.00303 (2015)
20. Bohannon, P., Fan, W., Flaster, M., et al.: A cost-based model and effective heuristic for repairing constraints by value modification. In: Proceedings of the 2005 ACM SIGMOD International Conference on Management of Data, pp. 143–154 (2005)
21. Song, S., Zhang, A., Wang, J., et al.: SCREEN: stream data cleaning under speed constraints. In: Proceedings of the 2015 ACM SIGMOD International Conference on Management of Data, pp. 827–841 (2015)
22. Zheng, Z., Milani, M., Chiang, F.: CurrentClean: spatio-temporal cleaning of stale data. In: 2019 IEEE 35th International Conference on Data Engineering (ICDE), 172–183. IEEE (2019)
23. Box, G.E.P., Jenkins, G.M., Reinsel, G.C., et al.: Time Series Analysis: Forecasting and Control. John Wiley & Sons, Hoboken (2015)
24. Brillinger, D.R.: Time Series: Data Analysis and Theory. Siam (1981)
25. Park, G., Rutherford, A.C., Sohn, H., et al.: An outlier analysis framework for impedance-based structural health monitoring. J. Sound Vibr. **286**(1–2), 229–250 (2005)
26. Konda, P., Das, S., Suganthan, G.P., et al.: Magellan: toward building entity matching management systems. Proc. VLDB Endowment **9**(12), 1197–1208 (2016)
27. Zhang, H., Diao, Y., Immerman, N.: Recognizing patterns in streams with imprecise timestamps. Proc. VLDB Endowment **3**(1–2), 244–255 (2010)
28. Yakout, M., Berti-équille, L., Elmagarmid, A.K.: Don't be SCAREd: use SCalable Automatic REpairing with maximal likelihood and bounded changes. In: Proceedings of the 2013 ACM SIGMOD International Conference on Management of Data, pp. 553–564 (2013)
29. Milne, D., Witten, I.H.: Learning to link with Wikipedia. In: Proceedings of the 17th ACM Conference on Information and Knowledge Management, pp. 509–518 (2008)
30. Chen, Z., Ji, H.: Collaborative ranking: a case study on entity linking. In: Proceedings of the Conference on Empirical Methods in Natural Language Processing. Association for Computational Linguistics, pp. 771–781 (2011)
31. Dredze, M., McNamee, P., Rao, D., et al.: Entity disambiguation for knowledge base population. In: Proceedings of the 23rd International Conference on Computational Linguistics. Association for Computational Linguistics, pp. 277–285 (2010)
32. Tan, C., Wei, F., Ren, P., et al.: Entity linking for queries by searching Wikipedia sentences. arXiv preprint arXiv:1704.02788 (2017)
33. Guo, Z., Barbosa, D.: Robust named entity disambiguation with random walks. Semant. Web **9**(4), 459–479 (2018)

34. Feng, J., Huang, M., Zhao, L., et al.: Reinforcement learning for relation classification from noisy data. In: Thirty-Second AAAI Conference on Artificial Intelligence (2018)
35. Zhang, T., Huang, M., Zhao, L.: Learning structured representation for text classification via reinforcement learning. In: Thirty-Second AAAI Conference on Artificial Intelligence (2018)
36. Chen, J., Jönsson, P., Tamura, M., et al.: A simple method for reconstructing a high-quality NDVI time-series data set based on the Savitzky-Golay filter. Remote Sens. Environ. **91**(3–4), 332–344 (2004)
37. Zhang, A., Song, S., Wang, J., et al.: Time series data cleaning: from anomaly detection to anomaly repairing. Proc. VLDB Endowment **10**(10), 1046–1057 (2017)
38. Chu, X., Ilyas, I.F., Papotti, P.: Holistic data cleaning: putting violations into context. In: 2013 IEEE 29th International Conference on Data Engineering (ICDE), pp. 458–469. IEEE (2013)
39. Köpcke, H., Rahm, E.: Frameworks for entity matching: a comparison. Data Knowl. Eng. **69**(2), 197–210 (2010)
40. Brunner, U., Stockinger, K.: Entity matching on unstructured data: an active learning approach. In: 2019 6th Swiss Conference on Data Science (SDS), pp. 97–102. IEEE (2019)
41. Mudgal, S., Li, H., Rekatsinas, T., et al.: Deep learning for entity matching: a design space exploration. In: Proceedings of the 2018 International Conference on Management of Data, pp. 19–34 (2018)
42. Meng, R., Xin, H., Chen, L., et al.: Subjective knowledge acquisition and enrichment powered by crowdsourcing. arXiv preprint arXiv:1705.05720 (2017)
43. Welinder, P., Branson, S., Perona, P., et al.: The multidimensional wisdom of crowds. In: Advances in Neural Information Processing Systems, pp. 2424–2432 (2010)
44. Kajino, H., Tsuboi, Y., Sato, I., et al.: Learning from crowds and experts. In: Workshops at the Twenty-Sixth AAAI Conference on Artificial Intelligence (2012)
45. Liang, D., Altosaar, J., Charlin, L., et al.: Factorization meets the item embedding: regularizing matrix factorization with item co-occurrence. In: Proceedings of the 10th ACM Conference on Recommender Systems, pp. 59–66 (2016)
46. Galárraga, L., Razniewski, S., Amarilli, A., et al.: Predicting completeness in knowledge bases. In: Proceedings of the Tenth ACM International Conference on Web Search and Data Mining, pp. 375–383 (2017)
47. Qi, F., Chang, L., Sun, M., et al.: Towards building a multilingual sememe knowledge base: predicting sememes for BabelNet synsets. arXiv preprint arXiv:1912.01795 (2019)
48. Qi, F., Huang, J., Yang, C., et al.: Modeling semantic compositionality with sememe knowledge. arXiv preprint arXiv:1907.04744 (2019)
49. Liu, S., Xu, J., Ren, X.: Evaluating semantic rationality of a sentence: a sememe-word-matching neural network based on HowNet. In: Tang, J., Kan, M.-Y., Zhao, D., Li, S., Zan, H. (eds.) NLPCC 2019. LNCS (LNAI), vol. 11838, pp. 787–800. Springer, Cham (2019). https://doi.org/10.1007/978-3-030-32233-5_61
50. Keogh, E., Chu, S., Hart, D., et al.: An online algorithm for segmenting time series. In: Proceedings IEEE International Conference on Data Mining, vol. 2001, pp. 289–296. IEEE (2001)
51. Gardner Jr., E.S.: Exponential smoothing: the state of the art-Part II. Int. J. Forecast. **22**(4), 637–666 (2006)
52. Rekatsinas, T., Chu, X., Ilyas, I.F., et al.: HoloClean: holistic data repairs with probabilistic inference. arXiv preprint arXiv:1702.00820 (2017)

53. Mayfield, C., Neville, J., Prabhakar, S.: ERACER: a database approach for statistical inference and data cleaning. In: Proceedings of the 2010 ACM SIGMOD International Conference on Management of Data, pp. 75–86 (2010)

54. Krishnan, S., Franklin, M.J., Goldberg, K., et al.: ActiveClean: an interactive data cleaning framework for modern machine learning. In: Proceedings of the 2016 International Conference on Management of Data, pp. 2117–2120 (2016)

55. Li, M., Li, J.: A minimized-rule based approach for improving data currency. J. Comb. Optim. **32**(3), 812–841 (2016)

56. Ngomo, A.-C.N., Auer, S.: LIMES: a time-efficient approach for large-scale link discovery on the web of data. In: Proceedings of the Twenty-Second international joint conference on Artificial Intelligence(IJCAI 2011), pp. 2312–2317 (2011)

57. Scharffe, F., Liu, Y., Zhou, C., RDF-AI: an architecture for RDF datasets matching, fusion and interlink. In: Proceeding of IJCAI, : Workshop on Identity, Reference, and Knowledge Representation (IR-KR). Pasadena (CA US), vol. 2009, p. 23 (2009)

58. Zhu, H., Xie, R., Liu, Z., Sun, M.: Iterative entity alignment via joint knowledge embeddings. In: Proceedings of International Joint Conference on Artificial Intelligence, pp. 4258–4264 (2017)

59. Zhang, Q., Sun, Z., Hu, W., et al.: Multi-view knowledge graph embedding for entity alignment. In: Proceedings of the Twenty-Eighth International Joint Conference on Artificial Intelligence, pp. 5429–5435 (2017)

60. Trisedya, B.D., Qi, J., Zhang, R.: Entity alignment between knowledge graphs using attribute embeddings. In: Proceedings of the AAAI Conference on Artificial Intelligence, vol. 33, pp. 297–304 (2019)

61. Bordes, A., Usunier, N., Garcia-Duran, A., et al.: Translating embeddings for modeling multi-relational data. In: Advances in Neural Information Processing Systems, vol. 26, pp. 2787–2795 (2013)

62. Wu, Y., Liu, X., Feng, Y., et al.: Relation-aware entity alignment for heterogeneous knowledge graphs. In: Proceedings of the AAAI Conference on Artificial Intelligence, pp. 5278–5284 (2019)

63. Wang, Z., Lv, Q., Lan, X., et al.: Cross-lingual knowledge graph alignment via graph convolutional networks. In: Proceedings of the 2018 Conference on Empirical Methods in Natural Language Processing, pp. 349–357 (2018)

64. Cao, Y., Liu, Z., Li, C., et al.: Multi-channel graph neural network for entity alignment. In: Proceedings of the 57th Annual Meeting of the Association for Computational Linguistics, pp. 1452–1461 (2019)

65. Sun, Z., Wang, C., Hu, W., et al.: Knowledge graph alignment network with gated multi-hop neighborhood aggregation. In: Proceedings of the AAAI Conference on Artificial Intelligence, vol. 34, no. 01, pp. 222–229 (2020)

Chinese Named Entity Recognition: Applications and Challenges

Qisen Xi[1], Yizhi Ren[1(✉)], Siyu Yao[1], Guohua Wu[1], Gongxun Miao[2], and Zhen Zhang[1]

[1] Cyberspace of School, Hangzhou Dianzi University, Hangzhou 310018, China
{xiqs,renyz,yaosy,wugh,zhangzhen}@hdu.edu.cn
[2] Zhongfu Information Inc., Jinan 250101, China
miaogx@zhonfu.net

Abstract. Chinese Named Entity Recognition (NER) is an important task in Chinese natural language processing, which has been widely used in automatic question answering, reading comprehension, knowledge graph, machine translation and other fields. With the development of natural language processing techniques and the enhancement of text mining, the acquisition of semantic knowledge in text area becomes very important, and named entity recognition is the foundation of information application technology such as relationship extraction, which has important significance. In this chapter, we first provide a comprehensive review of traditional approaches. Then, we present the differences of between Chinese NER and NER, and describe the details of its application. We also introduce the challenge of Chinese entity recognition. Last, we compare recent works, give a vision about future work and propose the application in the Multi-dimensional Data Association and inTelligent Analysis (MDATA) model.

Keywords: MDATA · Named entity recognition · Chinese named entity recognition

1 Introduction

Named entities generally refer to entities with specific meaning or strong referentiality in the text, which usually person name, locations name, organization name, date and time, proper nouns, etc. Academically, the named entities generally include 3 categories (entity category, time category, number category) and 7 subcategories (person's name, location name, organization name, time, date, currency, percentage). Named entity recognition is the process about extracts the above entities from input text, and can identify more types of entities.

In practical applications, the NER model usually only needs to identify the person's name, place name, organization name, date and time, and some systems will also provide proper noun results (such as abbreviations, conference name, product name, etc.). In addition, in some application scenarios, entities in a specific field will be given, such as book titles, song titles, and journal titles.

© Springer Nature Switzerland AG 2021
Y. Jia et al. (Eds.): MDATA: A New Knowledge Representation Model, LNCS 12647, pp. 51–81, 2021.
https://doi.org/10.1007/978-3-030-71590-8_4

Formally, in NER model, given a sequence of tokens s $= <w_1, w_2, ..., w_N>$, the output list of tuples is $<I_s, I_e, t>$, each of which is a named entity mentioned in s. In this tuples, the start and the end indexes of a named entity is represented as $I_s \in [1, N]$ and $I_e \in [1, N]$ [1], and the entity type is represented as t. In Fig. 1, it shows an example about a NER process. Inputing a sentence in the NER model, and after recognition, output the three entities Person, Time and Location.

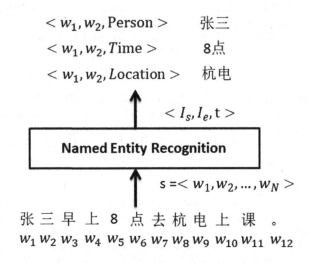

Fig. 1. A named entity recognition task

2   Background

We introduced the development and conventional methods of NER in recent years. And then introduced the application of NER.

2.1   Development of NER Method

As to the techniques applied in NER, there are four main streams [1]: (1) rule-based approaches, (2) unsupervised learning approaches, (3) machine learning approaches, and (4) deep learning approaches.

Rule-Based Approaches. Rule-based approaches, which do not need annotated data, but rely on manual rules. Such as specific domain dictionaries, including the Synonymous Lin dictionary, Syntactic vocabulary template and Regular expression.

Unsupervised Learning Approaches. It is mainly based on the method of clustering. According to the text similarity, different clusters are obtained, representing different entity category groups. Commonly used features or auxiliary information include vocabulary resources, corpus statistical information (TF-IDF), shallow semantic information (NP-chunking), etc.

Machine Learning Approaches. There are some methods for NER, such as Hidden Markov Models (HMMs), Decision Tree (DT), Maximum Entropy Model (MEM), Maximum Entropy Markov Models (HEMMs), support vector machine (svm) and conditional random fields (CRFs).

Deep Learning Approaches. With the development of deep learning, NER based on deep learning has continuously achieved SOTA results. Compared with traditional methods, deep learning has the following advantages:

1) Powerful vector representation ability;
2) Powerful computing power;
3) Non-linear mapping ability from input to output;
4) The ability of learning high-dimensional latent semantic information;
5) End-to-end training method.

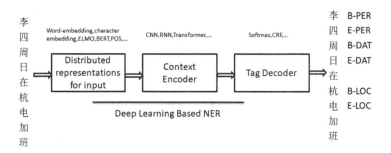

Fig. 2. Deep learning based NER

Figure 2 shows the based model. The model consists of distributed representations for input, context encoder, tag decoder.

(1) Distributed representations for input. The distributed representation of the input refers to embedding the original input sequence, or adding some features used in traditional shallow supervised models in addition to embedding. Word embedding such as Glove, Word2Vec, Random Init, which is the more common input presentation layer, that is the vector representation of the word is directly found through the index of the word. This Character embedding is also often

used in English, that is, the character sequence of the word is encoded with the sequence coding models, such as RNN, CNN and Transformer, to obtain the character level representation of the word. The pretrained Contextual Embeddings like ELMo and BERT is another commonly input representation layer. The last type is other features, such as POS, gazetters, linguistic dependency. From the results of recent years, it is better to combine different models to embedding, which can represent the deeper characteristics of the input information.

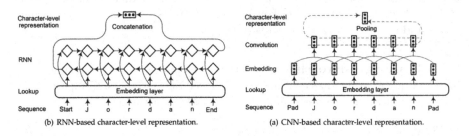

(b) RNN-based character-level representation.   (a) CNN-based character-level representation.

Fig. 3. The CNN and RNN based model in distributed representations [1]

(2) Context encoder. Through the operations distributed representations for input in the part, we use the Lookup Table to find the embedding of the corresponding characters, words, etc., and then convert the original text into a low-level, dense semantic vector. The context encoder part will perform further operations on the transformed semantic vector, encoding the original features, and then represent the semantic information of the sentence. Context encoding is mainly divided into several methods: CNN, RNN, Transformer, etc. As a semantic coding tool, CNN can extract information about adjacent key characters through the operation of the convolution kernel, similar to the idea of N-gram. However, it cannot extract the long dependency relationship of words, and is generally used as a part of feature extraction to combine with features extracted from other network structures, RNN can model the dependency on the input through the hidden layer, and the output represents the semantics of the sentence, but due to its loop structure, it will run slower [1]. In recent years, the proposal of Transformer has proposed a new method for Context encoder. Transformer mostly uses a self-attention mechanism. GPT, Bert, XLNET, ALBERT, etc. developed on this basis have achieved SOTA effects in the current NER field.

(3) Tag decoder. Tag decoder is the final stage in a NER model. In the tag encoder stage, the semantic representation of the sentence is decoded into the tag sequence of each character in the sentence. There are about four methods of Tag decoder: Softmax, CRF, RNNs, Pointer Network. Softmax treats the NER problem as a classification problem and predicts the label of each character in the sentence separately. However, this processing method usually has a poor

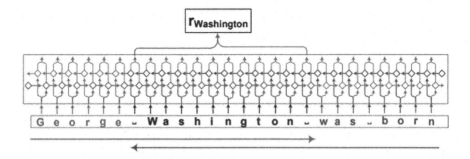

Fig. 4. The sentence "Washington" in contextual encoder [1]

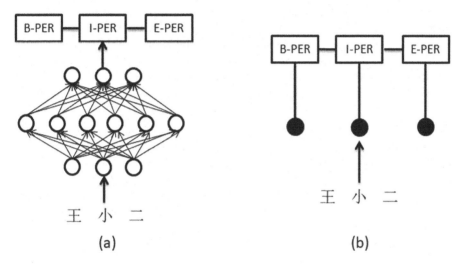

Fig. 5. Tag decoders: Softmax, CRF

effect because it does not take the association relationship and sequence information between the tags into account. CRF regards the label to be predicted as a sequence, this is currently the best way. The information of the tag sequence can be fully considered. The RNNs model regards the label to be predicted as a text sequence. Generally use RNNs as basic components to form a Sequence-to-Sequence structure.

2.2 Applications of Chinese NER

Currently, Chinese Named Entity Recognition (CNER) has made great achievements in the public domain, such as in the dataset of People's Daily. However, only a small number of entity types (three types) exists in these datasets. With the development of professional domain, the requirement for knowledge graph construction and question answering system is becoming more and more urgent in the professional domain. Chinese named entity recognition in the professional field is particularly important. Professional domain data are different from public, because they have all kinds of entities.

Business. The "information explosion" caused by the advent of big data era, which makes it easy for people to obtain a large amount of information, but at the same time, it also brings many problems, such as complicated sources of information, disorder data, is difficult to distinguish between true from false. These issues make it difficult to fully understand the business. The enterprise-related knowledge required by users is usually stable and common in the industry, but this knowledge usually exists in different forms (such as graphics, documents, etc.), and the storage location is sparse and the distribution platform is widely dispersed, so the search is time-consuming. It is very important to find the potential relationships between various information in the enterprise, such as real-time financial announcements and news on the Internet. Under this premise, the Bi-LSTM-CRF model [2] is applied in the named entity recognition tasks to help users excavate and organize business information, so as to realize the named entity recognition of three types of entities in the business domain.

Mechanical Applications. Manufacturing is focused on production experience, which is particularly essential for mining and reusing industry knowledge. With the continuous development of manufacturing and technology, more and more researchers are focusing on using advanced technology to mine manufacturing data to help manufacturing production. It is necessary to obtain better performance NER from the manufacturing domain text and manufacturing knowledge, to feed back into actual production. In [3], it combined ALBERT-AttBiLSTM-CRF and transfer learning to solve the CNER task.

Social Media. Due to the informality of language and the strong noise in social media texts, named entity recognition in Chinese social media is an important but difficult task. Most of the previous methods on NER have focused on supervised learning in-domain, which is limited by the scarce annotated data in social media. A BiLSTM-CRF is proposed based on the characteristics of radical level feature and self-concern to solve the clinical Chinese NER problem [4]. Afterwards, a unified feature model for the NER problem in Chinese social media, which can learn from foreign corpus and unannotated texts in the domain [5]. The unified model includes two methods for cross-domain learning and semi-supervised learning.

Military. Considering the structural characteristics of military equipment names, it proposed a deep neural network model recognition method based on word vectors and state features in [6]. In view of the difficulty of constructing feature templates in military texts, an entity recognition framework based on BiLSTM-CRF is introduced in [7]. They combined words and character vectors as input to improve the performance of the model. Yin et al. described an annotation strategy that considers fuzzy entity boundaries, combined with domain expert knowledge, and constructed Military Corpus based on microblog data [8]. Under the guidance of the word vector expression layer of the bidirectional encoder, the model is used to obtain word-level characters under the guidance of BERT. Under the direction of BiLSTM, the layer extracts contextual features, forms a feature matrix, and finally uses CRF to generate the optimal tag sequence.

Spatial-temporal Network. Geographical relationship extraction is to identify the semantic relationship between two geographical concepts or entities from the text, such as temporal relationship, spatial relationship, attribute relationship, state relationship, etc. Existing research focuses on temporal and spatial relationship extraction. Since each language has a set of vocabulary systems that can fully show spatial relationships, it is difficult to extract spatial relationships. The method of pattern matching can realize the extraction of named entities in sentence units. At the same time, by constructing a geographic relationship knowledge base that combines ontology, facts, and synonyms, it can be used to filter the results of geographical relationship extraction [9].

The spatial information described in natural language mainly includes addresses, coordinates, and spatial relationships, etc. Address information can be extracted by referring to the geographical entity recognition method. On this basis, with the reference to the standard address database, the mapping relationship between the spatial information described by natural language and the geographic coordinates is established with the help of geocoding technology. In addition, when performing named entity recognition on text, attributes are also required value standardization [10]. First, according to a unified concept classification system, semantic web alignment technology is used to map geographic knowledge concepts to solve the problem of inconsistencies in the granularity and level of geographic knowledge; Second, comprehensive consideration of geographic entity types, text similarity and attribute characteristics, etc., establish each concept. The hierarchical geographic entity linkage solves the ambiguity of geographic entity knowledge in different data sources; Finally, using techniques such as conflict detection and truth discovery, the knowledge of relationships between different geographic entities is removed, associated and merged [11].

3 Problem Definition

3.1 The Difference Between Chinese NER and NER

Compared with English, NER on Chinese text faces more challenges. It is known that Asian languages like Chinese are naturally logographic. There are no conventional linguistic features (like capitalization) available for NER. Moreover, Chinese characters and words have complex relations. Given no delimiter between characters, a word can be comprised of a single character or multi-character (i.e. n-char). Meanwhile, the meaning of Chinese vocabulary can be inferred by its constituent characters. For instance, the meaning of confidence in Chinese can be derived by self and belief. Furthermore, Chinese characters often have hieroglyphic forms. The same etyma often indicates similar semantics. Besides, to build a new large NER dataset reflecting new words and memes over Chinese text is often expensive and labor-intensive [12].

3.2   Challenge in Chinese NER

Chinese NER (CNER) challenges are more difficult than NER. NER have obvious formal signs, for example, the first letter of each word in the entity should be capitalized, so it is relatively easy to identify the entity boundary. The focus of the task is to determine the type of entity. Due to the particularity of Chinese, there is no similarity between text and space identifiers or capital letters in English texts, such as clear boundaries, it cannot distinguish the boundary of the words and the boundary of the Chinese entities clearly, makes the CNER task more complex, and relative to the entity type annotation subtasks, entity boundary recognition is more difficult.

The first step of traditional CNER is word segmentation, which determines the boundary of words, and then builds a model for recognition according to the semantic features of words. This method not only requires manual design and construction of a large number of input features for experiments to obtain the optimal combination of features, which will take a lot of time and effort, but also relies heavily on the effect of Chinese word segmentation, and accumulates the error of word segmentation in the entity recognition process, affecting the final recognition effect. From segmentation to NER pipeline, however, can suffer the potential issue of error propagation, since NEs are an important source of OOV in segmentation, and incorrectly segmented entity boundaries lead to NER errors [13]. As shown in Fig. 6, for example, inputting a sentence in the NER pipeline, because of the characteristics of Chinese word segmentation, the word segmentation may be wrong. After that, no matter how the sequence is labeled, the correct entity cannot be extracted.

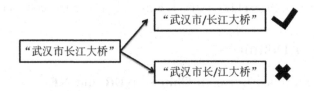

Fig. 6. Ambiguity of Chinese word segmentation

In addition, there are many types of Chinese named entities, and new ones are emerging. The structure of Chinese named entities is quite complex. There is no certain limit on the length of some types of named entities, and different entities have different structures. For example, there are a lot of nesting, aliases, acronyms and other problems in organization names, so there are no strict rules to follow. Among people's names, there are also very long names of ethnic minorities or translated foreign names, and there is no uniform word form specification. Therefore, the recognition recall of such named entities is relatively low. At the same time, in different domains and scenarios, the extensions of the named entities are also different. Correctly labeling these named entity types usually involves contextual semantic analysis, which makes it difficult to identify Chinese named entities.

4   Related Methods

Our aim in developing this taxonomy is to provide a clearer angel of current approaches to CNER, and to identify gaps in these techniques which will help us to identify directions for future research. Based on the level of granularity, most of the models can be divided into three categories: word-based model, character-based model, and lexical-based model.

4.1   Word Based Chinese NER

Some studies have proposed some Chinese NER methods, which usually embed a large amount of text through traditional word embedding methods such as Word2Vec. Recent studies have shown the importance of some deep learning methods such as LSTM and pre-training methods (BERT). There are also studies that have proposed new training methods such as CW2VEC [15].

Word Segmentation. Word segmentation has been pursued with considerable efforts in the Chinese NLP community. And word segmentation is the foundation of Word-based Chinese NER (Table 1).

In [34], it considered the domain adaptation problem for joint segmentation and POS-tagging. Trained using the Chinese Treebank, the accuracy of the baseline system on the test data of the Internet literature was greatly reduced. He applied self-training and unsupervised clustering to improve the accuracy of the target-domain, both of which require relatively small changes to the supervised baseline system, and use completely unannotated target-domain data.

A novel discriminative learning algorithm is proposed in [35], which takes advantage of the knowledge in the massive natural annotations on the Internet. Natural annotations implied by structural information are used to reduce the searching space of the classifier, then the constraint decoding in the pruned searching space gives predictions not worse than the normal decoding does. Annotation differences between the outputs of constraint decoding and normal decoding are used to train the enhancement of the classifier, linguistic knowledge in the human-annotated corpus and the natural annotations of web text are thus integrated together. Experiments on Chinese word segmentation indicate

Table 1. Taxonomy of Chinese NER

Taxonomy	Work	Input representation	Context decoder	Tag encoder
Word-based	[14]	LSTM	Chinese social media NER	Chinese social media NER
	[15]	CW2VEC	LSTM	CRF
	[16]	BERT	–	CRF
	[17]	WORD2VEC	CNN	CRF
Character-based	[18]	Tag	–	CRF
	[19]	Character-based	–	CRF
	[20]	Character-based	–	CRF
	[21]	Character pre-trained embedding	BiLSTM + Attention	CRF
	[22]	Transformer	Transformer	CRF
	[23]	BERT	GRU	CRF
	[24]	Comprehensive-embedding	BiLSTM + Attention	CRF
	[25]	BERT	BiLSTM	CRF
	[12]	Conv-GRU	Bi-directional GRU	CRF
	[26]	BiLSTM	fuseBiLSTM	CRF
Lexction-based	[13]	Lattice	LSTM	CRF
	[27]	Lattice	CNN	CRF
	[28]	Lattice	GNN	CRF
	[29]	LSTM	GAT + fusion	CRF
	[30]	GNN	LSTM	CRF
	[31]	Word-character embedding	WC-LSTM	CRF
	[32]	ExSoftword	Bi-LSTM/CNN/ Transformer	CRF
	[33]	FlatLattice	Self-attention + FFN	CRF

the enhanced word segmenter achieves significant improvement on testing sets of different domains, in spite of using a single classifier with only local features.

In [36], it investigates techniques for adopting freely available data to help improve the performance on Chinese word segmentation. This work proposed a simple but robust method for constructing partial segmentation from different free data sources, including unlabeled data and the Wikipedia. This technology models the task of Chinese word segmentation as a character sequence labeling problem, which is to give each character in a sentence a word-boundary tag. He used four tags, b, m, e and s, which represent the beginning, middle, end of a multi-character word, and a single character word, respectively. A manually segmented sentence can be expressed as a tag sequence, as shown in Fig. 7. And two major sources of freely available annotations are also studied: lexicons and natural annotations in Fig. 8.

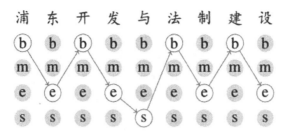

Fig. 7. The segmentation problem. B, m, e, s stand for the beginning middle, end of a multi-character word, and a single character word [36]

In [37], it solved the field adaptation problem of Chinese novel segmentation by using information extraction (IE) technology to automatically mine specific noun entities in novels. His method does not use any target domain annotations, such as domain dictionaries or small-scale annotated target domain sentences. Semi-supervised word segmentation under the same settings is usually performed by merging the target domain statistics into the source news domain training, but this method needs to use the news domain to retrain the statistical model of each target domain. There are a lot of novels on the Internet, from the point of view of training time and cost. In contrast, the proposed model uses novel specific nouns as plug-in resources, as resources for models trained on the extended annotated news corpus, and does not require retraining for every novel.

The flowchart of the proposed method is shown in Fig. 9. It consists of a training process and a testing process. Given an annotated news corpus (which he called the Gen corpus), the training process is performed only once, thus generating a set of models for analyzing different novels without retraining. The testing process refers to the segmentation process of the novel. It is carried out separately for each novel.

An adversarial multi-standard learning is proposed in [38] for CWS by integrating shared knowledge from multiple sub-standards. In particular, he treats each segmentation criterion as a task, and proposes three different shared-private models under the framework of multi-task learning, where the shared layer is used to extract criteria-invariant features, and a private layer is used to extract the criteria specific features. Inspired by the success of adversarial strategies on domain adaptation, he further utilizes adversarial strategies to ensure that the shared layer can extract common foundations and conditional invariant features that apply to all criteria.

Regarding heterogeneous criteria as multiple "related" tasks, it can improve each other's performance while sharing information. In order to take advantage of the shared information between these different criteria, three shared models of CWS tasks are proposed, as shown in Fig. 10. The feature layers of these three models include a private (criterion-specific) layer and a shared (criterion invariant) layer. The difference among the three models is the information flow

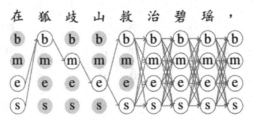

(a) "在 (at) 狐岐山 (Huqi Mountain) 救治 (save) 碧
瑶 (Biyao)", where "狐岐山" matches a lexicon word.

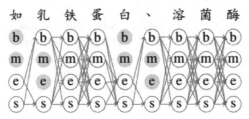

(b) "如 (e.g.) 乳铁蛋白 (lysozyme)、 溶菌酶 (lactoferrin)",
where "乳铁蛋白" is a hyperlink.

Fig. 8. Examples of annotated data [36]

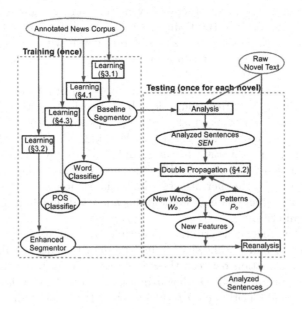

Fig. 9. Flowchart of the proposed method

between the task layer and the shared layer. In addition, these three models also share an embedding layer.

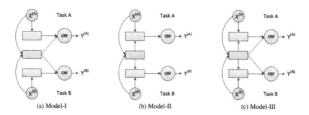

Fig. 10. Three shared-private models for multi-criteria learning. The yellow blocks are the shared BiLSTM layer, and the yellow circles denote the shared embedding layer [38] (Color figure online)

A new type of neural network model based on BiLSTM is proposed in [39], which combines a global recurrent structure designed to model boundary features dynamically. This structure can learn to use the target domain corpus and extract the correlation or irrelevance between characters, which is the reminiscence of discrete boundary features such as Accessor Variety.

Named Entity Recognition. In [14], it proposed a model that allows joint training of learned representations, integrating the best Chinese word segmentation system using an LSTM neural model that learns representations, with the best NER model of Chinese social media, and the model supports log-bilinear CRF training neural representation.

Unlike rule-based methods that utilize rigid features or component level information, stroke-level information is used in [15] to learn Chinese word embeddings. Stroke n-grams is a minimalist method that captures the semantic and morphological level information of Chinese words.

In addition, BERT obtains the semantic vectors according to the context of the word dynamically, thereby obtaining a successful answer. Therefore, fine-tuning of the pre-trained BERT model on the basis of an additional output layer can generate some state-of-the-art technology models for various downstream tasks.

An effective Chinese word segmentation method is proposed in [16], which uses BERT and adds a domain projection layer on the top through multi-criteria learning. They are used to capture heterogeneous segmentation criterias and common underlying knowledge. And they visualized the attention score to illustrate linguistic in CWS. For practical purposes, acceleration techniques are applied to improve the word segmentation speed. It includes knowledge extraction, quantification and compiler optimization.

In [17], it labels entities with the word size. Each word is represented as a low-dimensional dense vector, which can capture the semantic relationship between

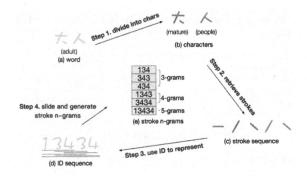

Fig. 11. Stroken embedding [15]

words. It is usually learned from unlabeled text, where Word2vec is selected as its training model, and the skip-gram is selected to predict the context of words in sentences.

4.2   Character Based Chinese NER

Research shows that character-based methods are better than word-based methods to address Chinese NER tasks. Many Chinese NER researches are based on word segmentation and even Part-Of-Speech (POS) tags. In fact, these steps are not necessary. Research shows that character-based methods are better than word-based methods in Chinese NER. He et al. proposed a character-based Conditional Random Field (CRF) model to solve segmentation tasks and NER tasks [18]. A sequence labeling method is proposed in [19] that can combine a variety of linguistic information and use local and global features. Local features are based on neighboring tokens, including the token itself. Global features are extracted from the entire document of other occurrences of the same tokens. He uses global features in a dictionary and compared the performance of character level and word level in NER task.

Compared the performance of character-level and word-level in the NER task, it is found that the performance of character-based name tagging is better than word-based Chinese tags. It studied the influence of word segmentation on Chinese and Japanese name marking in [20]. In addition, the work found that the performance of character-based Chinese name tagging is better than word-based Chinese. Cao et al. proposed a novel adversarial transfer learning framework to make full use of the boundary information shared by tasks and prevent the task-specific functions of CWS [21]. Since arbitrary characters can provide important cues in predicting entity types, he uses self-attention to clearly capture the long-distance dependence between two markers. The architecture of the proposed model is shown in Fig. 12. The model is mainly composed of five components: embedding layer, shared dedicated feature extractor, self-attention, task-specific CRF and task discriminator.

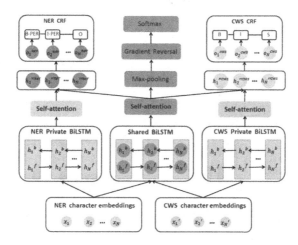

Fig. 12. Adversarial generative network based Chinese NER [21]

TENER is proposed in [22], which is a NER architecture adopting adapted Transformer Encoder to model the character-level features and word-level features, utilising relative positional encoding to endow the Transformer with the ability of direction and distance awareness.

In [23], it proposed a neural network model for Chinese named entity recognition and achieved more advanced results. The work uses GRU blocks to learn long-distance dependence, which has shorter training time and fewer parameters. At the same time, he uses BERT to learn contextual semantic information to construct character embedding. And add Chinese character radical information in the Chinese character embedding, which can make better use of internal semantic information.

A multi-level context model is divided into 4 layers in [24].

1) Splicing character-embedding, word-embedding, pos-embedding to obtain comprehensive embedding;
2) Connecting the integrated embedder to the BiLSTM neural network and obtain the top hidden unit;
3) Connecting the obtained hidden unit to the attention mechanism for processing;
4) Using CRF to decode the data of the upper layer.

In [25], it proposed a BERT with enhanced character embedding model (ECEM). Character embedding can extract useful features and feed them into the BiLSTM layer. As shown in Fig. 14, the entire algorithm consists of four parts. Data preprocessing is the first part. The purpose is to re-divide the corpus, divide it according to the character level, and use the BIO method to tokenize again. The enhanced character embedding layer is constructed to convert each character into context-level embedding and stroke-level embedding through BERT and CW2VEC respectively. The third part connects the deeper context

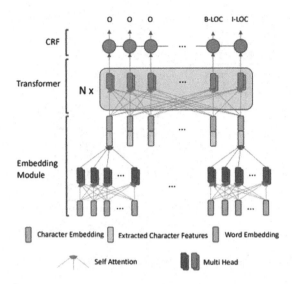

Fig. 13. Transformer Encoder for Name Entity Recognition(TENER) [22]

information output by the two BiLSTMs as the final representation of the characters. The fourth part uses CRF to predict sequence labels.

In [12], it proposed a exploiting multiple-character named entity recognition model (EC-CNER). Specifically, he derives character representations based on multiple embeddings of different granularities from root, character to word level. And he uses convolution operation to derive character representation based on local radical level context information. Similarly, the Conv-GRU network is designed to capture the semantic representation of characters based on the local context and remote dependencies of the characters. As shown in Fig. 15, these character representations with different angles are concatenated in series and fed into the BiGRU-CRF marker for sequence marking.

A char-subword-word representation form with a tree structure is constructed by making full use of characters, subwords and segment words [26]. Based on this representation, he further proposed a hierarchical LSTM (HiLSTM) framework to capture and learn the information in the char-subword-word representation.

4.3 Lexicon Based Chinese NER

However, gold-standard segmentation is rarely available in NER datasets, and word segmentation errors negatively impact the identification of named entities.

In recent years, Chinese NER papers mostly use Lexicon matching, adding word information to word-level sentences. Recently, facts have proved that the lattice structure has great benefits for using word information and avoiding the error propagation of word segmentation. We can use a word Lattice structure to intuitively show that every time a word is matched, a new word is formed for the word nodes, and then connect edges according to the range it spans.

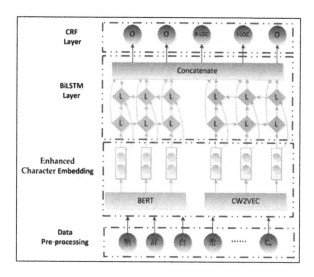

Fig. 14. Enhanced character embedding model (ECEM) [25]

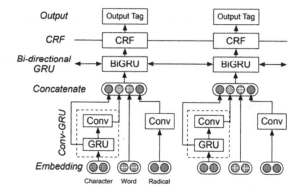

Fig. 15. Exploiting multiple-character named entity recognition model (ME-CNER) [12]

However, in order to cope with this Lattice structure, a small part of the existing conventional model needs to be modified to make it compatible with this structure. The first idea is to form a new vector representation for each word node, and send it to the context encoder together with the word vector, and modify the context encoder accordingly to enable it to encode this structure. The second idea is to add the dictionary matching information to the vector representation, which is equivalent to modifying the input representation layer.

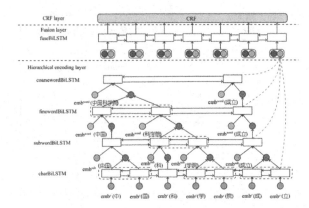

Fig. 16. Char-subword-word representation [26]

In recent years, most of the research on Chinese NER revolves around these two ideas. Recent research can be divided into two categories. The first category is Dynamic Architecture. The input structure will dynamically change, and the context encoder also needs to dynamically modify the structure to character-ize the input structure. Corresponding idea one. The second category is Adapt Embedding, which modifies the input presentation layer, corresponding to the second idea.

Dynamic Architecture. There are many different dynamic architectures. We first introduce the adapt basic architecture.

The lattice structure LSTM model for Chinese NER is studied in [13], which encodes the input character sequence and all potential words matching the lexi-con. As shown in Fig. 17, it constructs a word character lattice by automatically matching large sentences. As a result word sequences in Fig. 17, such as Yangtze River Bridge, Yangtze River and Bridge can be used to disambiguate potential relevant named entities in a context, such as the person name.

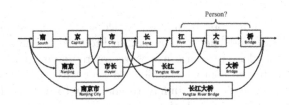

Fig. 17. Word character lattice [13]

Then, in order to solve the exponential character path in the lattice, the structure uses the lattice LSTM structure to automatically control the flow of information from the beginning to the end of the sentence. As shown in Fig. 18, the gating unit is used to dynamically route information from different paths to each character. After training on NER data, lattice LSTM can learn to automatically find more useful words from the context, so as to obtain better NER performance.

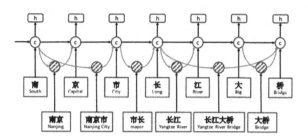

Fig. 18. Lattice LSTM structure [13]

Although the previous work using RNN to merge dictionaries has achieved great success, these methods still have two problems and are still difficult. First, RNN-based methods cannot take full advantage of GPU parallelism due to the loop structure, which limits their computational efficiency. Specifically, the lattice LSTM uses two recursive conversion calculations on the entire length of the input, one for each character in the sentence, and the other for the potential words in the dictionary. Therefore, their speed is limited. Second, it is difficult for them to deal with conflicts between potential words that are merged into the dictionary: a character may correspond to several potential words in the dictionary, and this conflict may mislead the model to make it predict different labels, as shown in Fig. 19. Due to the nature of sequential processing in RNN, it is difficult to determine which word is correct based on previous input alone [27]. Another more serious problem is that such inter-word conflicts are ubiquitous in Chinese NER, and these ambiguities cannot be resolved without referring to the entire sentence context and high-level information.

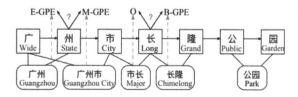

Fig. 19. Example of word character lattice. RNN models may suffer from conflicts between potential words [27].

In order to solve this problem, a new type of convolutional neural network with a rethinking mechanism is proposed in [27]. The proposed method uses CNN to deal with the first problem to process the entire sentence and all possible words in parallel. The intuition is that when the window size of the convolution operation is set to 2, all possible words can be easily merged into the corresponding positions. As shown in Fig. 20, words with a certain length correspond to different positions in certain layers. In this way, characters coupled with potential words can be processed in parallel. The second problem is solved by using a rethinking mechanism. Most existing Chinese NER models only use the feedforward structure to learn features. After seeing the entire sentence, they had no chance to modify the conflicting dictionary information. By adding a feedback layers, this rethinking mechanism can use advanced semantics to improve the weight of embedded words and resolve potential conflicts among words.

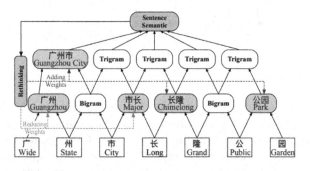

Fig. 20. Schematic of CNN model incorporating lexicons with a rethinking mechanism [27].

Another type of dynamic architecture can be summarized as graph-based methods. Since RNN and CNN are hard to model long-distance dependencies. Another line is to convert lattice into graph and use a graph neural network (GNN) to encode it.

In [28], it proposed a dictionary-based graph neural network (LGN), which implements Chinese NER as a node classification task. Through careful connection, the model breaks the serialization processing structure of RNN, and has a better interaction effect between characters and words. Dictionary knowledge links related characters to capture local components. At the same time, a global relay node is designed to capture remote dependencies and advanced functions. LGN follows a neighborhood aggregation scheme in which the node representation is calculated by recursively aggregating its incoming edge and global relay nodes. Due to multiple iterations of aggregation, the model can use global context information to repeatedly compare ambiguous words to make better predictions. Figure 21 and Fig. 22 show schematic diagrams of graph construction and aggregation in LGN.

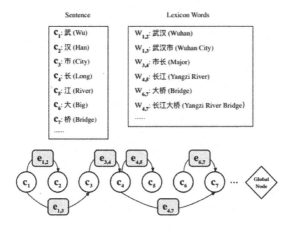

Fig. 21. Illustration of graph construction [28]

A character-based collaborative graph network is proposed in [29], including coding layer, layer, fusion layer and decoding layer. Specifically, there are three word-character interaction graphs in the graphics layer. The first one is the C-graph, which is used to integrate self-matching lexical words. It simulates the connection between characters and self-matching vocabulary words. The second is the transition graph (T-graph), which establishes a direct connection between the character and the nearest contextual matching word. It helps to meet the challenge of directly integrating words in the closest context. The third is the L-graph, which is inspired by the L-graph LSTM. L-graph captures partial information from matching lexical words and the nearest context lexical words through multiple jumps implicitly. The construction of these graphs does not require external NLP tools, which can avoid error propagation problems. In addition, these diagrams complement each other well, and a fusion layer is designed for the collaboration between these diagrams. Figure 23 shows this model.

In [30], it proposed a novel multi-digraph structure, which can explicitly simulate the interaction between characters and geographical name dictionaries. The model is combined with the adapted Gated Graph Sequence Neural Network (GGSNN) and the standard two-way LSTM-CRF (BiLSTM-CRF), which can learn the weighted combination of information from different geographical name dictionaries and resolve matching conflicts based on contextual information.

The overall architecture of the model is shown in Fig. 24. Specifically, the model consists of multi-digraph, adapted GGNN embedding layer and BiLSTM-CRF layer. The multiple graphs explicitly model the text together with NE Gazetteer information. Then, the improved GGNN structure is used to convert the information in this graphical representation into a feature representation space. The encoded feature representation is then fed to the standard BiLSTM-CRF to predict the final structured output.

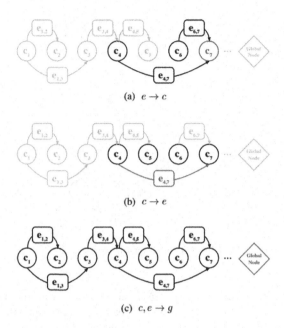

Fig. 22. Aggregation in LGN [28]

Although the sequence structure is still important for NER and the graph is universal, the gap between them cannot be ignored. These methods need to use LSTM as the bottom encoder to carry the sequential perceptual bias, which complicates the model.

Therefore, FLAT (Flat Lattice Transformer) is proposed for Chinese NER [33]. The transformer uses fully connected self-attention to model the long-distance dependences in the sequence. In order to preserve location information, Transformer introduces the location representation of each token in the sequence. Inspired by the concept of position representation, he designed a novel position code for the lattice structure, as shown in Fig. 25. In detail, the method assigns two position indexes for tokens (characters or words): head position and tail position, through these position indexes, it can reconstruct the lattice from a set of tokens. Therefore, he can directly use Transformer to completely model the lattice input. Transformer's self-attention mechanism allows characters to directly interact with any potential word, including self-matching words. For a character, its self-matching word means the word that contains the word. Figure 26 shows the overall architecture of FLAT.

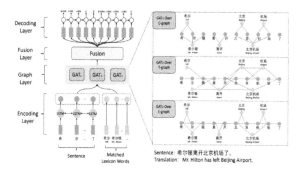

Fig. 23. Main architecture of a Collaborative Graph Network for integrating lexical knowledge in Chinese NER [29]

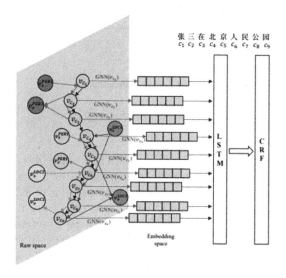

Fig. 24. Multi-digraph structure [30]

Adapt Embedding. As pointed out in [32], the model architecture of Lattice-LSTM is very complicated. In order to introduce dictionary information, Lattice-LSTM adds multiple additional edges between non-adjacent characters in the input sequence, which greatly slows down its training and inference speed. In addition, it is difficult to transfer the structure of Lattice-LSTM to other neural network architectures.

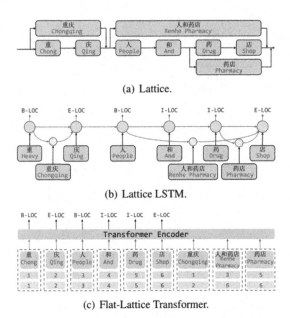

(a) Lattice.

(b) Lattice LSTM.

(c) Flat-Lattice Transformer.

Fig. 25. An encode position in FLAT [33]

A simpler method is then proposed in [32] to realize the idea of Lattice-LSTM, which is to merge all matching words of each character into a character-based NER model. The primary principle of the model design is to achieve fast reasoning speed. To this end, Ma suggests to encode the dictionary information in the character information and design an encoding scheme to retain as many dictionary matching results as possible. Compared with Lattice-LSTM, this method avoids the use of complex model architecture, and it is easy to implement. In addition, the method can quickly adapt to any appropriate neural network NER model by adjusting the character representation layer. Furthermore, ablation studies show that this method has advantages in merging more complete and unique lexicon information and introducing more effective word weighting strategies.

As shown in Fig. 27, the overall architecture of the proposed method is as follows. First, the architecture maps each character of the input sequence to a dense vector. Next, it constructs the SoftLexicon function and adds it to the representation of each character. Then, these enhanced character representations are put into the sequence modeling layer and CRF layer to obtain the final prediction.

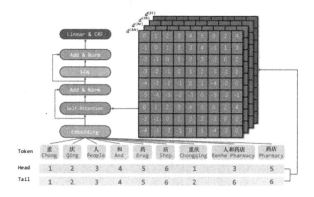

Fig. 26. The overall architecture of FLAT [33]

As shown in the figure, the gate mechanism sometimes fails to choose the right path. As shown in Fig. 28, the wrong choice may cause the lattice model to degenerate into a word-based partial model, and suffer from word segmentation errors. In addition, due to the change of word length, the length of the entire path is not fixed. In addition, each character has a variable-size candidate word set, which means that the number of incoming and outgoing paths is not fixed. In this case, the lattice LSTM model loses the ability of batch training, so the efficiency is very low.

To address the above problems, a novel word-character LSTM(WC-LSTM) is proposed in [31] to integrate word information into character-based model. To prevent this model from degenerating into a partial word-based model, the method assigns word information to a single character and ensures that there are no shortcut paths between characters. Specifically, word information is assigned to its end character and start character in forward WC-LSTM and backward WC-LSTM respectively. The method introduces four strategies to extract fixed-sized useful information from different words, which ensures that the proposed model can perform batch training without losing word information.

The architecture of the proposed model is shown in Fig. 29. Same as the widely used neural Chinese NER, it uses LSTM-CRF as the main network structure. The difference between this model and the standard LSTM-CRF model mainly lies in the embedding layer and LSTM, which can be summarized as follows. First, it expressed Chinese sentences as a series of character-word pairs to integrate word information into each character. Second, in order to enable the model to be batch-trained and meet different application requirements, it introduced four coding strategies to extract fixed-size but different information from words. Finally, it used chain structure word character LSTM to extract features from characters and words for better prediction.

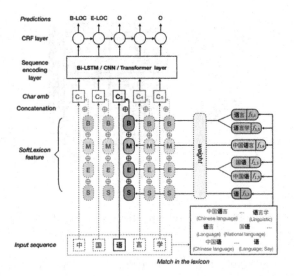

Fig. 27. The overall architecture of Ma's model [32]

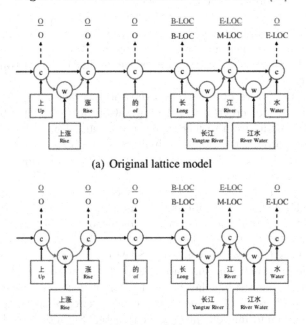

Fig. 28. An example of the lattice model degenerates into a partial word-based model [31]

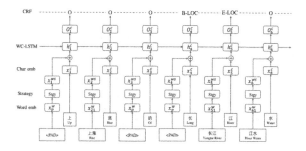

Fig. 29. The architecture of unidirectional model [31]

5 Challenges and Ideas When Combining with MDATA

In recent years, with the development of deep learning, the accuracy of Chinese NER has gradually improved. In MDATA, we added spatiotemporal attributes and spatiotemporal relations R to the knowledge graph. This spatio-temporal characteristic includes time and place, which enhances the traceability of the knowledge graph. However, the addition of temporal and spatial attributes will increase the difficulty of Chinese NER recognition. For example, in the epidemic situation, in the applied knowledge map of epidemiological history investigation, the fine-grained requirement for entity recognition is to be able to identify specific passing places and specific transportation vehicles, such as XX hotel, G79, D2242, etc. This is a certain degree of difficulty for Chinese NER. Therefore, in MDATA, based on this spatiotemporal relationship and attributes, multiple joint extraction models can be used to extract entities, relationships and attributes. The design purpose of this joint extraction model is to allow the spatiotemporal relationship R and spatiotemporal attributes to assist entity recognition while performing named entity recognition.

After named entity recognition and spatiotemporal relationship extraction, the generated data needs to be integrated, and triples are the best way to describe the integration. A triple is a tuple composed of (entity 1, relationship, entity 2). In the relationship extraction task, when extracting the relationship between any two entities 1 and 2, if they have a relationship, they can be constructed as Triad. For example, a sentence "Zhang San takes a train from Beijing to Wuhan at 10 o'clock on February 1, 2020 Beijing time". Based on this joint extraction model of temporal and spatial attributes, the triplet that can be constructed is ("Zhang San", "Take the train", "Train G79"), and include spatial-temporal attributes in both relationships and attributes. Fig. 30 shows the process.

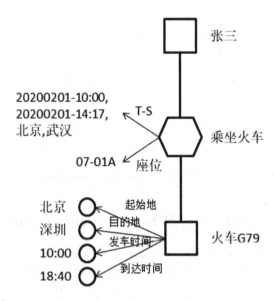

Fig. 30. Example of Multi-dimensional Data Association and in Telligent Analysis (MDATA)

6   Chapter Summary

The task of Chinese named entity recognition (NER) has always been a research hotspot in the field of natural language processing (NLP). It mainly uses sequence annotation to obtain entities with specific meaning in text. From the early method based on rules and dictionaries, through the traditional machine learning method and deep learning method, to the pre training language model in recent two years, researchers have made continuous attempts and explorations.

In this chapter we have presented a survey of historical and current state-of-the-art techniques for CNER. We have identified a classification method based on fine-grained CNER that allowed us to characterize CNER techniques, and to generate a taxonomy of such techniques. This proposed taxonomy can be used as a comparison and analysis tool for current CNER techniques. The entity composition in different fields is different, and the external knowledge of named entities in different application backgrounds is not the same. How to fully consider the characteristics of the domain and integrate them into the model, and how to use the domain resources to specifically identify Chinese named entities needs further study [7].

Named-entity recognition (NER) is a subtask of information extraction that seeks to locate and classify named entities mentioned in unstructured text into predefined categories. How to effectively apply the extracted information to the task of data mining and analysis is very important. Knowledge graph which represents a collection of interlinked descriptions of entities can effectively solve this problem. By embedding the extracted entities into knowledge graph, the relationship between entities can be clearly judged. In this chapter, we propose a knowledge graph with spatiotemporal concept, which can be applied to all walks of life efficiently.

References

1. Li, J., Sun, A., Han, J., Li, C.: A survey on deep learning for named entity recognition. IEEE Trans. Knowl. Data Eng., 1 (2020). https://doi.org/10.1109/TKDE.2020.2981314
2. Li, Y., Xin, Y., Fu, Y.: Chinese named entity recognition in business domain based on Bi-LSTM-CRF
3. Yao, L., Huang, H., Wang, K.-W., Chen, S.-H., Xiong, Q.: Fine-grained mechanical Chinese named entity recognition based on ALBERT-AttBiLSTM-CRF and transfer learning. Symmetry 12(12), 1986 (2020)
4. Yin, M., Mou, C., Xiong, K., Ren, J.: Chinese clinical named entity recognition with radical-level feature and self-attention mechanism. J. Biomed. Inf. 98, 103289 (2019)
5. He, H., Sun, X.: A unified model for cross-domain and semi-supervised named entity recognition in Chinese social media. In: Thirty-First AAAI Conference on Artificial Intelligence (2017)
6. You, F., Zhang, J., Qiu, D.: Weapon name recognition based on deep neural network. J. Comput. Syst 27, 239–243 (2018)
7. Yang, Z.: Research on Chinese named entity recognition technology and application in inspection and quarantine. PhD thesis (2019)
8. Xuezhen, Y., Hui, Z., Junbao, Z., Wanwei, Y., Zelin, H.: Multi-neural network collaboration for Chinese military named entity recognition. J. Tsinghua Univ. (Sci. Technol.) 60(8), 648–655 (2020)
9. Gao, C., Yu, L.: A knowledge-based method for filtering geo-entity relations. J. Geoinf. Sci. 21(9), 1392–1401 (2019)
10. Ballatore, A., Bertolotto, M., Wilson, D.C.: A structural-lexical measure of semantic similarity for geo-knowledge graphs. ISPRS Int. J. Geoinf. 4(2), 471–492 (2015)
11. Zhang, X., Zhang, C., Wu, M., Lv, G.: Spatiotemporal features based geographical knowledge graph construction. SCIENTIA SINICA Informationis 50(7), 1019–1032 (2020)
12. Xu, C., Wang, F., Han, J., Li, C.: Exploiting multiple embeddings for Chinese named entity recognition. In: Proceedings of the 28th ACM International Conference on Information and Knowledge Management, pp. 2269–2272 (2019)
13. Zhang, Y., Yang, J.: Chinese NER using lattice LSTM. arXiv preprint arXiv:1805.02023 (2018)
14. Peng, N., Dredze, M.: Improving named entity recognition for chinese social media with word segmentation representation learning. arXiv preprint arXiv:1603.00786 (2016)
15. Cao, S., Lu, W., Zhou, J., Li, X.: cw2vec: learning Chinese word embeddings with stroke n-gram information. In: AAAI, pp. 5053–5061 (2018)
16. Huang, W., Cheng, X., Chen, K., Wang, T., Chu, W.: Toward fast and accurate neural Chinese word segmentation with multi-criteria learning. arXiv preprint arXiv:1903.04190 (2019)
17. Wen, G., Chen, H., Li, H., Hu, Y., Li, Y., Wang, C.: Cross domains adversarial learning for Chinese named entity recognition for online medical consultation. J. Biomed. Inf. 112, 103608 (2020)

18. He, J., Wang, H.: Chinese named entity recognition and word segmentation based on character. In: Proceedings of the Sixth SIGHAN Workshop on Chinese Language Processing (2008)
19. Liu, Z., Zhu, C., Zhao, T.: Chinese named entity recognition with a sequence labeling approach: based on characters, or based on words? In: Huang, D.-S., Zhang, X., Reyes García, C.A., Zhang, L. (eds.) ICIC 2010. LNCS (LNAI), vol. 6216, pp. 634–640. Springer, Heidelberg (2010). https://doi.org/10.1007/978-3-642-14932-0_78
20. Li, H., Hagiwara, M., Li, Q., Ji, H.: Comparison of the impact of word segmentation on name tagging for Chinese and Japanese. In: LREC, pp. 2532–2536 (2014)
21. Cao, P., Chen, Y., Liu, K., Zhao, J., Liu, S.: Adversarial transfer learning for Chinese named entity recognition with self-attention mechanism. In: Proceedings of the 2018 Conference on Empirical Methods in Natural Language Processing, pp. 182–192 (2018)
22. Yan, H., Deng, B., Li, X., Qiu, X.: TENER: adapting transformer encoder for name entity recognition. arXiv preprint arXiv:1911.04474 (2019)
23. Gong, C., Tang, J., Zhou, S., Hao, Z., Wang, J.: Chinese named entity recognition with Bert. In: Proceedings of the 2019 International Conference on Computer Intelligent Systems and Network Remote Control (CISNRC), pp. 8–15 (2019)
24. Johnson, S., Shen, S., Liu, Y.: CWPC_BiAtt: character-word-position combined BiLSTM-attention for Chinese named entity recognition. Information 11(1), 45 (2020)
25. Jia, B., Wu, Z., Wu, B., Liu, Y., Zhou, P.: Enhanced character embedding for Chinese named entity recognition. Meas. Control 53(9–10), 1669–1681 (2020)
26. Gong, C., Li, Z., Xia, Q., Chen, W., Zhang, M.: Hierarchical LSTM with char-subword-word tree-structure representation for Chinese named entity recognition. Sci. China Inf. Sci. 63(10), 1–15 (2020). https://doi.org/10.1007/s11432-020-2982-y
27. Gui, T., Ma, R., Zhang, Q., Zhao, L., Jiang, Y.-G., Huang, X.: CNN-based Chinese NER with lexicon rethinking. In: IJCAI, pp. 4982–4988 (2019)
28. Gui, T., Zou, Y., Zhang, Q., Peng, M., Fu, J., Wei, Z., Huang, X.-J.: A lexicon-based graph neural network for Chinese NER. In: Proceedings of the 2019 Conference on Empirical Methods in Natural Language Processing and the 9th International Joint Conference on Natural Language Processing (EMNLP-IJCNLP), pp. 1039–1049 (2019)
29. Sui, D., Chen, Y., Liu, K., Zhao, J., Liu, S.: Leverage lexical knowledge for Chinese named entity recognition via collaborative graph network. In: Proceedings of the 2019 Conference on Empirical Methods in Natural Language Processing and the 9th International Joint Conference on Natural Language Processing (EMNLP-IJCNLP), pp. 3821–3831 (2019)
30. Ding, R., Xie, P., Zhang, X., Lu, W., Li, L., Si, L.: A neural multi-digraph model for Chinese NER with gazetteers. In: Proceedings of the 57th Annual Meeting of the Association for Computational Linguistics, pp. 1462–1467 (2019)
31. Liu, W., Xu, T., Xu, Q., Song, J., Zu, Y.: An encoding strategy based word-character LSTM for Chinese NER. In: Proceedings of the 2019 Conference of the North American Chapter of the Association for Computational Linguistics: Human Language Technologies, Volume 1 (Long and Short Papers), pp. 2379–2389 (2019)
32. Peng, M., Ma, R., Zhang, Q., Huang, X.: Simplify the usage of lexicon in Chinese NER. arXiv preprint arXiv:1908.05969 (2019)
33. Li, X., Yan, H., Qiu, X., Huang, X.: FLAT: Chinese NER using flat-lattice transformer. arXiv preprint arXiv:2004.11795 (2020)

34. Liu, Y., Zhang, Y.: Unsupervised domain adaptation for joint segmentation and POS-tagging. In: Proceedings of COLING 2012: Posters, pp. 745–754 (2012)

35. Jiang, W., Sun, M., Lü, Y., Yang, Y., Liu, Q.: Discriminative learning with natural annotations: Word segmentation as a case study. In: Proceedings of the 51st Annual Meeting of the Association for Computational Linguistics (Volume 1: Long Papers), pp. 761–769 (2013)

36. Liu, Y., Zhang, Y., Che, W., Liu, T., Wu, F.: Domain adaptation for CRF-based Chinese word segmentation using free annotations. In: Proceedings of the 2014 Conference on Empirical Methods in Natural Language Processing (EMNLP), pp. 864–874 (2014)

37. Qiu, L., Zhang, Y.: Word segmentation for Chinese novels. In: Twenty-Ninth AAAI Conference on Artificial Intelligence, pp. 2440–2446 (2015)

38. Chen, X., Shi, Z., Qiu, X., Huang, X.: Adversarial multi-criteria learning for Chinese word segmentation. arXiv preprint arXiv:1704.07556 (2017)

39. Huang, S., Sun, X., Wang, H.: Addressing domain adaptation for Chinese word segmentation with global recurrent structure. In: Proceedings of the Eighth International Joint Conference on Natural Language Processing (Volume 1: Long Papers), pp. 184–193 (2017)

Joint Extraction of Entities and Relations: An Advanced BERT-based Decomposition Method

Changhai Wang and Aiping Li[✉]

National University of Defense Technology, Changsha 410073, China
1625324713@qq.com, liaiping@nudt.edu.cn

Abstract. Joint extraction of entities and relations is an important task in the field of Natural Language Processing (NLP) and the basis of many NLP high-level tasks. However, most existing joint models cannot solve the problem of overlapping triples well. We propose an efficient end-to-end model for joint extraction of entities and overlapping relations in this chapter. Firstly, the BERT pre-training model is introduced to model the text more finely. Next, we decompose triples extraction into two subtasks: head entity extraction and tail entity extraction, which solves the problem of single entity overlap in the triples. Then, We divide the tail entity extraction into three parallel extraction sub-processes to solve entity pair overlap problem of triples, that is the relation overlap problem. Finally, we transform each extraction sub-process into a sequence tag task. We evaluate our model on the New York Times (NYT) dataset and achieve overwhelming results (Precise = 0.870, Recall = 0.851, and F1 = 0.860) compared with most of the current models. The experimental results show that our model is effective in dealing with triples overlap problem.

Keywords: MDATA · Entity and relation extraction · BERT

1 Introduction

With the advent of big data era, information extraction technology has become increasingly important. As a key component of information extraction technology, entity relation extraction aims to extract some triples ⟨head entity, relation, tail entity⟩ containing two entities and their relations from unstructured natural language texts to convert texts into structured information. Entity relation extraction can be used to construct large-scale knowledge graph and is also the basis of machine translation, machine reading comprehension, intelligent dialogue, search engine and so on.

Traditional entity relation extraction normally developed on the basis of pipelines. Works of entity relation extraction can be divided into two sub-tasks: the first task identifies all entities in the text sequence [1]; while the second task extracts relations based on the identified entities [2]. With the continuous

© Springer Nature Switzerland AG 2021
Y. Jia et al. (Eds.): MDATA: A New Knowledge Representation Model, LNCS 12647, pp. 82–98, 2021.
https://doi.org/10.1007/978-3-030-71590-8_5

updating of various neural networks, a series of efficient pipeline models appear. However, the pipeline method has the defect of error propagation that the error of entity recognition will be passed to the next step of relation extraction, which seriously affects the effect of the model [3].

In order to overcome the error propagation, following works proposed joint learning modela. Using a single model to jointly extract entities and relations can better integrate the information between entities and relations, which achieve excellent results in entity relation extraction task. The feature-based joint extraction models [3–6] requires complex feature engineering, costing a lot of manpower. On the contrary, the end-to-end joint extraction models [7–9] based on neural network can extract features by itself.

The biggest challenge of joint extraction model is the triplet overlap. According to the triplet overlap degree, it classified the triplets in the text sequence into three categories [9], including *Normal, Single Entity Overlap (SEO)* and *Entity Pair Overlap (EPO)*. As shown in Fig. 1, Normal means that all triples of a sentence have no overlapped entities. *SEO* means that some triples of a sentence have an overlapped entity but no overlapped entity pairs, and *EPO* means that some triples of a sentence have overlapped entity pairs. Unfortunately, most of the existing joint extraction models cannot deal with the three kinds of triple overlap at the same time. For example, The tagging scheme proposed in [8] can only extract *Normal* triples and cannot solve any triple overlap problem.

In order to meet the above challenges, we propose an efficient end-to-end joint extraction model to solve the problem of triple overlap as much as possible. Inspired by a recent work [10], we transform the triple extraction problem into multiple sequence tag problems, and propose a better extraction scheme.

Our model is mainly composed of four parts: first of all, the sentence features are encoded by feature extraction; next, extract the head entity through the sequence tag method; then, randomly select a head entity and fuse its features into sentence features; finally, the sequence tag method is used to label the sentences with relation type, and the relation and tail entities are jointly

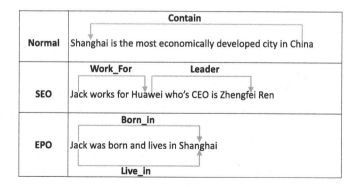

Fig. 1. Examples of normal, Entity Pair Overlap (EPO) and Single Entity Overlap (SEO) classes

extracted. Head entity extraction and tail entity extraction are divided into two steps, which can solve the *SEO* problem. In order to solve the *EPO* problem, we carry out multiple tags (EPO_None_Tagging, EPO_Two_Tagging and EPO_Three_Tagging) when extracting relations and tail entities.

The main contributions of this chapter are as follows:

- We propose an end-to-end neural network model to implement joint extraction of entities and relations by transforming the triple extraction problem into multiple sequence tag problems.
- Our joint extraction model can solve the problem of triples overlap. The problem of *SEO* is solved by extracting head entity and tail entity by parts. The *EPO* problem can be dealt with by introducing EPO-Two-Tagging and EPO-Three-Tagging.
- By testing on the NYT dataset with results of Precise(0.870), Recall (0.851), F1(0.860), our model beats almost all existing models.

2   Related Work

With the rise of knowledge graph, being the most important step in the construction of knowledge base, entity relation extraction has become a research hotspot. At present, there are two main frameworks for supervised entity relation extraction: pipeline methods and joint methods.

The pipeline methods divide entity relation extraction into two subtasks: Named Entity Recognition (NER) and Relation Extraction (RE).

NER is a basic task of natural language processing, which belongs to the task of sequence tag. Classic NER models are based on artificial features, using techniques including Maximum Entropy (ME) [11], Support Vector Machine (SVM) [12], Hidden Markov (HM) [13] and Conditional Random Field (CRF) [14] to classify entities. Later, many models were developed with the deep learning technique, which greatly improve the effect of NER, including BILSTM+CRF [15], DNN+R [16] and so on.

In [16], it assumed that real-world information can be used to improve the effect of named entity recognition in the corresponding field; based on the Japanese chess game state data and commentary, a deep model of DNN+R is trained, which proves that the effect of the model is much better than the separate DNN model. Relation extraction (RE) is to identify the relation of the sentence marked with entity pairs, and extract the triples that have relations. In [17], it used CNN for relation extraction for the first time, and used CNN to extract sentence features, which avoids complex data preprocessing and improves the performance of the model. Making use of the advantages of CNN and RNN, a method combining neural network and traditional feature engineering is proposed in [18], which is assisted by traditional feature engineering. Although the pipeline method is more flexible and there is no need to worry about the triplet overlap problem, the result of the pre-task will affect the post-task and cause error propagation.

The joint methods overcome error propagation issue and use a single model to jointly extract entities and relations, but they face new challenges, for example the triple overlap. In [8], it proposed a joint extraction model based on a novel tagging scheme, which compresses entities and relations into a sequence tag task, but the defect is that it cannot deal with triple overlap. A seq2seq model named CopyRE is proposed in [9], which is based on the replication mechanism to generate triples. In principle, it can solve the problem of triplet overlap; but the seq2seq model has a large loss. In [19], it pointed out that CopyRE [9] is a very good entity relation extraction model based on the seq2seq structure, but CopyRE has the problems that head and tail entities cannot be distinguished and multi-tokens entities cannot be matched. Then, it explained the principle of CopyRE in detail and reasoned for the above problems of CopyRE; the fully connected layer with the ReLU activation function is used to solve the problem of the indistinguishability between head and tail entities, and the multi-task learning combined with NER is used to solve the problem that the multi-character entities cannot be matched.

In [20], it proposed a sequence tag model based on positional attention, in which each word in a sentence is marked with a sequence; the current word is marked with its entity type, and other word markers are marked with the relation type of the current word. Applying the graph convolution network to entity relation extraction, an end-to-end joint extraction model of entities and relations in which linear structure is used to extract sequential features of the sentence and dependency structure is used to extract regional features of the sentence is presented in [21]. The prediction results of overlapping relations is much better than the previous sequential methods by using the graph-based method. In [22], it proposed a novel scheme to convert entity relation extraction into multi-turn machine reading comprehension. At the same time, it also provided a new extraction idea: first extracting the head entity, second binding extracting the tail entity and the relation on the basis of the head entity.

3 Preliminary

3.1 Task Description

The entity relation extraction task is actually a triple extraction task. For supervised entity relation extraction, the data examples are as follows:
{
    "tokens":
        ["A", "French", "court", "sentenced", "six", "Algerian-French", "men", "to", "prison", "terms", "of", "up", "to", "10", "years", "on", "Tuesday", "for", "their", "role", "in", "a", "2001", "plot", "to", "attack", "the", "United", "States", "Embassy", "in", "Paris", ",", "closing", "the", "books", "on", "one", "of", "France", "'s", "most", "serious", "terrorist", "cases", "."]
    "spo_list":
        ["Paris", "/location/administrative_division/country", "France"]

["France", "/location/location/contains", "Paris"]
["France", "/location/country/administrative_divisions", "Paris"]
"spo_details":
[31, 32, "LOCATION", "/location/administrative_division/country", 39, 40, "LOCATION"]
[39, 40, "LOCATION", "/location/location/contains", 31, 32, "LOCATION"]
[39, 40, "LOCATION", "/location/country/administrative_divisions", 31, 32, "LOCATION"]
}

The task of entity relation extraction inputs a text sentence and outputs all the triples involved in the sentence. The form of entity relation triples is (s, p, o), where s refers to the head entity of the triple, that is, the subject, which is a fragment in the text sentence; o refers to the tail entity of the triple, that is, the object, which is also in the text sentence A fragment of; and p refers to the relation between the head entity s and the tail entity o, that is the predicate. The data set will preset a series of relations, namely the predicate list. In the task, we need to identify what is the relation between two entities. In a word, it can be understood that identifying the relation between s and o is p, or finding the most appropriate relation p that s and o hold.

3.2   Problem Analysis

By analyzing the task data, it is not difficult to find that this task is an one-to-many information extraction task. Though pipeline models are more flexible without the overlap problem, but there is error propagation. There is no error transmission in the joint extraction model, but the problem of triple overlap is a major difficulty. By observing the sample data, the characteristics of the sample can be summarized as follows:

- The extraction result will show that one s corresponds to multiple (p, o), that is, an entity is a case of multiple head entities , such as if we have a sentence: "Jack's teachers include Jane and Smith", triples <Jack, teacher, Jane> and <Jack, teacher, Smith> will be extracted.
- The extraction result will produce multiple (s, p) corresponding to one o, that is, an entity is a case of multiple tail entities. For example, the sentence "David is the father of Jane and Smith" corresponds to triples: <Jane, father, David> and <Smith, father, David>.
- The extraction result may show that the head entity $s1$ of triple $(s1, p1, o1)$ is the tail entity $o2$ of another triple $(s2, p2, o2)$, that is, an entity is either some triples' head entities or other triples' tail entities. For example, "Jane is David's son and Jack's teacher" can extract to triples <Jane, father, David> and <Jack, teacher, Jane>.
- The extraction result may also show a pair of (s, o) corresponding to multiple p, that is, there are multiple relations between the two entities. For example, "David is both Jane's father and her teacher" can extract <Jane, father, David> and <Jane, teacher, David>.

The above four overlapping problems can be classified into two categories. The first three (one s corresponding to multiple (p, o) problems, multiple (s, p) corresponding to one o problem, one $s1$ of a triple $(s1, p1, o1)$ is $o2$ of another triple $(s2, p2, o2)$) are essentially one entity in multiple triples. They are single entity overlap(SEO) problem. In fact, they account for a large proportion in the triple overlap problem. The fourth (a pair of (s, o) corresponds to multiple p) is essentially a pair of entities with multiple relations. It can be classified as entity pair overlap (EPO) problem which accounts for a small proportion.

Innovations. In traditional solution, the pipeline model, a sequential annotation model is firstly used to recognize named entity; then the relation between entities is extracted by the relation recognition model. Except suffering the error propagation and time consuming issue, this scheme cannot deal with the case that a pair of (s, o) corresponds to multiple p.

The joint extraction model does not have the error propagation issue, but the model lacks flexibility. And it also have difficulty in dealing with triple overlap. For example, the aforementioned joint extraction model based on marking strategy proposed in [8] combines entity types, entity locations and relation types into a single tag type, and convert the problem into a sequence marking task. However, this model can nether solve the three SEO problems nor the EPO problem, so that the effect of the model is poor. Though, later CopyRE is proposed in [9], which used the seq2seq model to directly generate triples and the triple overlap problem can be completely solved from the principle; the effect is still poor.

In order to improve the effect of entity relation extraction, we can draw the following experiences through the above analysis of data samples and existing models:

- Select the joint extraction model to avoid the error propagation problem of the pipeline model
- The task finally needs to be transformed into a sequence labeling problem. The current generation model is not effective in handling information extraction problems.
- In the case of ensuring the effect of the model, it is necessary to solve the overlapping problems of various triples as much as possible
- More attention should be pay to the improvement of coding work. It is the foundation of the deep learning model and determines the success or failure of the model

4   Method

In this section, we describe our proposed method in detail. First, we introduce the tagging scheme, and the designed end-to-end model is then described.

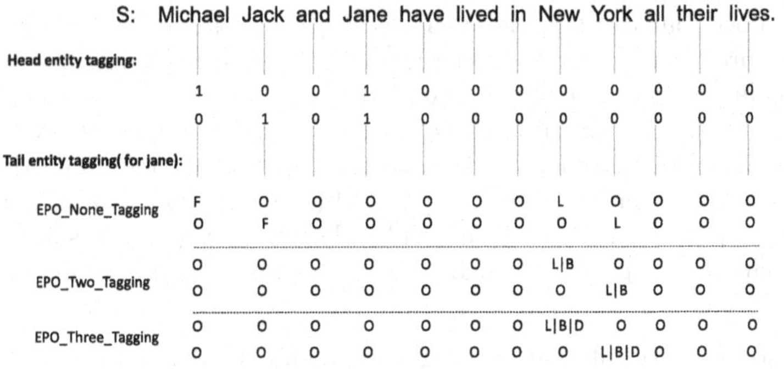

S: Michael Jack and Jane have lived in New York all their lives.

Head entity tagging:												
	1	0	0	1	0	0	0	0	0	0	0	0
	0	1	0	1	0	0	0	0	0	0	0	0

Tail entity tagging(for Jane):

EPO_None_Tagging	F	0	0	0	0	0	0	L	0	0	0	0
	0	F	0	0	0	0	0	0	L	0	0	0
EPO_Two_Tagging	0	0	0	0	0	0	0	L|B	0	0	0	0
	0	0	0	0	0	0	0	0	L|B	0	0	0
EPO_Three_Tagging	0	0	0	0	0	0	0	L|B|D	0	0	0	0
	0	0	0	0	0	0	0	0	L|B|D	0	0	0

Fig. 2. An instance of our tagging scheme. F stands for Friend_is, L for Live_in, B for Born_in, D for Death_in, L|B for Live_in and Born_in, L|B|D for Live_in, Born_in and Death_in.

4.1 The Tagging Scheme

Inspired by the method in [10], we propose a tagging scheme to solve triples overlap problem. As shown in Fig. 2, our tagging scheme is composed of two steps: one is extracting the head entity, the other is extracting the relation and tail entity for each recognized head entity.

Head entity extraction mainly includes two classifiers. One is used to mark the start position of the header entity. If the current word is the beginning of the head entity, it is marked as 1, otherwise it is marked as 0. The other is used to mark the end position of the header entity, and its marking process is similar to the former. Different from Yu [10], we only mark out head entities without entity classification.

For each identified head entity, relation and tail entity extraction also consist of two classifiers. One is used to mark the start position of the tail entity, and if the current word is the beginning of the tail entity, it is marked with the corresponding relation type, otherwise it is marked as O. The other is used to mark the end position of the tail entity, and the marking process is similar to the former. Notice that we marked the tail entity three times with different policies: EPO-None-Tagging, EPO-Two-Tagging, EPO-Three-Tagging. EPO-None-Tagging means that when extracting tail entities, the relation overlap between entity pairs is not considered. EPO-Two-Tagging means to extract entity pairs with two overlapping relations. EPO-Three-Tagging means extracting an entity pair with three overlapping relations. At this step, EPO-None-Tagging is only adopted in [10], so that they cannot solve the *EPO* problem.

In Fig. 2, we show an example of our tagging scheme. 'Michael' and 'Jack' are the start and end words of the header entity 'Michael Jack', respectively. In the header entity extraction, Michael is marked as 1 in the start tag sequence and Jack is marked as 1 in the end tag sequence. When extracting the relation and tail entities for the head entity 'Jane', EPO-None-Tagging extracts triples (⟨ Jane, Friend_is, Michael Jack⟩, ⟨Jane, Live_in, New York⟩), EPO-Two-Tagging extracts triples (⟨Jane, Live_in, New York⟩, ⟨Jane, Born_in, New York⟩), and EPO-Three-Tagging extracts triples (⟨Jane, Live_in, New York⟩, ⟨Jane, Born_in, New York⟩, ⟨Jane, Death_in, New York⟩). It is noticeable that our extraction scheme can get four different triples for the head entity Jane, while Yu's [10] scheme can only get two of them: (⟨Jane, Friend_is, Michael Jack⟩, ⟨Jane, Live_in, New York⟩).

4.2   The End-to-End Model

Our model consists of four modules: encoder, head entity extraction, head entity selection, relation and tail entity extraction. BERT [23] and BiLSTM are used to encode the source sentence. The head and tail entities are extracted step by step.

Encoder. The encoding module contains four steps: first, using Wordpiece to divide the source sentence to generate the tokens required by BERT; next, BERT encodes the sentence to generate the sentence sequence embedding; then, encode the part-of-speech information by BIO tagging to generate the part-of-speech tag embedding; finally, integrate sentence sequence embedding and part-of-speech embedding to generate sentence representations by BiLSTM.

WordPiece. To encode sentences, we need to divide the source sentences first. As shown in Fig. 3, given a sentence $S = [w_1, w_2...w_m]$, we use Wordpiece to split it into $X = [x_1, x_2...x_n]$. Now fine pre-training models, such as OpenAI GPT [24] and BERT, adopt WordPiece when processing raw data. In English, many words have the same prefix and suffix, which makes the vocabulary larger, the training speed slow down, and the training quality decrease. For example, a verb has a verb prototype, a verb present tense, and a verb past tense (walk, walking, walked). Normally, 1000 verbs require 3000 tokens to represent the above three forms. WordPiece splits the words, for example walk, ing, ed, then 1000 verbs only need 1002 tokens to represent the above three forms. By splitting English words, WordPiece can reduce the size of the vocabulary list, speed up the training speed, and generate higher quality word embedding. BERT adopts Wus [25] WordPiece scheme.

Sentence Encoding. We employ BERT to encode sentence $X = [x_1, x_2...x_n]$ into sentence sequence embedding $E^w = [e_1^w, e_2^w...e_n^w]$. It should be noted that

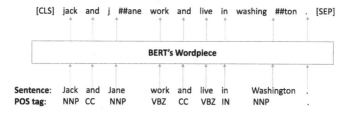

Fig. 3. An example of Wordpiece in BERT

the use of WordPiece in the last step will destroy the label of the training data. However, in practice, we need to correct the label for the training data. The infrastructure of the BERT model is a stacked Transformer [26] structure, which was proposed by Google in 2017. Abandoning the previous complex sequence model, Transformer is a network structure based on attention mechanism, which not only speeds up the training speed, but also greatly improves the quality of feature extraction. There are two tasks in BERT pre-training: Masked Language Model (MLM) and Next Sentence Prediction (NSP). When training BERT, these two tasks are trained at the same time. The goal of MLM is to build a language model, randomly mask 0.15 of the tokens during the training process, and then predict the masked tokens. Bert adds the NSP task that inputs two sentences A and B to predict whether B is the next sentence of A, which makes the model learn the connection between the two sentences. BERT truly implements bidirectional modeling of context, adding sentence-level information to make model more elaborate.

Part-of-Speech Encoding. Using BERT to encode sentences, we waste the part-of-speech tagging information provided by the dataset. WordPiece destroys the part-of-speech tagging sequence. For example, the source sentence has the word Jane with part-of-speech tag NNP. After WordPiece, the word Jane becomes two fragments (j and ##ane). In order to make full use of part-of-speech tagging information, we encode part-of-speech tags by using BIO tagging. For example, the previous j is encoded as BNNP, and ##ane is encoded as INNP. Given the part-of-speech tag sequence $P = [p_1, p_2...p_m]$ corresponding to the source sentence S, we use BIO tagging to encode it into $E^p = [e_1^p, e_2^p...e_n^p]$ according to the situation of WordPiece.

Sentence Presentation. Through the above modules, we have obtained sentence encoding $E^w = [e_1^w, e_2^w...e_n^w]$ and part-of-speech encoding $E^p = [e_1^p, e_2^p...e_n^p]$. LSTM [27] with natural sequence characteristics, perfectly meets the requirements of text processing, and solves the problem of long-term dependence of RNN. It has been proved that it can effectively capture the semantic information of each word. We choose a bi-directional LSTM to encode sentence features. At each step t where $t \in [1, n]$, BiLSTM employs a forward LSTM to generate the forward state and employs a backward LSTM to generate the backward state. The forward state and the backward state extract the forward and backward information of the sentence, respectively. We stack the forward state and the backward state to get the global information of the current word. Then, we get the final expression of the sentence $h^s = [h_1^s, h_2^s...h_n^s]$.

$$h_t^{forward} = LSTM^{forward}(h_{t-1}, [e_t^w, e_t^p]) \tag{1}$$

$$h_t^{backward} = LSTM^{backward}(h_{t-1}, [e_t^w, e_t^p]) \tag{2}$$

$$h_t^s = [h_t^{forward}, h_t^{backward}] \tag{3}$$

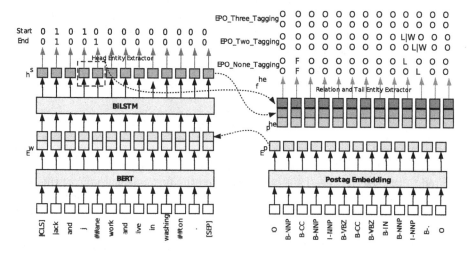

Fig. 4. The overall structure of our model. BERT and BiLSTM are used to encode the source. The head and tail entities are extracted step by step.

Head Entity Extractor. This module directly decodes the characteristic representation $h^s = [h_1^s, h_2^s h_n^s]$ of the sentence $X = [x_1, x_2 x_n]$ to identify all the potential head entities in the sentence. We use two binary classifiers: the first classifier marks a classification tag y_i^{start} for token x_i to detect whether x_i is the beginning of a header entity; the second classifier marks a classification tag y_i^{end} for token x_i to detect whether x_i is the end of a header entity. When extracting the header entity, the operation for each token is as follows:

$$p_i^{start} = softmax(w^{start} \cdot h_i^s + b^{start}) \tag{4}$$

$$y_i^{start} = argmax p_i^{start} \tag{5}$$

$$p_i^{end} = softmax(w^{end} \cdot h_i^s + b^{end}) \tag{6}$$

$$y_i^{end} = argmax p_i^{end} \tag{7}$$

If y_i^{start} is 1, the token x_i is proved to be the beginning of a header entity, and vice versa. If y_i^{end} is 1, the token x_i is proved to be the end of a header entity, and vice versa.

Head Entity Selection. In the previous step, all potential head entities of the sentence $X = [x_1, x_2 x_n]$ were extracted. When extracting tail entities, we need to select a head entity first, and fuse the head entity feature fhe and sentence feature $h^s = [h_1^s, h_2^s h_n^s]$. As shown in Fig. 4, the details of feature fusion are as follows:

$$h^{rt} = [h^s : f^{he} : p^{he}] \tag{8}$$

where h^{rt} represents the feature obtained by fusion and is used to predict the relation and tail entity. f^{he} represents the feature representation of the selected head entity. p^{he} marks which head entity is selected.

Assuming that the start position of the selected head entity is k and the end position is j, the representation of the head entity f^{he} is as follows:

$$f^{he} = (h_k^s + ... + h_j^s)/(j - k + 1) \qquad (9)$$

Relation and Tail Entity Extractor. This module extracts the tail entity related to the selected head entity by decoding the fusion feature h^{rt} of the sentence and the head entity. As shown in Fig. 4, we perform three tail entity extraction operations (EPO-None-Tagging, EPO-Two-Tagging, EPO-Three-Tagging) for each selected head entity. EPO-None-Tagging means that when extracting the tail entity, it does not consider overlapping with the head entity. EPO-Two-Tagging means extracting the tail entity that has a two-fold relation with the head entity. EPO-Three-Tagging means extracting the tail entity that has a triple relation with the head entity.

For each tail entity extraction, we use two multi-classifiers: the first classifier marks a relation category label y_i^{start} for token x_i and detects whether x_i is the beginning of a tail entity; the second classifier marks a relation category label y_i^{end} for token x_i and detects whether x_i is the end of a tail entity. Taking EPO-None-Tagging as an example, the operation for each token is as follows:

$$p_i^{start} = softmax(w_{None}^{start} \cdot h_i^{rt} + b_{None}^{start}) \qquad (10)$$
$$y_i^{start} = argmax p_i^{start} \qquad (11)$$
$$p_i^{end} = softmax(w_{None}^{end} \cdot h_i^{rt} + b_{None}^{end}) \qquad (12)$$
$$y_i^{end} = argmax p_i^{end} \qquad (13)$$

If $y_i^{start} = k$ and $k \neq 0$, token x_i is proved to be the beginning of a tail entity that has the k-th relation with the selected head entity, and vice versa. If $y_i^{end} = k$ and $k \neq 0$, token x_i is proved to be the end of a tail entity that has the k-th relation with the selected head entity, and vice versa.

5   Experiments

In this section, we show the experiments that are conducted to evaluate our proposed method.

5.1   Dataset

In order to evaluate the performance of the model, we use the widely used New York Times (NYT) dataset. In 2010, Riedel produced the NYT dataset through remote supervision [28]. For the training set, it is marked automatically by the remote supervision algorithm, and for the test set, in order to improve the quality, manual labeling is used. The remote supervision algorithm is based on the following hypothesis: for a triplet ($\langle$ head entity, relation, tail entity $\rangle$) in an existing knowledge base, if there is a sentence in the external document base containing the entity pair, the corresponding relation is reflected to a certain extent. On the basis of this assumption, based on a small labeled knowledge base and an external document base, remote supervision can label the sentences in the document base and generate labeled samples automatically. Remote monitoring can avoid the high cost of manual labeling, but there are many interference factors. In order to reduce the noise of the original NYT data set, a higher quality NYT data set is created in [9] by deleting data samples with a length of more than 100 and data samples without any triples.

Table 1. NYT dataset description

Dataset	NYT
Relation type	24
Entity type	3
Number of training sets	56195
Number of test sets	5000

As shown in Table 1, we used the NYT dataset which was processed in [9], including 3 entity types and 24 relation types, among which there are 56195 training samples and 5000 test set samples. According to the classification of triple overlap, this chapter divides the text sentence into: normal sentence, single entity overlapping sentence and entity pair overlapping sentence. Specifically, the training set of the NYT dataset includes 37,011 normal sentences, 14,735 single-entity overlapping sentences, and 9782 entity-pair overlapping sentences; the test set of the NYT dataset includes 3266 normal sentences Sentences, 1297 single entity overlapping sentences and 978 entity pair overlapping sentences.

5.2   Experiment Settings

In our experiment, the model was developed using TensorFlow framework with TensorFlow version 1.15; the model was trained on a single RTX2070. The pre-training model BERT is to migrate the "BERT-Base, Cased" released by Google. Its Transformer encoder has 12 layers, each layer has a feature dimension of 768, anTd each layer uses a 12-head attention mechanism, including a total of 110m parameters. The dimension of word vector embedding is 768, and the dimension of part of speech information embedding is 91 recovery. The sentence feature dimension of BiLSTM is 859. This model uses the mini-batch mechanism to train the model. The number of data per batch is 10. To prevent overfitting, we set the dropout to 0.5. We use the Adam optimizer and set the initial learning rate to $2e^{-5}$ and the learning decay rate to 0.96^n.

Table 2. Experimental parameter setting

Experimental parameters	Value
BERT	BERT-Base, Cased
Word embedding	768
Part-of-speech embedding	91
Sentence features	859
Optimizer	Adam
Batch-size	10
Learning rate	$2e^{-5}$
Learning decay rate	0.96^n

The model in this chapter has two main steps (head entity extraction, relation and tail entity extraction), and joint training is carried out using parameter sharing. Because the head entity and tail entity are extracted step by step, and the tail entity has three parallel extractors, multiple loss functions appear in the model. The loss function L_{head} is the optimization objective of the head entity extractor. The loss function L_{tail}^{None} is the EPO_None_Tagging optimization objective, and the loss function L_{tail}^{Two} is the EPO_Two_Tagging optimization objective, and the loss function L_{tail}^{Three} is the EPO_Three_Tagging optimization objective. The loss function of the joint model is as follows:

$$L = \lambda L_{head} + \mu_1 L_{tail}^{None} + \mu_2 L_{tail}^{Two} + \mu_3 L_{tail}^{Three} \tag{14}$$

where λ, Mu_1, μ_2 and Mu_3 are super parameters that reflect the importance of each small objective function.

Regarding evaluation indicators, following two existing works [8,9], we use Precision (Prec, precision rate), Recall (Rec, recall rate) and F1 to evaluate experimental results. For the predicted results, only if the entity pairs and relations of a triple are correct, can it be considered to be a correct result. Precision refers to the fraction of correct predicted triples in all predicted triples. Recall refers to the fraction of correct predicted triples in all correct triples. F1 is used to balance precision and recall, reflecting the comprehensive performance of the model.

If we run the model of this chapter once, we can only get all the potential head entities of the text sentence and all the triples corresponding to one of the head entities. In the model training, each training sample will use all the head entities involved in the sample and sample a head entity to get all the corresponding triplets as the training target. During the training, the sample will be fed to the model many times, and the final model will see all the triples of the sample.

Table 3. Comparison of experiment results

	Prec	Rec	F1
NovelTagging	62.4	31.7	42.0
CopyRMultiDecoder	61.0	56.6	58.7
GraphRel2p	63.9	60.0	61.9
CopyMTL	72.7	69.2	70.9
ETL-Span	84.1	74.6	79.1
Our model	**87.0**	**85.1**	**86.0**

In model testing, all the potential head entities of a sentence can be obtained by running the model once, and then all the triples of the test sample can be obtained by traversing the potential head entities and executing the model.

5.3 Experiment Results

In this section, we compare the results of our models with Noveltagging [8], Copyr [9], GraphRel2p [21], copyMTL [19] and ETL-span [10]. Based on the performance comparison of each model on the NYT dataset, we will prove the effect of the models in this chapter.

As shown in the Table 3, the model in this chapter is significantly better than other models with higher accuracy, recall rate and F1 score, achieving relatively ideal results. Compared with the ETL-Span model, the accuracy of the model in this chapter has increased by 2.9%, the recall rate has increased by 10.5%, F1 has increased by 6.9%, and the effect has improved significantly.

Table 4. The influence of different tail entity extractors on experiment results

	Prec	Rec	F1
only EPO_None_tagging	86.1	69.1	76.7
+ EPO_Two_tagging	86.7	80.5	83.5
+ EPO_Three_tagging	87.0	85.1	86.0

In order to deal with the problem of entity-pair overlap, the model in this chapter uses three parallel extractors in relation and tail entity recognition. As shown in Table 4, if the model only uses EPO_ None_Tagging, without considering the EPO problem, the recall rate of the model is 69.1; considering the EPO problem, the model increases the recall rate of EPO_ Two_Tagging, to 80.5 (+11.4); the model increases the recall rate of EPO_Two_Tagging and EPO_Three_Tagging, to 85.1 (+11.4 + 4.6). After adopting EPO_Two_Tagging and EPO_Three_Tagging, the recall rate is greatly improved, which proves that the model in this chapter is effective in dealing with the problem of entity-pair overlap.

6   Connections with the MDATA Model

MDATA is a dynamic knowledge representation framework. Compared with the traditional knowledge graph, it not only contains a series of ⟨head entity, relation, tail entity⟩, but also contains the temporal and spatial information of triples. Entity relation extraction is the basis for building a knowledge graph or the MDATA graph, but MDATA puts forward higher requirements for this task. It needs to extract five components such as {head entity, relation, tail entity, time, space} and involves more complicated relations extracted from those components. The model in this chapter is still based on the extraction of triples, but it has certain guiding significance for the extraction of quintuples. If the decomposition strategy of this article is refined and divided into multiple steps, we may have more progress on the problem of quintuple extraction.

7   Chapter Summary

In the chapter, we introduce an end-to-end joint entity and relation extraction model. The model solves the SEO problem by extracting the head entity and tail entity separately, and can also deal with the EPO problem by introducing EPO-Two-Tagging and EPO-Three-Tagging. Compared with most models, our model has achieved outstanding results on the NYT dataset.

However, the overlapping problem in information extraction is far from being solved. In the future, under MDATA framework, we can further extract the structured information with temporal and spatial information, namely the five-element ancestor (head entity, relation, tail entity, time, space).

References

1. Shaalan, K.: A survey of Arabic named entity recognition and classification. Comput. Linguist. **40**(2), 469–510 (2014)
2. Rink, B., Harabagiu, S.M.: UTD: classifying semantic relations by combining lexical and semantic resources. In: Erk, K., Strapparava, C. (eds.) Proceedings of the 5th International Workshop on Semantic Evaluation, SemEval@ACL 2010, Uppsala University, Uppsala, Sweden, 15–16 July 2010, pp. 256–259. The Association for Computer Linguistics (2010)
3. Li, Q., Ji, H.: Incremental joint extraction of entity mentions and relations. In: Proceedings of the 52nd Annual Meeting of the Association for Computational Linguistics, ACL 2014, 22–27 June 2014, Baltimore, MD, USA, Volume 1: Long Papers, pp. 402–412. The Association for Computer Linguistics (2014)
4. Miwa, M., Sasaki, Y.: Modeling joint entity and relation extraction with table representation. In: Moschitti, A., Pang, B., Daelemans, W. (eds.) Proceedings of the 2014 Conference on Empirical Methods in Natural Language Processing, EMNLP 2014, 25–29 October 2014, Doha, Qatar, A meeting of SIGDAT, a Special Interest Group of the ACL, pp. 1858–1869, ACL (2014)
5. Ren, X., et al.: Cotype: joint extraction of typed entities and relations with knowledge bases. In: Barrett, R., Cummings, R., Agichtein, E., Gabrilovich, E. (eds.) Proceedings of the 26th International Conference on World Wide Web, WWW 2017, Perth, Australia, 3–7 April 2017, pp. 1015–1024. ACM (2017)

6. Yu, X., Lam, W.: Jointly identifying entities and extracting relations in encyclopedia text via A graphical model approach. In: Huang, C., Jurafsky, D. (eds.) COLING 2010, 23rd International Conference on Computational Linguistics, Posters Volume, 23–27 August 2010, Beijing, China, pp. 1399–1407. Chinese Information Processing Society of China (2010)

7. Miwa, M., Bansal, M.: End-to-end relation extraction using LSTMS on sequences and tree structures. In: Proceedings of the 54th Annual Meeting of the Association for Computational Linguistics, ACL 2016, 7–12 August 2016, Berlin, Germany, Volume 1: Long Papers, The Association for Computer Linguistics (2016)

8. Miwa, M., Bansal, M.: End-to-end relation extraction using LSTMS on sequences and tree structures. In: Proceedings of the 54th Annual Meeting of the Association for Computational Linguistics, ACL 2016, 7–12 August 2016, Berlin, Germany, Volume 1: Long Papers, The Association for Computer Linguistics (2016)

9. Zeng, X., Zeng, D., He, S., Liu, K., Zhao, J.: Extracting relational facts by an end-to-end neural model with copy mechanism. In: Gurevych, I., Miyao, Y. (eds.) Proceedings of the 56th Annual Meeting of the Association for Computational Linguistics, ACL 2018, Melbourne, Australia, 15–20 July 2018, Volume 1: Long Papers, pp. 506–514. Association for Computational Linguistics (2018)

10. Yu, B., et al.: Joint extraction of entities and relations based on a novel decomposition strategy. In: Giacomo, G.D., Catalá, A., Dilkina, B., Milano, M., Barro, S., BugarínBugarín, A., Lang, J. (eds.). ECAI 2020–24th European Conference on Artificial Intelligence, 29 August–8 September 2020, Santiago de Compostela, Spain, 29 August - 8 September 2020 - Including 10th Conference on Prestigious Applications of Artificial Intelligence (PAIS 2020), vol. 325 of Frontiers in Artificial Intelligence and Applications, pp. 2282–2289. IOS Press (2020)

11. Borthwick, A., Grishman, R.: A maximum entropy approach to named entity recognition. Ph. D. thesis, Citeseer (1999)

12. Isozaki, H., Kazawa, H.: Efficient support vector classifiers for named entity recognition. In: 19th International Conference on Computational Linguistics, COLING 2002, Howard International House and Academia Sinica, Taipei, Taiwan, 24 August - 1 September 2002 (2002)

13. Bikel, D.M., Miller, S., Schwartz, R.M., Weischedel, R.M.: Nymble: a high-performance learning name-finder, CoRR, vol. cmp-lg/9803003 (1998)

14. McCallum, A., Li, W.: Early results for named entity recognition with conditional random fields, feature induction and web-enhanced lexicons. In: Daelemans, W., Osborne, M. (eds.) Proceedings of the Seventh Conference on Natural Language Learning, CoNLL 2003, Held in cooperation with HLT-NAACL 2003, Edmonton, Canada, 31 May - 1 June 2003, pp. 188–191. ACL (2003)

15. Huang, Z., Xu, W., Yu, K.: Bidirectional LSTM-CRF models for sequence tagging, CoRR, vol. abs/1508.01991 (2015)

16. Tomori, S., Ninomiya, T., Mori, S.: Domain specific named entity recognition referring to the real world by deep neural networks. In: Proceedings of the 54th Annual Meeting of the Association for Computational Linguistics, ACL 2016, 7–12 August 2016, Berlin, Germany, Volume 2: Short Papers, The Association for Computer Linguistics (2016)

17. Zeng, D., Liu, K., Lai, S., Zhou, G., Zhao, J.: Relation classification via convolutional deep neural network. In: Hajic, J., Tsujii, J. (eds.) COLING 2014, 25th International Conference on Computational Linguistics, Proceedings of the Conference: Technical Papers, 23–29 August 2014, Dublin, Ireland, pp. 2335–2344. ACL (2014)

18. Nguyen, T.H., Grishman, R.: Combining neural networks and log-linear models to improve relation extraction, CoRR, vol. abs/1511.05926 (2015)

19. Zeng, D., Zhang, H., Liu, Q.: CopyMTL: copy mechanism for joint extraction of entities and relations with multi-task learning. In: The Thirty-Fourth AAAI Conference on Artificial Intelligence, AAAI 2020, The Thirty-Second Innovative Applications of Artificial Intelligence Conference, IAAI 2020, The Tenth AAAI Symposium on Educational Advances in Artificial Intelligence, EAAI 2020, New York, NY, USA, 7–12 February 2020, pp. 9507–9514. AAAI Press (2020)

20. Dai, D., Xiao, X., Lyu, Y., Dou, S., She, Q., Wang, H.: Joint extraction of entities and overlapping relations using position-attentive sequence labeling. In: The Thirty-Third AAAI Conference on Artificial Intelligence, AAAI 2019, The Thirty-First Innovative Applications of Artificial Intelligence Conference, IAAI 2019, The Ninth AAAI Symposium on Educational Advances in Artificial Intelligence, EAAI 2019, Honolulu, Hawaii, USA, 27 January - 1 February 2019, pp. 6300–6308. AAAI Press (2019)

21. Fu, T., Li, P., Ma, W.: Graphrel: modeling text as relational graphs for joint entity and relation extraction. In: Korhonen, A., Traum, D.R., Màrquez, L. (eds.) Proceedings of the 57th Conference of the Association for Computational Linguistics, ACL 2019, Florence, Italy, 28 July- 2 August 2019, Volume 1: Long Papers, pp. 1409–1418. Association for Computational Linguistics (2019)

22. Li, X., et al.: Entity-relation extraction as multi-turn question answering. In: Korhonen, A., Traum, D.R., Màrquez, L. (eds.) Proceedings of the 57th Conference of the Association for Computational Linguistics, ACL 2019, Florence, Italy, 28 July- 2 August 2019, Volume 1: Long Papers, pp. 1340–1350. Association for Computational Linguistics (2019)

23. Devlin, J., Chang, M., Lee, K., Toutanova, K.: BERT: pre-training of deep bidirectional transformers for language understanding. In: Burstein, J., Doran, C., Solorio, T. (eds.) Proceedings of the 2019 Conference of the North American Chapter of the Association for Computational Linguistics: Human Language Technologies, NAACL-HLT 2019, Minneapolis, MN, USA, 2–7 June 2019, Volume 1 (Long and Short Papers), pp. 4171–4186. Association for Computational Linguistics (2019)

24. Radford, A., Narasimhan, K., Salimans, T., Sutskever, I.: Improving language understanding by generative pre-training (2018)

25. Wu, Y., et al.: Google's neural machine translation system: bridging the gap between human and machine translation, CoRR, vol. abs/1609.08144 (2016)

26. Vaswani, A., et al.: Attention is all you need. In: Guyon, I., et al. (eds.) Advances in Neural Information Processing Systems 30: Annual Conference on Neural Information Processing Systems 2017, 4–9 December 2017, Long Beach, CA, USA, pp. 5998–6008 (2017)

27. Hochreiter, S., Schmidhuber, J.: LSTM can solve hard long time lag problems. In: Mozer, M., Jordan, I., Petsche, T. (eds.) Advances in Neural Information Processing Systems 9, NIPS, Denver, CO, USA, 2–5 December 1996, pp. 473–479. MIT Press (1996)

28. Riedel, S., Yao, L., McCallum, A.: Modeling relations and their mentions without labeled text. In: Balcázar, J.L., Bonchi, F., Gionis, A., Sebag, M. (eds.) ECML PKDD 2010. LNCS (LNAI), vol. 6323, pp. 148–163. Springer, Heidelberg (2010). https://doi.org/10.1007/978-3-642-15939-8_10

Entity Alignment: Optimization by Seed Selection

Xiaolong Chen, Le Wang, Yunyi Tang, Weihong Han, Zhihong Tian, and Zhaoquan Gu$^{(\boxtimes)}$

Cyberspace Institute of Advanced Technology, Guangzhou University, Guangzhou 510006, China
18981651893@163.com, 2111806047@e.gzhu.edu.cn,
{wangle,hanweihong,tianzhihong,zqgu}@gzhu.edu.cn

Abstract. The knowledge representation framework of MDATA requires the fusion of multi-source and multi-dimensional data. The main steps of data fusion are entity alignment and disambiguation. The method of entity alignment mainly includes the similarity calculation of entity description text and entity embedding. The embedding-based entity alignment method usually uses pre-aligned entities as seed data, and aligns the entities in different knowledge graphs through seed entity constraints. This method relies heavily on the quality and quantity of seed entities. In this chapter, we introduce an algorithm to optimize the selection of seed entities, and select seed entity pairs through the centrality and differentiability of entities in the knowledge graph. In order to solve the problem of insufficient number of high-quality seed entities, an iterative entity alignment method is adopted. We have done experiments on DBP15K dataset, and the experimental results show that the proposed method can achieve good entity alignment even under weak supervision.

Keywords: MDATA · Entity alignment · Knowledge graph · Seed selection

1 Introduction

In the information explosion society, in order to make better use of different information, different organization have established different knowledge graph (KG), which extract and standardize the knowledge in the information and store it in the form of relational graph, for example, Freebase [1], DBpedia [2], Meituan brain, etc. DBpedia extracts structured data from Wikipedia entries and constructs an open domain knowledge graph to enhance the search function of Wikipedia. Freebase is an encyclopedia-like website similar to Wikipedia, and its entries are in the form of structured data which facilitates the related query between data. The Meituan brain organizes the data relationships among businesses, users and items in the form of a knowledge graph for its recommendation applications. However, these knowledge graphs are constructed independently, so

© Springer Nature Switzerland AG 2021
Y. Jia et al. (Eds.): MDATA: A New Knowledge Representation Model, LNCS 12647, pp. 99–116, 2021.
https://doi.org/10.1007/978-3-030-71590-8_6

that the representation and content of these knowledge graphs are different for the same entity. However, in collaborative applications of multiple knowledge graphs, it is necessary to consider whether the entities in different knowledge graphs have the same semantics.

Entity alignment refers to mapping the same entity with different representations in different knowledge graphs into one entity. For example, former US President Barack Hussein Obama is expressed as *m.02mjmr* in Freebase and *Barack Obama* in DBpedia, but they essentially point to for the same entity. Entity alignment also plays a vital role in MDATA (Multi-dimensional Data Association and intelligent Analysis) model. MDATA is a new knowledge representation model that introduces the temporal and spatial characteristics of entities and enriches the representation of knowledge. It is mainly oriented to the fusion and analysis of multi-source knowledge; it will have multiple subgraphs to represent knowledge, and each subgraph adopts traditional knowledge representation methods for calculation and implementation, which is an important basis for realizing large search in ubiquitous network space. Therefore, entity alignment is an important operation step in both the application scenarios that MDATA faces or the processing of its own subgraphs.

To solve this problem, there are three main methods: string similarity calculation, artificial semi-supervision, and entity embedding. The string similarity calculation method is to calculate the similarity between the entity name and its attribute string, which has problems such as low alignment accuracy and difficult expansion; manual semi-supervision uses crowdsourcing or reliable external information to perform entity alignment, although the accuracy is high, there are problems and challenges with high labor and time costs; the entity embedding method uses the knowledge graph embedding algorithm to represent the entity in the low dimensional vector space, and uses the distance calculation of the entity vector to achieve entity alignment. However, this method mainly considers the attribute or structure of the entity, and does not do the corresponding research on seed selection in embedding. There is a problem that the alignment accuracy is not high due to the insufficient number or quality of seeds.

Therefore, we propose an entity alignment method based on seed selection optimization. In the process of seed selection, we mainly consider the centrality and differentiability of entities in two knowledge graph. The aligned seed entities with high centrality and differentiability are the priority of high-quality seeds. In order to alleviate the problem of insufficient seed entities caused by this method, this chapter introduces a method of iterative generation of aligned entities to solve the problem of insufficient high-quality labeled seed pairs. Finally, the entities of the multi-knowledge graph are represented in a unified low-dimensional vector space, and the aligned entities are located close in the vector space. In general, the main contributions and components of this study are as follows:

1. We formally define the selection problem of seeds for entity alignment;
2. we used a pre-aligned seed selection algorithm for multi-knowledge graph, and used selected high-quality seed entities as label data to learn the joint representation of multi-knowledge graph;

3. We adopt a semi-supervised method of seed alignment iterative generation to effectively solve the problem of lack of high-quality seeds, which is used for entity representation learning of multi-knowledge graph;
4. We have done experiments on multiple datasets, and the experimental results show that the method proposed in this chapter can effectively construct entity representation of multi-knowledge graph, and achieve better effect on entity alignment task through fewer high-quality seed entities, which proves the effectiveness of this method.

The rest of the chapter is organized as follows. The next section introduces the background of the entity alignment. Section 3 introduces some related works in the filed. In Sect. 4, we describe the proposed method, which improves the entity alignment performance. Section 5 shows the experimental results and the challenges brought by the MDATA model is discussed in Sect. 6. Finally, we summarize the chapter in Sect. 7.

2 Background

The study of knowledge graph be traced back to the study of expert system, which solidified the expert knowledge in various fields in the form of knowledge base. Since the expert system in various fields was independent and the knowledge was highly symbolic, there were few studies on entity alignment at that time. Later, it gradually evolved into the form of the semantic web, representing the knowledge graph in RDF, OWL, etc., mainly involving the alignment of ontology and concept level, and the alignment of ontology and concept level mainly used rules, crowdsourcing and string similarity calculations and other related methods. Nowadays, with the rapid increase of various types of information and the increase of various data organization methods and knowledge bases, the knowledge graph pays more attention to the information and processing of the entity itself. Therefore, compared with the previous expert system and the semantic web, it has also developed more methods are used for entity alignment, and the related methods are briefly introduced below.

2.1 Crowdsourcing and Rules Based Alignment

The methods of crowdsourcing and rules based alignment methods are more derived from manual operations to achieve alignment, such as verifying the alignment results obtained by the system through manual crowdsourcing. For example, it used manual crowdsourcing to construct a knowledge graph in [3]. In [4], it used a combination of machine entity alignment results with crowdsourced problem selection and reasoning to achieve entity alignment. Some rule-based methods mainly focus on solidification of manual knowledge in the form of rules, such as the formation of dictionary library. In this respect, wordNet based on English knowledge and "Big word Forest" based on Chinese knowledge are included. In terms of rule matching, an entity alignment method is proposed in [5], which is based on WordNet and fuzzy formal concept analysis. There are also methods for entity matching and alignment based on regular expressions. This kind of method has high accuracy, but it often consumes a lot of time and labor cost, and the scalability is not high, so it cannot adapt to today's explosive demand for knowledge.

2.2 Similarity Calculation

The string similarity calculation method mainly realizes the alignment operation by comparing the similarity of the text description of the entities, including the similarity of entity names and the similarity of entity attributes. For example, it directly use string matching to calculate the similarity between entities in [6]. Attribute-based distribution is used to assign weights to attributes, and then it uses the text similarity of the weighted attributes to perform entity alignment [7]. In [8], it proposes an improved string comparison algorithm for ontology alignment of the knowledge graph. The string matching algorithm considers the length of the longest common substring of the two strings and the length of the unmatched string. The method based on string similarity calculation is simple to use and easy to understand, but this method has the problem of low accuracy, and it is not suitable for describing multi-knowledge graphs with large differences, such as cross-language knowledge graphs.

2.3 Entity Embedding

Knowledge graph embedding methods mainly include translation model and graph neural network model, this kind of method mainly through the multi-knowledge graph joint training, in the unified low-dimensional vector space represents the multi-knowledge graph entity, relationship, etc., such methods usually use pre-aligned seed entity pairs as label data to train and learn the multi-knowledge graph, or learning by using the neighbor structure information of knowledge graph. For example, it generated a projection matrix in [9] by training and learning a priori seed alignment entities, and transformed the vector representation in one knowledge graph into the vector space of another knowledge graph through the projection matrix. The combination of structure embedding and attribute embedding of knowledge graphs is used to align the entities of two cross-language knowledge graphs in [10], and it also realized the embedding of multi-knowledge graphs in the same vector space through seed entities. MTransE [11] carried out entity alignment through TransE [12] algorithm, specifically using a single network embedded loss function and vector mapping loss function sum together to train. In [13], it generated new aligned entities as training data according to the existing aligned seed entities to solve the problem of insufficient training data. Afterwards, it also used the newly generated aligned entities as aligned seed entities for the next round of training [14]. In order to prevent error propagation, soft alignment was introduced in [15], which realized knowledge graph embedding by adversarial learning and then perform entity alignment.

This method does not need to know pre-aligned entities or only needs a small number of pre-aligned entities to achieve a better alignment effect.

As for the methods based on graph neural network, for example, it uses graph convolution neural network in [16] to embed and align the knowledge graph. At the same time, the attribute information of entities is introduced to improve the effect of cross language entity alignment. In [17], it regarded the alignment between cross-language knowledge graphs as the matching problem between two graphs, and used GCN to generate the embedding of two graphs, and calculated the matching value of two graphs through the embedded value to realize the KG alignment. Node-level embedding is provided in [18], which used graph convolution network (GCNs) to encode information about node neighbors, and directly modeled the equivalence relationship between entities.

3   Related Work

Since this article is mainly based on the knowledge graph entity vector optimized by seed selection for alignment, we analyze the existing entity alignment methods based on embedding and seed entities.

The projection matrix is used in [9] to map the vector representations of the two knowledge graphs to the same vector space, in which the seed alignment entity was used as the bridge between the two knowledge graphs to represent the learning connection, and the projection matrix was calculated as a constraint during training, but the method mainly use the structural information of the knowledge graph, the semantic and content information of the entity is not used.

In [10], it used a combination of structure embedding and attribute embedding to align the same entities in different language knowledge graphs. The structure embedding was mainly "entity-relation-entity" information, and the attribute embedding was mainly "entity-relationship-attribute" information, but attribute embedding does not use the true value of the attribute, only uses the type information of the attribute, and also uses the seed alignment entity to constrain the loss function of attribute embedding and structure embedding.

Entity alignment based on the embedding representation of the knowledge graph is performed in [14], including knowledge embedding, joint embedding, and iterative alignment. The knowledge embedding is based on the triple facts in KGs to learn translation-based entity embedding and Relation embedding, joint embedding learning mapping the knowledge embeddings of various KGs to the joint semantic space based on the seed set of known aligned entities. The iterative alignment method iteratively aligns new entities, and continuously discovers those aligned entities with higher confidence to update the joint knowledge embedding.

In [19], it considered the local and global information of the entity to be input into the GCN for embedding learning of the knowledge graph, and also combined the iterative learning of seed alignment entities to continuously add newly aligned entities to the training to solve the problem of seed alignment entities. This method assumes that the same entities in multiple kgs have similar neighbors and attribute names. The attribute information considered here is mainly attribute names instead of attribute values. At the same time, the most common attributes (defined as an attribute that appears in more than 80% of entities) are discarded because they appear together with many entities and there is no difference. Among the remaining attributes, the k most common attributes are selected because they can better distinguish the entity. For the attribute feature vector of an entity be marked as:

$$x_a^i = \frac{n_i}{\sum\limits_{j=1}^{k} n_j} \tag{1}$$

Neither the embedded-based approach nor the seed-entity approach takes into account the impact of the selection of seed-entity on the representation of entity vectors when using seed-entity as training data, for example, seed entities with high weight or influence have greater influence on their neighbors. Therefore, this chapter considers the selection of seed entities, selects high-quality seed entities for the embedded training of the knowledge graph, and combined with the weakly supervised iterative alignment method, the knowledge graph alignment effect is better under the condition of only a few high quality seed entities.

4   Iterative Entity Alignment Method

In this section, we mainly introduce our proposed method for entity alignment. First, we introduce the problem definition formally. Then we introduce node centrality as an important property in our method. Afterwards, the propose iterative entity alignment is described in detail.

4.1   Problem Definition

Firstly, we give the formal definition of knowledge graph and entity alignment, which can be expressed in the following three formal ways.

First, we describe a knowledge graph (KG) as a set of knowledge facts that are described by a triple (s, p, o), where $s \in E, o \in E$ represent two entities and $p \in R$ represents the relation between the entities. The set E represents the set of all entities in the KG, while set R is the set of all relations in the KG.

We define $S = \{s\}, O = \{o\}, P = \{p\}$ as the corresponding sets. Notice that, s is the head entity of a fact, p is the relation between two entities, and o is the tail entity.

Considering two knowledge graphs, for any fact $(s, p, o) \in KG$ and $(s', p, o) \in KG'$, if these facts represent the same meaning, we should align the entities such as $s = s'$, i.e. $(s, p, o) \equiv (s', p, o)$. Hence, the entity alignment problem can be regarded as finding the same entity in different knowledge graphs.

In some entity alignment methods, a previously known set of aligned entities (S, S') is referred to as a seed entity, while an unknown set of aligned entities

(X, X') is represented as an unaligned entity. We mainly use the seeds of known entity set as the training set. After training the embedded model by the aligned entities, the embedded model can embed the entities of two knowledge graph in the same low dimensional vector space. Then, the entities with similar distance in the vector space are regarded as similar entities. We can use this method forecast the unaligned entity and find out some new alignment entities.

In the training process, in addition to the pre-aligned seed entity set, the aligned entity set also needs to be negatively sampled to construct a negative data set. In this chapter, we consider the seed entity with high centrality. Hence, we consider more about its neighbor when we take negative sampling. That is, we are to replace one of the entities of the seed entity pairs with the neighbor with high impact. Then the following objective functions are optimized in the training process:

$$L = s_p + \omega s_n \tag{2}$$

$$s_p = \sum_{t \in T^+} C(t) - \mu_1 \tag{3}$$

$$s_n = \sum_{t \in T^-} \mu_2 - C(t) \tag{4}$$

where S_p is the calculated score of the positive sample set, S_n is the calculated score of the negative sample set, ω is the super parameter for the balance equation, T^+ is the positive sample set, T^- is the negative sample set, μ_1 and μ_2 are also super parameters, and $C(t)$ is the score of the difference between the predicted result and the real result.

As $S_p \propto object$, the calculated result of the positive sample S_p should be as small as possible; when $S_n \propto (-object)$, that is, the calculated result of the negative sample S_n should be as large as possible. In order to facilitate the optimization calculation, we take the negative value of S_n. Finally, the objective function is optimized such that the score is as small as possible until convergence.

The relationship between S_p, S_n and the objective function can be roughly expressed by the following Fig. 1 and Fig. 2.

4.2   Node Centrality

Node centrality is a common and important concept in network science, which is used to measure the impact and importance of nodes in the network. Common centrality measurement methods include degree centrality, eigenvector centrality, Katz, PageRank, etc. The degree centrality is measured by the out degree and in degree of nodes. The larger the degree is, the more other nodes are connected to the node. Hence, more neighbors can be affected as shown in Fig. 3. Based on the degree centrality, the centrality of eigenvectors centrality also considers the importance of neighbor nodes, which is formally expressed as follows:

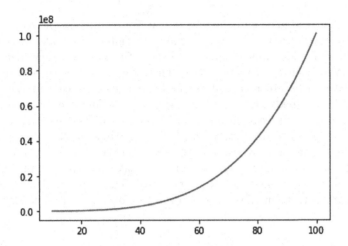

Fig. 1. S_n is inversely proportional to object

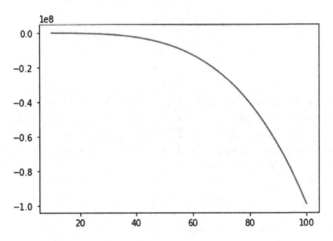

Fig. 2. S_p is proportional to object

$$c(v_4) = \frac{1}{\lambda}[c(v_1) + c(v_2) + c(v_3)] \tag{5}$$

The importance of node v_4 is determined by the importance of its neighbors v_1, v_2, v_3. Katz assigns each node the same initial centrality value based on the eigenvector centrality to solve the problem that the eigenvector centrality can't deal with the directed acyclic graph. PageRank is an improvement of Katz. On the basis of Katz, suppose that the out degree of a node is n, we attach $\frac{1}{n}$ of the starting node's central measurement value to each out edge. Through multiple iterations until the central value converges, the central value of each node is obtained.

In this chapter, degree centrality and eigenvector centrality are used to select seed entities. The specific method is to select the seed entity with the highest score as the training set from the pre-aligned DBP15K data set. In our designed algorithm, we use degree centrality and eigenvector centrality, while the remaining seed entity is added to the test set for testing.

4.3   Iterative Entity Alignment

In this chapter, we mainly introduce the method of iterative entity alignment, which uses the improved bootstrapping method. Bootstrapping algorithm infers a method in statistics, which uses limited sample data to re-establish a new sample that can represent the distribution of the parent sample. Specifically, there are samples that are put back in the original samples, which are sampled n times; a new sample is formed every time. Repeating the operation, many new samples are formed. Through these samples, a distribution of samples can be calculated. The bootstrapping method is based on many statistical assumptions, so that the accuracy of sampling will affect whether the hypothesis is true or not.

Applying the idea of bootstrapping method to entity alignment comes from the following ideas. Since it takes a lot of manual labour and time to construct pre-aligned seed entities from different knowledge graphs, the number of seed entity sets that can be used for model training is very small. Obviously, a small number of seed entity in the aligned sets directly affect the performance of training model. Hence, a method which can only use few seeds entities is needed for training.

The process of applying bootstrapping in training is to take the newly generated alignment entities as a part of the training set. After obtain new aligned entities, they can participate in the next round of training. However, similar as bootstrapping, there also exists the problem of error propagation, that is, the newly generated alignment entities cannot be guaranteed to be correct, which will directly cause data pollution to the training set, and could affect the accuracy of subsequent model.

Therefore, a novel method is adopted, where the generated aligned entities can be modified or deleted in the subsequent iteration when conflicts occur. Specifically, when the same entity has different entity labels (aligned entities) in different iteration rounds, we select the entity with higher confidence as the new aligned entity. This is important to note that, the proposed method in this chapter mainly aims at the entity alignment of one-to-one entity. An illustrative example of selecting a new aligned entity is shown in Fig. 4. We use the following formula to select or change the new alignment entity:

$$\Delta^t_{(x,y,y')} = \Pi(y|x; \Theta^t) - \Pi(y'|x; \Theta^t) \tag{6}$$

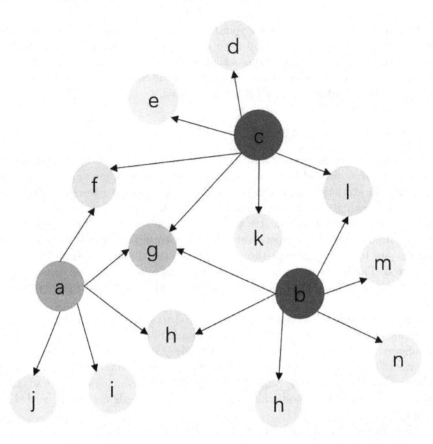

Fig. 3. The color of the node changes from bright to dim to indicate the decrease of the centrality of the node (here is the main example of degree centrality) (Color figure online)

where $Theta^t$ represents the embedded vector of the entity of the t-th round, $\Pi(y|x;\Theta^t)$ indicates that the entity aligned with x in the previous round is y. $\Pi(y'|x;\Theta^t)$ indicates that the entity aligned with x in the current round is y', $\Delta^t_{(x,y,y')} > 0$ indicates that y and x are aligned with a higher degree of confidence, and we choose y as the aligned entity of x. The iteration process can be described as Algorithm 1.

The following three figures illustrate the iterative update process of the seed alignment data. Figure 4 shows the alignment of entities in the previous round. For example, "trump" and "Donald" have the same attributes or neighbors of "president", "D.C", and "trader", so they are judged to be aligned entities in the round. Figure 5 shows that in this round of training, "trump" and "Donald" have the same attributes or neighbors as "W.h", "president", "D.C", and "trader". Compared with the previous round, "trump" and "Donald" have higher confidence in the alignment, hence "trump" and "Donald" are deleted in the seed

---

Algorithm 1: Use bootstrapping for iterative entity alignment

---

Input: Seed entities selected by centrality algorithm, seed(x,y)
Output: New alignment entity, new(x,y), $origin\ new(x,y) = seed(x,y)$
  1: Negative sampling of seed entities, $neg(x, y')$
  2: Combine negative samples and seed entities to get training dataset,
     $trainingdata = new(x, y) \cup neg(x, y')$
  3: Entity vector representation obtained by embedding training, x_v, y_v, y'_v
  4: compute $\triangle^t_{(x_v, y_v, y'_v)}$
  5: if $\triangle^t_{(x_v, y_v, y'_v)} > 0$
  6:    Delete (x,y') from new(x,y)
  7:    Add (x,y) to new(x,y)
  8: else
  9:    new(x,y) remains unchanged
 10: If the threshold is reached or the set number of iterations is exceeded
 11:    return new(x,y)
 12: else
 13:    Execute step 1

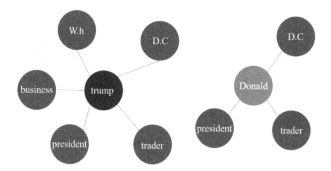

Fig. 4. In the last round, x and y had the same three properties or neighbors, x and y being the seeds of alignment

set of iterative alignment. Then, "trump" and "Donald" are new aligned seed entity pairs to participate in the next round of iteration training, as shown in Fig. 6. Therefore, the high quality seed set would be selected and updated, which reduces the error propagation in the updating process.

In the process of implementation, all entities are initialized randomly and are assigned with an initial embedding. Training is carried out by random gradient descent method. In the case of negative sampling, n neighbors of entities are randomly selected. Notice that, during the sampling process, the neighbors that have been sampled already are no longer sampled.

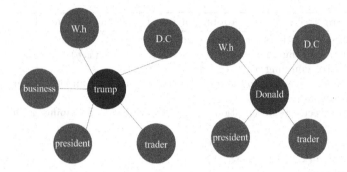

Fig. 5. In this round, x and y prime have four of the same properties or neighbors, and x and y prime are the seeds of alignment

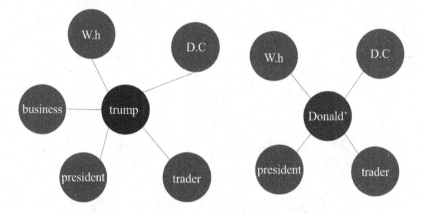

Fig. 6. In the next round, x and y are removed from the seed set, and x, y' are the new aligned seeds

5 Experiment

In the experiment, we implement the proposed method by python3.6 and tensorflow. The node centrality and neighbor selection algorithms are implemented using networkx. The CPU version is Hygon C86 7159 16-core Processor with 252G of memory.

5.1 Datasets

The dataset we use is DBP15K, which is based on multiple versions of DPedia and consists of three datasets: chinese-english (zh-en), japanese-english (ja-en), and French (fr-en). In each dataset, there are 15,000 known aligned entity pairs.

The dataset in the experiment is the data collected in [10]. Each entity must participate in at least one relational triplet, and then only the triples involving the entities in alignment are extracted. Each entity has only one aligned entity. The data are shown in Table 1.

Table 1. Datasets of DBP15K after collation

Dataset	Ent	Rel	Rel triple
fr	19661	903	105998
en	19993	1208	115722
ja	19814	1299	77214
en	19780	1153	93484
zh	19388	1701	70414
en	19572	1323	95142

5.2   Experiment Setting

On the basis of the sorted data set, the data from the top 1/2 to 1/3 of the original training set were selected as the training set while the seed entity pairs were selected by the central algorithm. The rest of the seed entities are selected as part of the test set, other parameters are also consistent with BootEA [13]. The number of training rounds is 500; the learning rate is 0.01; ω is the super parameter used to balance the objective function, which is set as 0.2; μ_1 is a hyperparameter to balance the accuracy of the positive sample results, which is set as 0.01; μ_2 is a hyperparameter to balance the negative sample results, which is set as 2.0; bootstrapping is performed once every 10 rounds of training, a total of 50 times.

In our experiment, we mainly compare our algorithm with BootEA, and the parameters of BootEA remain unchanged as [13]. In our comparison, Hits@k and average reciprocal ranking (MRR) were mainly selected as the evaluation indexes of the model results. Hits@k was used to compare the proportion of correctly aligned entities among the top k candidates. MRR was the average of the reciprocal ranking. Higher values of Hits@k and lower MRR indicate better alignment. The experimental parameter settings are shown in Table 2.

5.3   Comparison of Experimental Results

Table 3 lists the results of comparison between our proposed degree centrality based entity alignment method and the BootEA algorithm on the DBP15K dataset. The comparison focuses mainly on hits@1, hits@5, hits@10, hits@50 and MRR. As we can see from the table, when the size of the optimized seed training set was close to the 2/5 of the original ones, approximate alignment effect could be achieved. Considering Hits@50, the proposed method has the most similar result, which was 6.9% lower than that of BootEA. In contrast, the training time was 21.1% less and the test time was 17.6% less than those of BootEA. The results show that the degree centrality optimization is effective in seed entity selection.

Table 4 shows the comparison between the model results optimized based on eigenvector centrality and BootEA. The same measurements are used, and the

Table 2. Experimental parameter settings

μ	ω	μ_1	μ_2	Epochs	Bootstrapping num
0.01	0.2	0.01	2.0	500	50

Table 3. Comparison of model results with BootEA (4500 pairs of dbp15k datasets) after degree centered optimization of seed entity set (1890 pairs of dbp15k datasets)

Method	Hits@1	Hits@5	Hits@10	Hits@50	MRR
BootEA	0.6139	0.783	0.8393	0.9321	0.691
Degree centrality	0.4997	0.6708	0.7366	0.8631	0.581

seed training set is nearly 1/3 of the original training set. We can conclude from the results that the results of hits@1 and hits@50 are closer to those of BootEA, but the training time of our proposed method is less than that of BootEA, which saves 47% time than BootEA. The results show that the eigenvector centrality might affect the performance of the model, but save more training time.

Table 4. Comparison of model results after eigenvector centrality optimization of seed entity set (1645 pairs of dbp15k data set) with BootEA (4500 pairs of dbp15k data set)

Method	Hits@1	Hits@5	Hits@10	Hits@50	MRR
BootEA	0.6139	0.783	0.8393	0.9321	0.691
Eigenvector centrality	0.4015	0.5507	0.6073	0.7262	0.473

Table 5 is a comparison of the results of degree centrality and eigenvector centrality after optimizing the seed training set. From the comparison results, we can see that the results of eigenvector centrality are in hits @ [1, 5, 10, 50], with the performance 9% to 14% lower than the degree centrality. In addition, the MRR index is about 11% lower than the degree centrality. However, the training model only take nearly half of the time that the degree centrality based method spends, and the test also only costs less time. It shows that the seed entity set of degree centrality selection is more representative than the data set of eigenvector centrality selection. Hence, it can be associated with more potential aligned entities.

Table 5. A comparison of the results of the model after the degree centered optimization of the seed entity set (1890 pairs of dbp15k datasets) and the model after the eigenvector centered optimization of the seed entity set (1645 pairs of dbp15k datasets)

Method	Hits@1	Hits@5	Hits@10	Hits@50	MRR
Degree centrality	0.4997	0.6708	0.7366	0.8631	0.581
Eigenvector centrality	0.4015	0.5507	0.6073	0.7262	0.473

In order to directly prove how much the seed set selected by the central algorithm improves the model, we randomly selected the same number of entity sets from the original training data set, except the central algorithm selection for training. Then we compared the model results of the seed set selected by the central algorithm with the results that are generated by randomly selecting seed set training. As shown in Table 6, it is easy to see that the performance of the degree centrality algorithm is improved by 15% to 55% compared with the method of random selection. Similarly, the performance of the eigenvector centrality algorithm can be improved by 3% to 24% compared with the method of random selection.

Table 6. Comparison of the results of the model after central optimization of seed entity set with those of the model after random selection of seed set

Method	Hits@1	Hits@5	Hits@10	Hits@50	MRR
Degree centrality	0.4997	0.6708	0.7366	0.8631	0.581
Eigenvector centrality	0.4015	0.5507	0.6073	0.7262	0.473
Random selection	0.3233	0.5087	0.5873	0.7521	0.413

Intuitively speaking, node centrality algorithm helps to select the entities with greater impact in the knowledge graph, which are usually associated with more neighbor entities. In the real world, there is an assumption that the entities directly connected to the surrounding of the same entity are likely to be similar. Hence, through the entities with high centrality, more similar entities can be found around it to help improve the effect of entity alignment. However, compared with degree of centricity, eigenvector centricity has a drawback as the neighbors of neighboring entities with high importance may not have so high similarity. That is to say, they are similar to the iterative entity alignment, but they have the problem of error propagation. The important neighbors of the important entities are also very similar, thus the alignment performance is lower than that of the seed entity set selected by the degree centrality algorithm. Because the important neighbor is selected, the size of the seed entity set could be smaller, and thus the training time could be less.

6   Challenges of Entity Alignment in the MDATA Model

The MADTA knowledge representation model introduces temporal and spatial characteristics into the original knowledge graph model, enriching the representation of the knowledge graph. The MDATA model could be expressed through a multi-level graph architecture, and each level of subgraph adopts traditional knowledge representation methods for calculation and implementation. This modification could ensure the computing power and feasibility of the MDATA model.

In the MDATA model, the entities are designed with temporal and spatial characteristics, expect the traditional properties. In the knowledge system, the name of each entity should be unique, and the two entities sharing the same name need to be merged into the same one. Different from traditional entity alignment in the knowledge graph, different entities may have different temporal and spatial characteristics, it is much more difficult to merge the entities due to these factors.

In addition, the relation defined in the MDATA model also contains the temporal and spatial connections of two entities. When the relation changes, such as the relation disappears during some period, the MDATA could describe the change of the relation clearly. Hence, the spatial and temporal characteristics of the MDATA model are reflected on both the entities and the relations. Traditional knowledge alignment (including the entity alignment) methods might make incorrect decision, especially when the entities or the relations might have different meanings in different time periods or in different counties.

Therefore, in the scene of the MDATA-oriented knowledge graph, entity alignment also needs to be improved accordingly. For example, it is important to use the MDATA representation model to achieve dynamic alignment between entities and discover the same entity in different time periods. This could be crucial to realize knowledge fusion based on the MDATA model. In addition, this can also help realize dynamic updating of the MDATA-oriented knowledge. These methods could greatly improve the application scope of entity alignment in the original knowledge graphs. Meanwhile, the MDATA model faces some new challenges. For example, it becomes difficult to effectively integrate spatial and temporal information into the existing entity alignment methods. This might be the biggest challenge in realizing dynamic entity alignment. One idea is to apply the existing dynamic knowledge graph representation model to entity alignment tasks, and another method might be proposing an efficient embedding method for the MDATA model. Considering the strong representation ability of the MDATA model, entity alignment for the MDATA model would be a necessary and important research direction.

7   Chapter Summary

In this chapter, we use the centrality algorithm to optimize the selection of seed entities to improve the effect of entity alignment. In order to solve the problem of insufficient data set of seed entities, we use the iterative entity alignment method, and integrate the seed selection algorithm based on the BootEA algorithm. The experimental results prove that the seed entity optimized based on the degree-centrality algorithm can achieve close to the BootEA algorithm when the training data is less, and effectively saves the time cost of model training. As for future work, we will try more methods that can affect the effect of entity alignment, including more different measures of centrality and the types of knowledge graph they apply to, also includes research on the effect of central error propagation on entity alignment prediction.

References

1. Bollacker, K., Evans, C., Paritosh, P., Sturge, T., Taylor, J.: Freebase: a collaboratively created graph database for structuring human knowledge. In: Proceedings of the ACM SIGMOD International Conference on Management of Data, pp. 1247–1250 (2008)
2. Auer, S., Bizer, C., Kobilarov, G., Lehmann, J., Cyganiak, R., Ives, Z.: DBpedia: a nucleus for a web of open data. In: Aberer, K., et al. (eds.) ASWC/ISWC -2007. LNCS, vol. 4825, pp. 722–735. Springer, Heidelberg (2007). https://doi.org/10.1007/978-3-540-76298-0_52
3. Vrandečić, D., Krötzsch, M.: Wikidata: a free collaborative knowledgebase. Commun. ACM **57**(10), 78–85 (2014)
4. Zhuang, Y., Li, G., Zhong, Z., Feng, J.: Hike: a hybrid human-machine method for entity alignment in large-scale knowledge bases. In: CIKM (2017)
5. Chen, R.C., Bau, C.T., Yeh, C.J.: Merging domain ontologies based on the Word-Net system and fuzzy formal concept analysis techniques. Appl. Soft Comput. **11**(2), 1908–1923 (2011)
6. Suna, Y., Maa, L., Wangb, S.: A comparative evaluation of string similarity metrics for ontology alignment. J. Inf. Comput. Sci. **12**(3), 957–964 (2015)
7. Zhang, X.H., Jiang, H.H., Di, R.H.: Property weight based co-reference resolution for linked data. Comput. Sci. **40**(2), 40–43 (2013)
8. Stoilos, G., Stamou, G., Kollias, S.: A string metric for ontology alignment. In: Gil, Y., Motta, E., Benjamins, V.R., Musen, M.A. (eds.) ISWC 2005. LNCS, vol. 3729, pp. 624–637. Springer, Heidelberg (2005). https://doi.org/10.1007/11574620_45
9. Hao, Y., Zhang, Y., He, S., Liu, K., Zhao, J.: A joint embedding method for entity alignment of knowledge bases. In: Chen, H., Ji, H., Sun, L., Wang, H., Qian, T., Ruan, T. (eds.) CCKS 2016. CCIS, vol. 650, pp. 3–14. Springer, Singapore (2016). https://doi.org/10.1007/978-981-10-3168-7_1
10. Sun, Z., Hu, W., Li, C.: Cross-lingual entity alignment via joint attribute-preserving embedding. In: d'Amato, C., et al. (eds.) ISWC 2017. LNCS, vol. 10587, pp. 628–644. Springer, Cham (2017). https://doi.org/10.1007/978-3-319-68288-4_37
11. Chen, M., Tian, Y., Yang, M., et al.: Multilingual knowledge graph embeddings for cross-lingual knowledge alignment. arXiv preprint arXiv:1611.03954 (2016)
12. Bordes, A., Usunier, N., Garcia-Duran, A., et al.: Translating embeddings for modeling multi-relational data. In: Advances in Neural Information Processing Systems, pp. 2787–2795 (2013)
13. Sun, Z., Hu, W., Zhang, Q., et al.: Bootstrapping entity alignment with knowledge graph embedding. In: Twenty-Seventh International Joint Conference on Artificial Intelligence, IJCAI (2018)

14. Zhu, H., Xie, R., Liu, Z., Sun, M.: Iterative entity alignment via joint knowledge embeddings. In: Proceedings of the 26th International Joint Conference on Artificial Intelligence (IJCAI 2017) (2017)
15. Qu, M., Tang, J., Bengio, Y.: Weakly-supervised knowledge graph alignment with adversarial learning. https://arxiv.org/abs/1907.03179 (2019)
16. Xiong, F., Gao, J.: Entity alignment for cross-lingual knowledge graph with graph convolutional networks. In: Proceedings of the 28th International Joint Conference on Artificial Intelligence, AAAI Press (2019)
17. Xu, K., Wang, L., Yu, M., et al.: Cross-lingual knowledge graph alignment via graph matching neural network. arXiv preprint arXiv:1905.11605 (2019)
18. Wang, Z., Lv, Q., Lan, X., et al.: Cross-lingual knowledge graph alignment via graph convolutional networks. In: Proceedings of the 2018 Conference on Empirical Methods in Natural Language Processing, pp. 349–357 (2018)
19. Pang, N., Zeng, W., Tang, J., et al.: Iterative entity alignment with improved neural attribute embedding. In: CEUR-WS, pp. 41–46 (2019)

Knowledge Extraction: Automatic Classification of Matching Rules

Yunyi Tang, Le Wang, Xiaolong Chen, Zhaoquan Gu[✉], and Zhihong Tian

Cyberspace Institute of Advanced Technology, Guangzhou University,
Guangzhou 510006, China
2111806047@e.gzhu.edu.cn, 18981651893@163.com,
{wangle,zqgu,tianzhihong}@gzhu.edu.cn

Abstract. With the fast development of information technologies, more massive amounts of data are produced in cyberspace. Traditional web search methods cannot satisfy users' demands timely and accurately, and it is an urgent task to develop big search techniques in cyberspace. MDATA (Multi-dimensional Data Association and Intelligent Analysis) is a knowledge representation model with temporal and spatial characteristics. Through the effective expression of temporal and spatial characteristics, it supports efficient updating of dynamic knowledge. Pattern matching is often used to extract the needed knowledge from massive data for constructing the MDATA. Pattern matching requires matching rules to acquire needed substrings from a string. In practical application scenarios, some matching rules can be divided into several categories. The same category of the matching rules has the same meaning, but with different expressions. Regular expressions can aggregate matching rules with consistent structure and strong regularity together. However, in practical scenarios such as cyber security knowledge, such homogeneous matching rules are rare, and most of them are random and disordered. For random matching rules, manually designing regular expressions to aggregate them becomes time consuming and laborious. In order to address the problem, we apply word embedding algorithm to automatic classifying matching rules. Word embedding is a kind of representation learning algorithms which is usually adopted in recommendation systems, relation mining, text similarity matching and so on. It can convert words into low-dimensional space vectors based on neural network models. However, word embedding algorithms take into account the relationship between semantic information and context, which needs a large number of data. When we only consider the matching rules in pattern matching, such data is insufficient to reflect the context relationship, which leads to the failure of deriving accurate results. In this chapter, we design an automatic classification method which only needs a small number of data to meet the practical requirement.

Keywords: MDATA · Cyberspace security · Knowledge extraction · Matching rule

© Springer Nature Switzerland AG 2021
Y. Jia et al. (Eds.): MDATA: A New Knowledge Representation Model, LNCS 12647, pp. 117–130, 2021.
https://doi.org/10.1007/978-3-030-71590-8_7

1   Introduction

MDATA effectively solves the problem that spatial and temporal characteristics cannot be expressed [1]. In order to extract knowledge from massive data that the MDATA model needs, pattern matching is used during the MDATA construction phase. In pattern matching, many matching rules have the same type, but they have different representations. In order to match these rules together, regular expression is often used to represent similar rules, which has a logical formula operating on strings. Such expression uses certain characters that are defined in advance. Then, these expressions could represent a filtering logic of strings which could extract such "regular string" from the texts. Through regular expressions, people can efficiently match, cut, replace, and acquire words with consistent structure and strong regularity [2].

However, in practical scenarios, the words and sentences are described with random expression and they are of disordered structure. Complex regular expressions are needed to integrate these words and sentences into a unified expression. When new expression methods appear, we need to design new regular expressions to match them, which is a main drawback.

For example, in cyber security scenarios, "System Command Access", "System Command Exec (Unix)" and "System Command Injection" are taken as a same class of matching rules, which can be uniformly expressed by regular expressions and can then be matched in strings. However, this approach has two problems:

1) The commonness of matching rules needs to be observed artificially;
2) If a new matching rule does not meet the previous commonality, people need to modify or even design a new regular expression to match it.

To address these problems, we design a method based on the word embedding algorithm in the chapter, which can realize automatic classification of practical matching rules. Word embedding algorithm uses neural network models to vector-quantize words in text, so that the words with high-dimension can be represented in vector space with low-dimension. The position of the vector in the space can reflect the similarity of the words in the text, which implies two similar words have closer position.

Word embedding algorithm is often used in recommendation system, relation mining, text similarity matching and other fields [3]. We uses the idea of Word2vec in the chapter, which can also be regarded as a kind of word embedding algorithm. We first modify the input data processing part of the Word2vec algorithm such that the matching rules can be embedded in the vector space without massive data, which does not need the contextual information. Then we aggregate the same type of matching rules by a classification algorithm. The proposed method could be utilized in many practical scenarios, especially the data is sparse in representing rich contextual information.

The following sections of this chapter are organized as follows. In Sect. 2, we review the embedding algorithms, and introduce their related applications. In Sect. 3, we introduce the specific principles of Word2vec. In addition, we introduce the symbols used in the algorithm and the main functions of the algorithm. In Sect. 4, we describe the details about how to apply Word2vec to the automatic classification of matching rules. We also show the experimental results in Sect. 5 to verify the correctness, effectiveness, and characteristics of the proposed method. The opportunities and challenges are discussed in Sect. 6. Finally, we summarize the chapter in Sect. 7.

2   Background

Recent progress in neural embedding methods for linguistic tasks have dramatically advanced NLP capabilities [4–7]. These methods attempt to map words and phrases to a low dimensional vector space. The converted vectors can capture semantic relations between the words and they have been widely adopted.

Word2vec is a word embedding method which is based on neural network models. The Word2vec algorithm aims to find out the relationship between a word and its surrounding words in a sentence. It can be trained efficiently in millions of dictionaries and billions of data sets to compute the vector of each word. The training result of the algorithm, namely word vector, can measure the similarity between the words well. Behind the algorithm, the model is a shallow neural network which transforms word's one-hot sparse representation into a dense vector representation. This is the core idea to get the vectorization representation of a word through its context. The method used to calculate the word vector normally contains two models: CBOW (continuous bag-of-words) and skip-gram. Two optimization methods are commonly adopted, hierarchical softmax and negative sampling [7–9].

Item2vec [10] applies Word2vec to recommendation systems and it is based on SGNS (Skip-gram with Negative Sampling) with minor modifications. The effectiveness of item2vec is demonstrated when compared to a SVD-based item similarity model. The model produces a better representation for items than the one obtained by the baseline SVD model, where the gap between the two becomes more significant for unpopular items. Item2vec treats items as words, and the items' sequence as the words' sequence in Word2vec. Namely, it compares different items to words in word2vec, then connects these items in series. This process is equivalent to connecting words to form a sentence for learning. In this way, whether it is training or constructing a training set, it can be carried out in the way of word2vec.

Deepwalk [11] treats the nodes in a graph as the words in Word2vec, and it uses the random walk method to obtain these nodes' sequences. Finally, Deepwalk compares them to words' sequences in a text. The Word2vec algorithm is used to embed these nodes into the vector space, and these node vectors can reflect the relationship between nodes in the graph. This method can be used in relational deduction, recommendation systems and other fields.

Deepwalk's random walk is based on the edges between nodes, and then it generates a sequence of nodes, where only the first-order neighbors of the nodes are considered. In fact, the first-order neighbors in the network are very sparse.

Therefore, LINE (Large-scale Information Network Embedding) [12] thinks that more neighbors should be considered to enrich the representation of nodes. So it adopts a second-order neighbor approach. The second-order neighbor is to take the common neighbors of two nodes into consideration. The more common neighbors, the higher the second-order neighbors of the two nodes. SDNE (Structural Deep Network Embedding) [13] redesigned the target function of Word2vec, which also aims to embed the nodes in the graph into the vector space.

Word2vec can also be combined with classification algorithm to classify text. In [14], it combined Word2vec with the SVM (support vector machine) [15] to classify text based on its semantic characteristics. Word2vec is also applied in [16] to determine whether people's comments on the Internet are positive, negative or neutral.

3   Related Methods of Word2vec

In this chapter, we use Word2vec related content, and we first briefly describe the implementation of Word2vec.

Word2vec encodes a limited vocabulary $W = [w_i]_{i=1}^{W}$ with one-hot. A word sequence $(w_i)_{i=1}^{K}$ is taken from the word sequence composed of vocabulary W. The training set is obtained by the word sequence and the window size c. Then the training set is brought into the neural network model for training. After the training, the weight matrix between the input layer and the hidden layer in the neural network represents the words in vocabulary W.

There are two kinds of neural network structures in Word2vec, one is Skip-gram and the other is CBOW [6].

CBOW has multiple inputs and one output which is showed in Fig. 1. Skip-gram has one input and multiple outputs which is showed in Fig. 2. We first introduce the Skip-gram model briefly [9].

The goal of Skip-gram is to maximize

$$\frac{1}{K}\sum_{i=1}^{K}\sum_{-c\leq j\leq c, j\neq 0} logp(w_{i+j}|w_i) \tag{1}$$

where c is the window size, $p(w_j|w_i)$ is obtained through the softmax function:

$$p(w_j|w_i) = \frac{exp(u_i^T v_j)}{\sum_{k\in I_w} exp(u_i^T v_k)}, \tag{2}$$

where u_i, v_i are the vectors that can reflect the target word and the background word, and the parameter m is selected according to the experience and the size of the data set, $I_W \triangleq \{1, ..., |W|\}$.

Since the vocabulary W is often too large, the denominator of the formula is difficult to calculate. The commonly used optimization methods are Negative Sampling and Hierarchical Softmax [9].

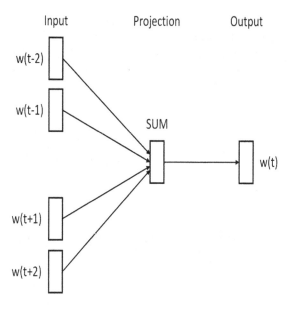

Fig. 1. CBOW

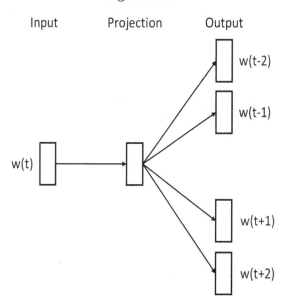

Fig. 2. Skip-gram

Negative sampling comes to alleviate the above computational problem by the replacement of the softmax function from Eq. (2) with

$$p(w_j|w_i) = \sigma(u_i^T v_j) \prod_{k=1}^{N} \sigma(-u_i^T v_k) \qquad (3)$$

where $\sigma(x) = 1/1 + exp(-x)$, and N is a parameter that determines the number of negative examples to be drawn per a positive example. A negative word w_i is sampled from the unigram distribution raised to the 3/4rd power. This distribution is found to significantly outperform the unigram distribution, empirically.

To overcome the imbalance between rare and frequent words, the following subsampling procedure is proposed. Given the input word sequence, we discard each word w with a probability

$$P(discard|w) = 1 - \sqrt{\frac{p}{f(w)}} \tag{4}$$

where $f(w)$ is the frequency of the word w and p is a prescribed threshold. This procedure is reported to accelerate the learning process and to improve the representation of rare words significantly [7]. Hierarchical softmax is an efficient way of computing softmax which is showed in Fig. 3. The model uses a binary tree to represent all words in the vocabulary. The V words must be leaf units of the tree. It can be proved that there are V-1 inner units. For each leaf unit, there exists a unique path from the root to the unit; and this path is used to estimate the probability of the word represented by the leaf unit [9].

At last, according to the target in Eq. (2), the network parameters are updated by back propagation method, and the final word vectors U, V are obtained.

4   Method

We first describe the practical problem we try to solve. Then, we describe the proposed method for automatic classification.

4.1   Problem Definition

To use regular expressions to match the matching rules, people need to design the rules artificially. After new and unmatchable rules appear, people need to design new rules to match. In response to this problem, we modified the input part of the Word2vec algorithm so that Word2vec can be used for automatic classification of matching rules.

In Algorithm 1, MR refers to the set of all matching rules and $MR1$ refers to the result of embedding a unique number in each matching rule; $Max(len(MR1))$ means to find the length of each element in $MR1$ and take its maximum value; id refers to the number corresponding to each matching rule and id.number refers to the total number of all Numbers, that is, the number of matching rules; $Vec1$ refers to the set of words vectorized in all matching rules and $Vec1.getvec(id)$ refers to taking the vectorized id from $Vec1$; Vec refers to the set of all matching rules' number which are vectorizd. The parameter m is the dimension of the embedded vector. w is the window size used to get the training set. $sliding\_window(MR1, m)$ refers to the use of m-sized sliding windows to

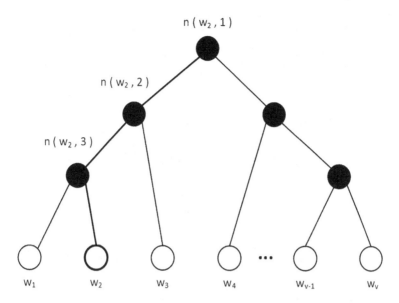

Fig. 3. An example binary tree for the hierarchical softmax model. The white units are words in the vocabulary, and the dark units are inner units. An example path from root to w_2 is highlighted. In the example shown, the length of the path $L(w_2) = 4$. $n(w, j)$ means the j-th unit on the path from root to the word w.

get the training set from $MR1$; $Skip - gram/CBOW(TrainingSet, m)$ refers to that the TrainingSet can be substituted into Skip-gram or CBOW network models for training, and the vector with dimension m can be obtained. It is worth noting that each matching rule number is unique and corresponds to the matching rule one to one. The relationship between MR, $Word2vec$, and Vec is $MR \rightarrow Word2vec \rightarrow Vec$.

The purpose of the whole algorithm is to represent all the matching rules in the form of vectors, which can reflect the similarity of the matching rules. In this way, these vectors can be substituted into machine learning classification or clustering algorithm to realize automatic classification of matching rules.

For example, $MR = ['aaaa', 'aaab', 'cdef']$. Through Word2vec algorithm, we obtain $Vec = [vector1, vector2, vector3]$, where each element in MR corresponds to each element in Vec, and in the vector space, the distance between $vector1$ and $vector2$ is close, and $vector3$ is far away from $vector1$ and $vector2$. This process is shown in Fig. 4

4.2   Automatic Classification of Matching Rules Using Word2vec

The purpose of automatic classification of matching rules is for a machine to observe the degree of similarity between the matching rules. The input is matching rule MR, and the output is Vec, where Vec is the vector corresponding to MR. The whole algorithm is shown in Algorithm 1.

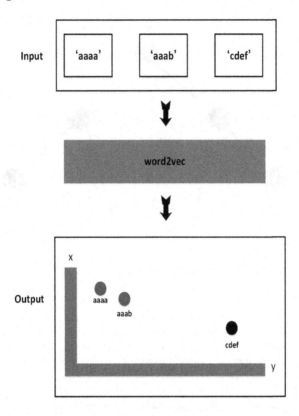

Fig. 4. Embedding example

The algorithm is described in the following steps:

1) The unique number of the matching rule is inserted into the corresponding matching rule to obtain $MR1$. For example, $MR = $ ['aaa', 'bbbb', 'ccc'], then the $MR1 = $ ['1aaa', '2bbbb', '3ccc'];

2) Setting the window size to the maximum length of the element in $MR1$. Where m refers to the dimension of the embedded vector, which is selected based on experience and the size of the data set;

3) The input of the algorithm is $MR1$, m, and w. the output is a set of vectors with the size of *id.number* and the vector dimension of the set is m. For example $MR1 = $ ['1aaa', '2bbbb', '3ccc'], $m = 2$. Then the input is $MR1$, $w = 5$, $m = 2$. The output is a set of vectors of size 3 and the dimension of these vectors is 2. Then we get the training set from $MR1$ through a sliding window of size w;

4) Substitute the training set and parameter m into Skip-gram or CBOW for training;

5) Extracting the numbered word vector from the trained word vector.

Algorithm 1: Automatic classification of matching rules using word2vec

Input: $MR1$, embedding size m, window size w
Output: maxtrix of vertex representations $Vec \in R^{id.number*m}$
1: $MR1$:Insert id in MR
2: window size $w=max(len(MR1))$
3: $TrainingSet = sliding\_window(MR1, w)$
4: $Vec1=Skip - gram/CBOW(TrainingSet, m)$
5: $Vec=Vec1.getvec(id)$
6: Return Vec

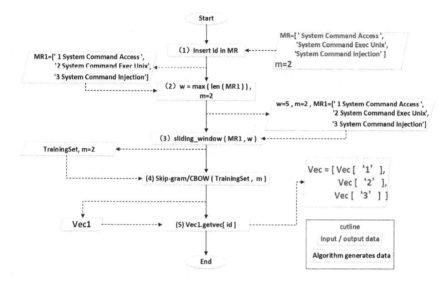

Fig. 5. Algorithm example

To better understand the algorithm, we depict the diagram of the example, as shown in Fig. 5.

First, we know that $MR = $ ['System Command Access', 'System Command Exec Unix', 'System Command Injection'].

Then $MR1 = $ ['1 System Command Access', '2 System Command Exec Unix', '3 System Command Injection'], and w is set to 5, because the longest length of $MR1$ is the second element, whose length is 5.

$MR1$ and w are used to obtain the training set. The training set and m are substituted into Skip-gram or CBOW to obtain the vector of all the words of $MR1$. The resulting vector $Vec1$ represents all the vectors of the words that are not repeated in $MR1$.

We take the vector corresponding to the number $Vec = [vec['1'], vec['2'], vec['3']]$. Each number represents a matching rule, and its distance in the vector space represents the similarity of the matching rule. The closer the distance, the higher the similarity.

5   Experiment

We implement the proposed algorithm by Python 3.7 and the compilation environment is Pycharm. The experimental parameters are fixed, and the Skip-gram network structure in Word2vec is used. For the optimization method, we select Hierarchical softmax in our experiment.

Firstly, in order to verify the correctness of the idea, we select some rules from cyber security and set $MR = [$'System Command Access', 'System Command ExecUnix', 'System Command Injection', 'HTTP Response Header Information Leakage']. Then $MR1 = [$'1 System Command Access', '2 System Command Exec Unix', '3 System Command Injection', '4 HTTP Response Header Information Leakage'], and $w = 6$ from $MR1$. For visualization purposes, let $m = 2$. In addition, since the number in front of each word only appears once in the training set, which is a rare word, the complete data set needs to be passed in the neural network for many times to ensure the embedding effect of the number, so *epoch* is set to 10000. Substitute the above parameters and data into Word2vec. Skip-Gram network structure and Hierarchical softmax optimization are used. After running 9 times, the result is visualized as Fig. 6.

It can be found that although the position of each point is different after each run, the distribution of Numbers '1', '2' and '3' is always concentrated. The number '4' is always a long way from the other numbers. This is because the matching rules represented by Numbers '1', '2' and '3' are very similar, while the matching rules represented by Numbers '4' are completely inconsistent with those represented by Numbers '1', '2' and '3', while '4' is very far away from the other numbers in the figure. It shows that similar matching rules are very close in the space represented by vectors.

Secondly, analyzing the effectiveness of the algorithm. Based on the understanding of the algorithm design, the algorithm has a good classification effect for data sets that have many identical words. In other words, the more identical words there are in each matching rule, the better the classification effect.

In order to verify the correctness of the above analysis, the mentioned conditions are quantified as *con*. Where a refers to that in the matching rules of the same category, the number of the same words between each matching rule is at least *con*. The data conditions and parameters are as follows:

1. The matching rules are divided into two categories, each of which has 100 matching rules, and the length of each matching rule is equal to 10;
2. The ratio of the training set to the test set is 7:3;
3. $w = 10$, $m = 2$, $epoch = 10000$. Skip-gram network structure and Hierarchical softmax optimization method are used;
4. Classification algorithm uses SVM, where the penalty parameter is set to 0.01.

The variation of classification accuracy with *con* is shown in Fig. 7. It shows that with the increase of con, the overall accuracy shows an increasing trend.

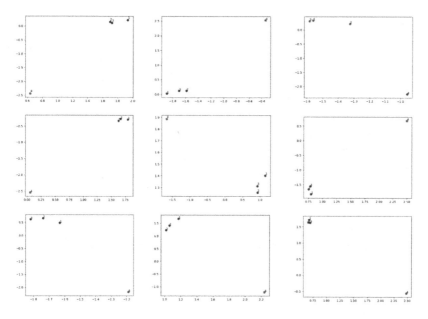

Fig. 6. The points in the figure represent the vectorized matching rules; the same color represents the agreed category; the horizontal and vertical coordinates represent the vectorized values. (Color figure online)

Finally, verifying the derivation of the algorithm. For matching rule A['abcd', 'bcde', 'cdef', 'defg', 'efgh'], it is obvious that if only the same word is used to match, A[0] and A[4] cannot be matched to the same rule, because there is no same word between 'abcd' and 'efgh'. Similarly, set the matching rule B['ijkl', 'jklm', 'klmn', 'lmno', 'mnop']. The following parameters are substituted into the algorithm, $w = 5$, $m = 2$, $epoch = 10000$, Skip-gram network structure is used and Hierarchical softmax optimization method is adopted. After that, K-Means clustering algorithm [17] is used and the number of clusters is set to 2 to obtain Fig. 8.

It can be seen from Fig. 8 that A[0] and A[4] are classified into a class, and B[0] and B[4] are classified into another class, indicating that this algorithm has certain derivation.

6   Opportunities and Challenges of Knowledge Extraction in the MDATA Model

MDATA model is represented by the multi-level graph architecture, and the subgraph of each level is calculated and implemented by the traditional knowledge representation method, which can guarantee the computing power and realizability of the MDATA model. By introducing temporal and spatial characteristics into the knowledge, MDATA model effectively solves the problem that

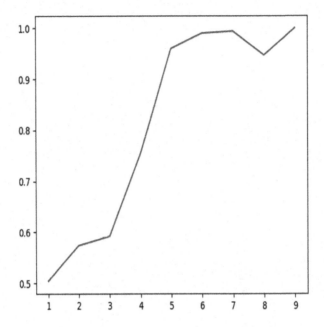

Fig. 7. The ordinate represents the accuracy, and the abscissa represents the value of con.

the temporal and spatial characteristics cannot be represented in a well-defined way. Through the effective expression of temporal and spatial characteristics, it supports the efficient updating of knowledge. MDATA model can efficiently represent knowledge with dynamic change and spatio-temporal characteristics, and has strong knowledge representation ability. Meanwhile, MDATA model is computable and easy to implement, which is an important basis for realizing large search in ubiquitous network space. In order to obtain a large amount of data needed to build MDATA model, entity recognition, relationship extraction, attribute extraction and other operations should be carried out on unstructured data. Using the traditional pattern matching method will consume a lot of manpower and material resources, so the method of representation learning is needed to realize the automatic classification of data content, so as to improve the efficiency of data acquisition.

7   Chapter Summary

In pattern matching, there exists many matching rules that belong to the same type, but they have different representations. These matching rules are likely to be expressed randomly and unstructured, and it would cost a lot of labor to group them together using traditional regular expression methods. In this chapter, the idea of word embedding is applied to the automatic classification of these matching rules. Each matching rule is embedded as a whole and expressed

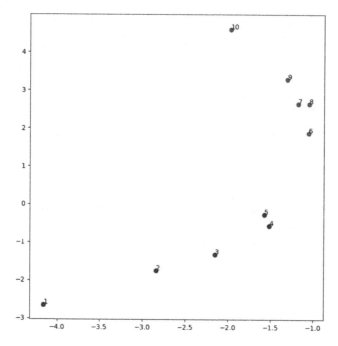

Fig. 8. The horizontal and vertical coordinates represent the vectorized values. Numbers 1–10 represent A[0:4] and B[0:4] in turn, and the same color represents belonging to the same category.

in the form of numbers. The content sequence in each matching rule is taken as a training set, and Word2vec algorithm is used for the training. The number vector output can reflect the similarity of the contents in the matching rules, and the number vector can be classified or clustered to classify the matching rules with similar contents. Finally, three experiments are designed to verify the correctness of the algorithm, its effectiveness in a certain situation and the characteristics of the algorithm. The experiment results also show that the algorithm can classify matching rules based on content similarity, which is not sensitive to the content order of matching rules. Moreover, if there exists a large amount of the same content in different types of matching rules, the classification effect will be greatly affected.

References

1. Jia, Y., Fang, B., Gu, Z., et al.: Network Security Situation Awareness. Electronic Industry Press (2020)
2. Friedl, J.E.F.: Mastering Regular Expressions - Powerful Techniques for Perl and Other Tools. Journal of the ACM (1997)
3. Mikolov, T.: Statistical language models based on neural networks. Brno University of Technology (2012)

4. Collobert, R., Weston, J.: A unified architecture for natural language processing: deep neural networks with multitask learning. In: Proceedings of ICML (2008)
5. Mnih, A., Hinton, G.E.: A scalable hierarchical distributed language model. In: Proceedings of NIPS (2009)
6. Barkan, O.: Bayesian neural word embedding. arXiv preprint
7. Mikolov, T., Chen, K., Corrado, G., Dean, J.: Efficient estimation of word representations in vector space. In: International Conference on Learning Representations (2013)
8. Mikolov, T., Sutskever, I., Chen, K., Corrado, G., Dean, J.: Distributed representations of words and phrases and their compositionality. In: Proceedings of the 26th International Conference on Neural Information Processing Systems (NIPS 2013), vol. 2, pp. 3111–3119 (2013)
9. Rong, X.: Word2vec parameter learning explained. Comput. Sci. (2014)
10. Barkan, O., Koenigstein, N.: Item2vec: neural item embedding for collaborative filtering. In: MLSP (2016)
11. Perozzi, B., Al-Rfou, R., Skiena, S.: DeepWalk: online learning of social representations. In: KDD (2014)
12. Tang, J., Qu, M., Wang, M., Zhang, M., Yan, J., Mei, Q.: LINE - large-scale information network embedding. In: MSRA (2015)
13. Wang, D., Cui, P., Zhu, W.: Structural deep network embedding. In: KDD (2016)
14. Lilleberg, J., Zhu, Y., Zhang, Y.: Support vector machines and Word2vec for text classification with semantic features. In: KDD (2016)
15. Saunders, C., Stitson, M.O., Weston, J.: Support vector machine. Comput. Sci. 1(4), 1–28 (2002)
16. Bai, X., Chen, F., Zhan, S.: A study on sentiment computing and classification of Sina Weibo with Word2vec. IEEE (2014)
17. Treshansky, A., McGraw, R.: An overview of clustering algorithms. In: Proceedings of SPIE (2001)

Network Embedding Attack: An Euclidean Distance Based Method

Shanqing Yu[1,2], Jun Zheng[2], Yongqi Wang[2], Jinyin Chen[1,2], Qi Xuan[1,2,3(✉)], and Qingpeng Zhang[4]

[1] Institue of Cyberspace Security, Zhejiang University of Technology, Hangzhou 310023, China
[2] College of Information Engineering, Zhejiang University of Technology, Hangzhou 310023, China
{yushanqing,2111903062,chenjinyin,xuanqi}@zjut.edu.cn, zjun2878@gmail.com
[3] PCL Research Center of Networks and Communications, Peng Cheng Laboratory, Shenzhen 518000, China
[4] City University of Hong Kong, Hong Kong 999077, China
qingpeng.zhang@cityu.edu.hk

Abstract. Network embedding methods are widely used in graph data mining. This chapter proposes a Genetic Algorithm (GA) based Euclidean Distance Attack strategy (EDA) to attack the DeepWalk-based network embedding to prevent certain structural information from being discovered. EDA disrupts the Euclidean distance between pairs of nodes in the embedding space by making a minimal modification of the network structure, thereby rendering downstream network algorithms ineffective, because a large number of network embedding based downstream algorithms, such as community detection and node classification, evaluate the similarity based on the Euclidean distance between nodes. Different from traditional attack strategies, EDA is an unsupervised network embedding attack method, which does not need labeling information.

Experiments with a set of real networks demonstrate that the proposed EDA method can significantly reduce the performance of DeepWalk-based networking algorithms, outperforming other attack strategies in most cases. The results also indicate the transferability of the EDA method since it works well on attacking the network algorithms based on other network embedding methods such as High-Order Proximity preserved Embedding (HOPE) and non-embedding-based network algorithms such as Label Propagation Algorithm (LPA) and Eigenvectors of Matrices (EM).

Keywords: MDATA · Network embedding · Euclidean distance attack

1 Introduction

Real-world complex systems can be represented and analyzed as networks. Network embedding map the nodes of a network into vectors in an Euclidean space, which largely facilitates the application of machine learning methods in graph data mining [1,2]. In this chapter, we focus on attacking the network embedding process, rather than one particular network algorithm. Since most network

© Springer Nature Switzerland AG 2021
Y. Jia et al. (Eds.): MDATA: A New Knowledge Representation Model, LNCS 12647, pp. 131–151, 2021.
https://doi.org/10.1007/978-3-030-71590-8_8

algorithms are based on network embedding, attacking the embedding process (instead of particular algorithms) could be a more generic approach that can be easily applied to various attack tasks. In this consideration, here we propose an Euclidean Distance Attack (EDA), aiming to disturb the distances between vectors in the embedding space directly. We think it is the distance between vectors that determine the performance of many downstream algorithms based on network embedding. Since we do not need to know the labels of training data, it can be considered as an unsupervised learning method. In particular, the main contributions of this chapter are as below:

- We propose a novel unsupervised attack strategy on network embedding, namely EDA, using the Euclidean Distance between embedding vectors as the reference.
- We adopt the Genetic Algorithm (GA) to search for the optimal solution for EDA. As compared with state-of-the-art baseline attack strategies, EDA performed the best in reducing the prediction accuracy of downstream algorithms for community detection and node classification tasks.
- We validate the transferability of EDA in reducing the performance on many other network algorithms.

The rest of the chapter is organized as follows. The next section introduces the background. In Sect. 3, we introduce the problem and we present some related methods in Sect. 4. Our method is presented in Sect. 5 including the experimental results. We discuss about the connection with the MDATA model in Sect. 6 and we finally summarize the chapter in Sect. 7.

2 Background

During the past a few decades, network science has emerged as an essential interdisciplinary field aiming at using network and graph as a tool to characterize the structure and dynamics of complex systems, including social networks, citation networks, protein networks and transport networks [3]. Network embedding solves the problem of high dimensions and sparseness of the original network data. It builds a bridge between machine learning and network science, enabling many machine learning algorithms to be applied in network analysis.

The network algorithm has developed rapidly and has been recognized by many people, but its robustness has not been widely verified, which is indispensable before generally applied. Moreover, while providing convenience to researchers, such network analysis algorithms may also bring the risk of privacy leakage, i.e., our personal information in the social network may be easily inferred by adopting such algorithms [4–6].

Recent studies on deep learning have shown that deep neural networks, especially those in the area of computer vision, seem to be susceptible to small perturbations despite the remarkable performances in many tasks [7–10]. These adversarial attacks usually target at specific algorithms and make the prediction accuracy drop sharply. Quite recently, it was also found that network algorithms in community detection [11], link prediction [12], and node classification [13–15] are also vulnerable to such adversarial attacks. Most of previous works focused on a specific task or particular algorithm which limit the practical significance of those research.

3 Problem

Network embedding attack, which aimed at making the node embedding representation as different as possible by slight perturbation on the original network, could be described mathematically as follows.

Given a undirected and unweighted network $G(V, E)$, where V denotes the set of nodes, and E denotes the set of links. The link between nodes v_i and v_j is denoted by $e_{ij} = (v_i, v_j) \in E$. In the process of perturbation, we denote the set of added links as $E^+ \subseteq \overline{E}$ and the set of deleted links as $E^- \subseteq E$, where $\overline{E}$ is the set of all pairs of unconnected nodes in G. Then, we get the adversarial network $\hat{G}(V, \hat{E})$ with the updated the set of links $\hat{E}$ satisfying the following formula.

$$\max \quad D(Emb(G), Emb(\hat{G})) \tag{1}$$
$$\text{s.t.} \quad \hat{E} = E \cup E^+ - E^- \tag{2}$$
$$|E^+| = |E^-| \tag{3}$$
$$|E^+| + |E^-| \ll |E| \tag{4}$$

where $D(Emb(G), Emb(\hat{G}))$ denotes the difference between the embedding representations of G and $\hat{G}$.

4 Related Methods

4.1 Network Embedding

With the development of machine learning technology, the feature learning for nodes in the network has become an emerging research task. The embedding algorithm transforms network information into the low-dimensional dense vector, which acts as the input for machine learning algorithms.

In the recent study, the first network embedding method was proposed in [16], namely DeepWalk, which introduced Natural Language Processing (NLP) model [17–19] into network and achieved great success in community detection [20–23] and node classification [24,25]. In [26], it developed Node2vec as an extension of DeepWalk. They utilized a biased random walk to combine BFS and DFS neighborhood exploration so as to reflect equivalence and homogeneity in the network structure. LINE was proposed in [27] that preserved both the first-order and second-order proximities to rich node representation. Moreover, it uses the adversarial framework for graph representation learning in [28].

For some specific tasks, such as community detection, a new Modularized Nonnegative Matrix Factorization (M-NMF) model os proposed in [29], which incorporates community structures into network embedding. Their approach is to jointly optimize the NMF-based model and the module-based community model so that the learned representation of nodes can maintain both microscopic and community structures. It formulated a multi-task neural network structure(PRUNE) in [30] to combine embedding vectors and the global node ranking. This model can more abundantly retain the information from the network structure.

These network embedding methods show the following advantages. Firstly, embedding can well obtain the structural information of the network; secondly, many approaches can be easily parallel to decrease the time consumption; thirdly, the representation vectors of nodes, obtained by the network embedding algorithms, can be used to support the subsequent network analysis tasks, such as link prediction, community detection, and node classification.

4.2   Adversarial Attacks

Given the importance of graph algorithm analysis, an increasing number of works start to analyze the robustness of machine learning models on graph [31] and graph neural networks model [32]. For instance, due to the connectivity and cascading effects in networks, the robustness and vulnerability of complex networks are analyzed in [33]. In [34], it developed a heuristic method, namely Disconnect Internally, Connect Externally (DICE). They added perturbations to the original network by deleting the links within community while adding the links between communities. An attack strategy against community detection, namely Q-Attack, is proposed in [11], which uses modularity Q, under particular community detection algorithm, as the optimization objective, aiming to disturb the overall community structure. In [12], it introduced an evolutionary method against link prediction using Resource Allocation Index (RA) to protect link privacy.

As for node classification, NETTACK is proposed in [13] to fool Graph Convolutional Networks (GCN) by generating adversarial networks. It further proposed Fast Gradient Attack (FGA) [14], which utilized the gradient of algorithm to design loss function. FGA model can generate adversarial network faster and make the target nodes classified incorrectly with quite small perturbations. Moreover, a greedy algorithm to attack GCNs is designed in [15] by adding fake nodes. This method generated adjacency and feature matrices of fake nodes to minimize the classification accuracy of the existing nodes. Those kinds of attack strategies are always effective in some cases since they are strongly targeted at specific algorithms.

Most current attack strategies belong to supervised learning, i.e., attackers can get actual labels of nodes or communities, and further utilize this information to design attack strategies. However, in many cases, it is difficult to get such information, making those supervised attack strategies less effective. To solve these problems, it analyzes adversarial vulnerability based on the structure of network only and derive efficient adversarial perturbations that poison the network [35]. What's more, it proposes an method based on projected gradient descent to attack unsupervised node embedding algorithms in [36].

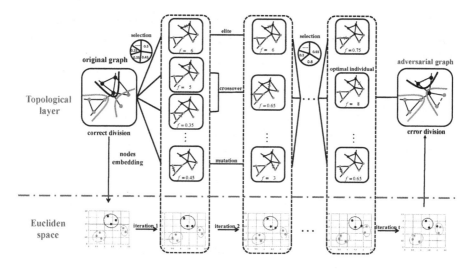

Fig. 1. The framework of EDA on a network. With the evolution of perturbation, the positions of nodes in the Euclidean space constantly changes, leading to the changing prediction results of node classification.

5 Our Method

5.1 Euclidean Distance Attack

In this section, we introduce *DeepWalk* briefly, based on which we propose the Euclidean distance attack (EDA) method. In particular, we turn the attack problem to a combinatorial optimization problem and then use Genetic Algorithm (GA) to solve it. Here, we choose DeepWalk because it is one of the most widely-used unsupervised network embedding methods and it can have good mathematical properties rooted at matrix factorizations [37].

DeepWalk. This chapter mainly focuses on undirected and unweighted networks. A network is represented by $G(V, E)$, where V denotes the set of nodes and, E denotes the set of links. The link between nodes v_i and v_j is denoted by $e_{ij} = (v_i, v_j) \in E$. The adjacency matrix of the network then is defined as A, with the element denoted by

$$a_{ij} = \begin{cases} 1 & (v_i, v_j) \in E \\ 0 & (v_i, v_j) \notin E. \end{cases} \tag{5}$$

Real-world networks are often sparse and high-dimensional, preventing the broad application of machine learning algorithms in graph data. To address these problems, network embedding is a family of methods to encode the topological properties in the graph data into low-dimensional features.

DeepWalk trains the vectors of nodes $R^{|V| \times n}$ by calculating the probability of generating the nodes on both sides from the center node, with the loss function represented by

$$\min_{R} \sum_{k=-w, k \neq 0}^{w} -\log P(v_{i+k} \mid v_i), \tag{6}$$

where the sequence $\{v_{i-w}, \cdots, v_{i-1}, v_{i+1}, \cdots, v_{i+w}\}$ is obtained by random walk within the window w around the center node v_i, and the probability $P(v_{i+k}|v_i)$ can be transformed by the following softmax function [38,39]:

$$P(v_{i+k} \mid v_i) = \frac{\exp(r_i r_{i+k}^T)}{\sum_{n=1}^{|V|} \exp(r_i r_n^T)}, \tag{7}$$

where r_i is the representation vector of node v_i.

EDA on Network Embedding. Many machine learning methods are based on the relative, rather than absolute, positions of samples in Euclidean space. Thus the Euclidean distance between samples playing a vital role in these methods. Moreover, due to the randomness of many network embedding algorithms, embedding vectors generated for the same node in different rounds might be different from each other. Regardless of such differences, the Euclidean distance between the same pair of nodes in the embedding space is approximately consistent. Those are the key motivation that drives us to propose the Euclidean Distance Attack (EDA): *Disturbing the Euclidean distance between pairwise nodes in the embedding space as much as possible with the minimal changes of the network structure.*

In particular, we calculate the distance between a pair of nodes v_i and v_j in the embedding space as follows:

$$d_{ij} = \mathbf{dist}(r_i, r_j) = ||r_i - r_j||_2, \tag{8}$$

based on which we can get the Euclidean distance matrix $D = [d_{ij}]_{|V| \times |V|}$ for the whole network, with each row denoted by D_i representing the Euclidean distances between node v_i and all the other nodes in the network.

Denote the adversarial network after our EDA as $\hat{G}$, and its corresponding Euclidean distance matrix in the embedding space as $\hat{D}$. We calculate the Pearson correlation coefficient between the distance vectors of the corresponding nodes in the original network and adversarial network:

$$\varphi(G, \hat{G}) = \sum_{i=1}^{|v|} |\rho(D_i, \hat{D}_i)| \tag{9}$$

Then, we focus on minimizing φ by changing a certain number of links in the network with the following objective function:

$$\min \varphi(G, \hat{G}). \tag{10}$$

Process of Perturbation. we perform network perturbation by adding and removing links. Furthermore, the perturbation is always excepted to be imperceptible when the attack methods are applied in real world scenarios. Thus EDA is designed to lower the performance of network embedding algorithms at a minimum cost, which means the perturbation should be as small as possible.

In the process of perturbation, we denote the set of added links as $E^+ \subseteq \overline{E}$ and the set of deleted links as $E^- \subseteq E$, where $\overline{E}$ is the set of all pairs of unconnected nodes in G. Then, we get the adversarial network $\hat{G}(V, \hat{E})$ with the updated the set of links $\hat{E}$ satisfying

$$\hat{E} = E \cup E^+ - E^- \tag{11}$$

Suppose u is the number of flipped links in the attack, the total complexity of instances in the searching space is equal to

$$O(u) = \mathcal{C}_{|E|}^u * \mathcal{C}_{|\overline{E}|}^u, \tag{12}$$

which could become huge as the size of the network or the number of flipping links grows. The search for the optimal solution is NP-hard, and thus we adopt the Genetic Algorithm (GA) to search for the optimal solution. The detailed procedure of EDA is presented in Algorithm 1.

Algorithm 1: Method of EDA

Input: *The original network* $G = (V, E)$
Output: *Adversarial network* $\hat{G}^*$

1 Initialize *the node vectors* $R^{|V| \times n}$ *and the distance matrix* D, with $d_{ij} = \mathbf{dist}(r_i, r_j)$;
2 **while** *not converged* **do**
3 $\quad$ $\hat{R}^{|V| \times n} = \mathbf{DeepWalk}(\hat{A}, n)$;
4 $\quad$ **for** $i = 1; i \leq |V|; i + +$ **do**
5 $\quad\quad$ **for** $j = 1; j < i; j + +$ **do**
6 $\quad\quad\quad$ $\hat{d}_{ij} = \sqrt{\sum_{q=1}^{n} (r_i^{\hat{q}} - r_j^{\hat{q}})^2}$;
7 $\quad\quad$ **end**
8 $\quad$ **end**
9 $\quad$ **for** $i = 1; i \leq |V|; i + +$ **do**
10 $\quad\quad$ $\rho_\tau + = \rho(D_i, \hat{D}_i)$;
11 $\quad$ **end**
12 $\quad$ $fitness = 1 - \frac{\rho_\tau}{|V|}$;
13 $\quad$ $\hat{G} = \mathbf{Genetic\,Algorithm}(G, fitness)$
14 **end**
15 **return** *Adversarial network* $\hat{G}^*$;

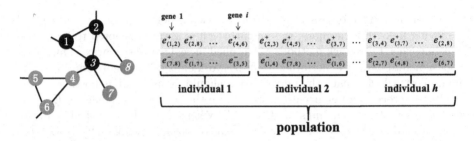

Fig. 2. Encoding of network. The individual solution includes i genes formed by adding and deleting links, and a population consists of h individuals. The sets of added and deleted links are represented in gray and yellow, respectively.

The Evolution of EDA. Here, we use the GA to find the optimal set of flipping links for EDA. Typically, the algorithm consists of three parts: encoding of the network, selection by fitness, crossover and mutation operation:

- **Encoding of network:** We directly choose the flipped links as genes, including the set of removed links E^- and the set of added links E^+. The length of each chromosome is equal to the number of added or deleted links. Figure 2 shows an overview of network encoding. Individuals are combinations of flipping links, representing different solutions of adversarial perturbations, and a population consists of h individuals.
- **Selection by fitness:** We use Eq. (13) as the fitness function of individual k in GA, capturing the relative changes of vector distances in the embedding space by the attack:

$$f(k) = 1 - \frac{\varphi(G, \hat{G})}{|V|}. \tag{13}$$

Then, the probability that individual k is selected to be the parent genes in the the next generation is proportional to its fitness:

$$p(i) = \frac{f(i)}{\sum_{j=1}^{h} f(j)}. \tag{14}$$

- **Crossover and mutation:** We then use the selected individuals of higher fitness as the parents to generate new individuals by adopting crossover and mutation operations, assuming that those better genes can be inherited in the process. In particular, single-point crossover between two individuals is used, with probability p_c, as shown in Fig. 3; while for mutation, we randomly select individuals from a population and randomly change their genes, with probability p_m, as shown in Fig. 4.

Overview of EDA. In Fig. 1, we divide the whole framework into two parts, the topological layer and the Euclidean space layer. In the topological layer,

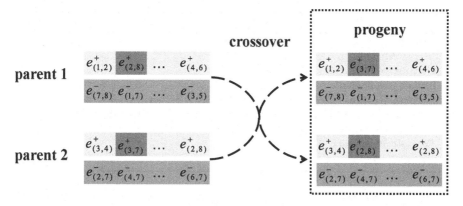

Fig. 3. An example of crossover operation, where link (2, 8) in parent 1 and link (3, 7) in parent 2 are exchanged to produce progeny.

$$e^+_{(1,2)} \quad e^+_{(2,8)} \quad \cdots \quad e^+_{(4,6)} \qquad \textbf{mutation} \qquad e^+_{(1,2)} \quad e^+_{(2,8)} \quad \cdots \quad e^+_{(3,7)}$$

$$e^-_{(7,8)} \quad e^-_{(1,7)} \quad \cdots \quad e^-_{(3,5)} \qquad -\;-\;-\;\longrightarrow \qquad e^-_{(7,8)} \quad e^-_{(1,7)} \quad \cdots \quad e^-_{(3,5)}$$

Fig. 4. An example of crossover operation, where a new link (3, 7) is generated by mutation.

we perturb the original network by adding or removing links, which can be observed directly in the figure. In the Euclidean space layer, the location of nodes are obtained by graph embedding algorithm. EDA method uses the Genetic Algorithm to iterate the initially generated perturbation, and finally blind the prediction algorithms.

For example, as shown in Fig. 1, one member (the node in black) in the original network that be divided into the black community from network embedding algorithm. However, after t times of evolutionary iterations, by flipping some links, this node is incorrectly divided into the blue community. Our strategy utilizes Genetic Algorithm to generate the optimal adversarial network through selection, crossover and mutation.

5.2 Experiments

To evaluate the effectiveness of EDA, we compare it with four baseline methods by performing multi-task experiments on several real-world networks.

Datasets. Here, we choose four commonly-used benchmark social networks to evaluate the performance of the attack strategies.

- **Zachary Karate Club (Karate)** [40]. The karate network is constructed by observing a university karate club, which consists of 34 nodes and 78 links.

Algorithm 2: Genetic Algorithm (GA)

Input: *The fitness of individuals* $f(k)$, $k = 1, 2, \ldots, h$ *and the parameters*
    h, p_c, p_m;
Output: *Adversarial network* $\hat{G}$
1 Initialize *individuals in population*;
2 *Elites* = **Retain**$(f(k), population)$; *Selection* = **Selection**$(f(k), individual)$;
    Crossover = **Crossover**$(p_c, Section)$; *Mutation* = **Mutation**$(p_m, Section)$;
3 population = *Elites* ∪ *Crossover* ∪ *Mutation*;
4 *Reconstruct network.*
5 return *Evolutionary network* $\hat{G}$;

Table 1. Basic structural features of three networks. $|V|$ and $|E|$ are the numbers of nodes and links, respectively; $\langle k \rangle$ is the average degree; C is the clustering coefficient and $\langle d \rangle$ is the average distance.

	Karate	Game	Citeseer	Cora
$|V|$	34	107	3312	2708
$|E|$	78	352	4732	5429
$\langle k \rangle$	6.686	6.597	3.453	5.680
C	0.448	0.259	0.128	0.184
$\langle d \rangle$	2.106	2.904	7.420	5.271

- **Game of Thrones (Game)** [41]. The TV sensation *Game of Thrones* is based on George Martin's epic fantasy novel series *A Song of Ice and Fire*. It is a network of character interactions in the novel, which contains 353 links connecting 107 characters.
- **The Citeseer dataset (Citeseer)** [42]. It is a paper citation network consisting of 3,312 papers and 4,732 citation links. These papers are divided into six classes.
- **The Cora dataset (Cora)** [42]. This dataset contains seven classes by combining several machine learning papers, which contains 2,708 papers and 5,429 links in total. The links between papers represent the citation relationships.

The basic topological properties of these networks are presented in Table 1.

Baseline Methods. We perform experiments on community detection and node classification to see how the proposed EDA degrades their performances. In particular, we compare the performance of EDA with that of the following baseline methods.

- **Randomly Attack (RA).** RA randomly deletes the existent links, while randomly adds the same number of nonexistent links. This attack strategy does not require any prior information about the network.
- **Disconnect Internally, Connect Externally (DICE).** DICE is a heuristic attack algorithm for community detection [34]. The attacker needs to

know the correct node labels in the network and then delete the links within community and add the links between communities.

- **Degree-Based Attack (DBA).** It has been found that many real-world networks follow the power-law distribution [43], in which a small fraction of nodes (usually named as hubs) have most connections. Since it is generally recognized that these hub nodes often have a huge impact on the connectivity of the network, here we also adopt another heuristic attack strategy named degree-based attack (DBA) [11]. In each iteration, we select the node of the highest degree and delete one of its links or add a link to the node with the smallest degree. Then, we update the degrees of these nodes. DBA is only based on the structure of the network, but not on the labels and attributes of the nodes.
- **Greedy Attack (GDA).** GDA is a method based on greedy algorithm. GDA calculates the fitness of each link from the candidate set, and selects the Top-K links as perturbation instead of using genetic algorithm.
- **Node Embedding Attack (NEA).** NEA is an attack strategy for network embedding proposed by Bojcheski et al. [35]. This method generates adversarial networks by maximizing the loss function of the adjacency matrix $\hat{A}$ and the matrix Z^* embedded from the adversarial network.

Parameter Setting and Convergence of GA. For DeepWalk and GA, there are many parameters. In our experiments, the parameter setting is empirically determined through balancing the performance and convergence speed shown in Table 2. Note that different parameter settings may lead to various performances of these network algorithms, but our attack strategies will be still effective in degrading them.

Figure 5 verifies the convergence of EDA. It can be seen from the experimental results of the genetic algorithm that iteration can be converged after 500 generations in most instances.

Attack on Community Detection. Community detection is one of the most common unsupervised learning problems in network science, aiming to identify the communities (a group of nodes that are closely connected) in a whole network. There are many community detection algorithms. Here, to validate the effectiveness of different attack strategies on network embedding, we would prefer to transfer nodes into vectors by DeepWalk and then realize the community detection by clustering these vectors in the embedding space by using K-means algorithm.

For each attack strategy, we flip the same number of links and then use the above community detection method to identify communities. We use the Normalized Mutual Information (NMI) to measure the performance [40].

NMI is used to evaluate the accuracy of a detected community. For two different categories of prediction C_p and reality C_t, it is defined as

$$\mathrm{NMI}(C_p, C_t) = \frac{\mathrm{MI}(C_p, C_t)}{\sqrt{H(C_p)H(C_t)}}, \tag{15}$$

Table 2. Parameters setting for DeepWalk and GA.

Item	Meaning	Value
l	Number of random walk	10
r	Size of window	5
w	Length of random walk	40
n	Size of representation	4/8/16/24
h	Number of population size	20
$n_{iteration}$	Number of iterations	1000
n_{elite}	Number of retained elites	4
$n_{crossover}$	Number of chromosomes for crossover	16
$n_{mutation}$	Number of chromosomes for mutation	16
p_c	Crossover rate	0.6
p_m	Mutation rate	0.08

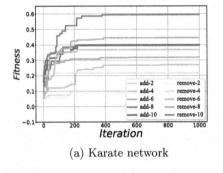

(a) Karate network

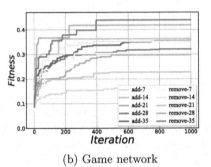

(b) Game network

Fig. 5. The above two figures are the EDA iteration diagrams of the karate network and the game network. The gray color represents the addition of the links, and the orange color represents the deletion of the links. (Color figure online)

where MI and H represent the Mutual Information and entropy, respectively, which are defined as

$$\text{MI}(C_p, C_t) = \sum_{i=1}^{|C_p|} \sum_{j=1}^{|C_t|} P(i,j) log(\frac{P(i,j)}{P(i)P'(j)}),\qquad(16)$$

$$H(C_p) = \sum_{i=1}^{|C_p|} P(i)log(P(i)),\qquad(17)$$

$$H(C_t) = \sum_{j=1}^{|C_t|} P'(j)log(P'(j)),\qquad(18)$$

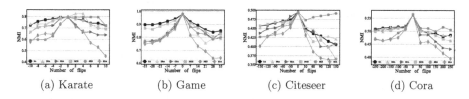

(a) Karate   (b) Game   (c) Citeseer   (d) Cora

Fig. 6. NMI as the functions of the percentage of attacked links for different attack strategies on community detection.

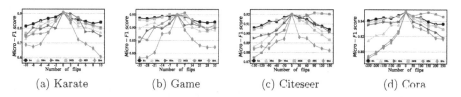

(a) Karate   (b) Game   (c) Citeseer   (d) Cora

Fig. 7. Micro-F1 score as the functions of the percentage of attacked links for different attack strategies on node classification.

respectively, where $|C_p|$, $|C_t|$ are the number of categories in the division of prediction and that of truth, respectively, $P(i) = |C_p^i|/|V|$, $P'(j) = |C_t^j|/|V|$, and $P(i,j) = |C_p^i \cap C_t^j|/|V|$. The value of NMI indicates the similarity between $|C_p|$ and $|C_t|$, thus, the larger value, the more similar the prediction and the truth are.

For baseline attack strategies, we carry out the experiments for 100 times and present the average result in Fig. 6. In each line chart, the highest value in the middle represented is the result without suffering from attack (flip-0). The left half is the result of removing links, and the right half is the result of adding links. In general, all proposed attack strategy can effectively reduce the accuracy of community detection. More specifically, heuristic attack strategies, such as DICE and DBA, are more effective than RA. GDA always has a good effect when there are fewer links flipping. In some cases, the performance of the NEA may be better than EDA. But in the majority of cases, our proposed EDA exhibits the best overall performance, with the lowest NMI in four networks.

Attack on Node Classification. Different from the community detection problem, node classification is a typical supervised learning in network science in which the label of some nodes are known. Again, here we would like to use DeepWalk to map nodes to vectors and then use Logistic Regression (LR) [44] to classify them, namely *DeepWalk+LR*. We use the same set of benchmark networks since their real communities are known beforehand. We randomly choose 70% of nodes as the training set and treat the rest as the test set, and use Micro-F1 and Macro-F1 to evaluate the classification results. We calculate the number of true positives (TP), false positives (FP), true negatives (TN), false negatives (FN) in the instances.

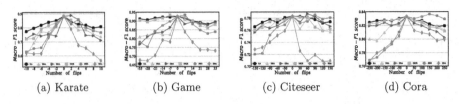

(a) Karate   (b) Game   (c) Citeseer   (d) Cora

Fig. 8. Macro-F1 score as the functions of the percentage of attacked links for different attack strategies on node classification.

Macro-F1 and Micro-F1 are then defined as

$$\text{Macro} - \text{F1} = \frac{\sum_{C_P \in C_T} F1(C_P))}{|C_T|}, \tag{19}$$

$$\text{Micro} - \text{F1} = \frac{2 * Pr * R}{Pr + R}, \tag{20}$$

respectively, where C_P, C_T are the category of in the division of prediction and that of truth, $F1(C_P)$ is the F1-measure for the label C_P, and Pr and R are calculated by

$$Pr = \frac{\sum_{C_P \in C_T} TP}{\sum_{C_P \in C_T} (TP + FP)}, \tag{21}$$

$$R = \frac{\sum_{C_P \in C_T} TP}{\sum_{C_P \in C_T} (TP + FN)}, \tag{22}$$

For multi-classification problems, Micro-F1 and Macro-F1 are used to evaluate the performance of the classification model.

Similarly, for each attack strategy, we flip the same number of links and then use the above two indicators to evaluate. For each case, we carry out the experiments for 100 times and present the average of results in Fig. 7 and Fig. 8. We find that both Micro-F1 and Macro-F1 decrease after each attack, regardless of the choice of the downstream classification algorithm (LR or KNN). In most cases, EDA still performs best, leading to the most significant drop of Micro-F1 and Macro-F1. The heuristic attack strategies DICE is more effective than RA, consistent with the results in community detection. However, it seems that in some instances, when the percentage of flipping links is relatively big, baseline methods may be more effective than EDA. It might be due to: GA has been recognized to tend to be trapped in local optimum. But still, in the majority of cases, our proposed EDA is significantly more effective than the other attack strategies.

Transferability of EDA. Generally, disturbing the distance matrix between node vectors in embedding space is equivalent to altering the similarity between nodes in the network, which will naturally affect other algorithms. We also examine the transferability of the proposed DeepWalk-based EDA method for other network algorithms.

In particular, we choose another network embedding method High-Order Proximity preserved Embedding (HOPE) [45] and two classic network algorithms, including Label Propagation Algorithm (LPA) [46] and Eigenvectors of Matrices (EM) [47], which are not based on network embedding. HOPE utilizes the generalized SVD to handle the formulation of a class of high-order proximity measurements. HOPE is widely used due to its high effectiveness and efficiency. LPA sets the label of a node identical to most of its neighbors through an iterative process, while EM directly uses the modularity matrix to study the community structure. We choose the two relatively large networks, i.e., Game and Cora, to explore the transferability of EDA.

The results are shown in Table 3. Although EDA is based on DeepWalk, it is still valid on HOPE-based node classification and community detection algorithms, i.e., HOPE+LR and HOPE+K-Means. Moreover, it is also valid on LPA and EM, which are not based on any network embedding algorithm. EDA still outperforms the other baseline attack strategies in most cases, suggesting that it has relatively strong transferability, i.e., we can generate small perturbations on the target network by EDA and destroy many network algorithms, no matter whether it is based on a certain network embedding method.

Visualization and Explanation Statistics of Flipping Links. To better understand how EDA works in reality, we visualize the perturbations of the added and deleted links to see how many of them are within the same communities or between different communities. Taking the karate club network as an example, we present its original network and the adversarial network after one-link attack, as shown in Fig. 9, where we can see that the added link is between two different communities while the deleted one is within the same community. To give more comprehensive results, we consider all the flipping links in all the experiments for experimental networks, and count the percentages of added links and deleted links within or between communities, respectively, as shown in Fig. 10. We find that most of the added links are between communities, while most of the deleted links are within the same community. This rule is quite interesting since EDA focuses on perturbing the network from embedding space without any prior knowledge of communities. One reason may be that the community is a critical structural property that matters the embedding results, and this is why EDA behaves quite well on attacking community detection algorithms.

The Position of Node Vector. Furthermore, to show what EDA does to network embedding, we also visualize node embedding vectors by t-sne method after the attack. For different percentages of rewiring links ranging from 1% to 7% in Karate club network, we obtain the nodes vectors of original and adversarial networks using DeepWalk, and then display the results in a two-dimensional space, as shown in Fig. 11. There are four communities represented by different colors. When there is no attack, the node vectors of different communities are separated, as shown in Fig. 11(a). As the number of rewiring links increases, the node vectors of different communities are being mixed gradually, and finally

Table 3. Transferability results on different attack strategies.

Dataset	Model	Metric	Baseline	R-7	R-14	R-21	R-28	R-35	A-7	A-14	A-21	A-28	A-35
Game	HOPE+LR	Micro-F1	Unattack	0.840	0.840	0.840	0.840	0.840	0.840	0.840	0.840	0.840	0.840
			RA	0.796	0.779	0.760	0.761	0.754	0.823	0.811	0.797	0.792	0.802
			Degree attack	0.810	0.717	0.727	0.715	0.704	0.844	0.826	0.830	0.786	0.779
			Greedy attack	0.835	0.721	0.802	0.782	0.703	0.848	0.839	0.761	0.820	0.750
			DICE	0.783	0.767	0.755	0.751	0.746	0.799	0.783	0.779	0.773	0.763
			NEA	0.724	0.727	0.799	0.711	0.798	0.823	0.784	0.771	0.819	0.787
			EDA*	**0.670**	**0.596**	**0.615**	**0.600**	**0.607**	**0.733**	**0.667**	**0.630**	**0.630**	**0.659**
		Macro-F1	Unattack	0.717	0.717	0.717	0.717	0.717	0.717	0.717	0.717	0.717	0.717
			RA	0.654	0.625	0.598	0.607	0.580	0.693	0.672	0.643	0.643	0.662
			Degree attack	0.670	0.555	0.551	0.548	0.535	0.720	0.691	0.693	0.626	0.612
			Greedy attack	0.714	0.553	0.705	0.682	0.537	0.725	0.724	0.592	0.717	0.598
			DICE	0.639	0.614	0.598	0.589	0.584	0.658	0.631	0.631	0.616	0.605
			NEA	0.545	0.532	0.669	0.521	0.663	0.683	0.619	0.607	0.695	0.637
			EDA*	**0.481**	**0.393**	**0.427**	**0.393**	**0.410**	**0.566**	**0.511**	**0.435**	**0.436**	**0.479**
	HOPE+K-Means	NMI	Unattack	0.496	0.496	0.496	0.496	0.496	0.496	0.496	0.496	0.496	0.496
			RA	0.460	0.451	0.443	0.433	0.427	0.472	0.468	0.464	0.460	0.473
			Degree attack	0.472	0.463	0.456	0.450	0.454	0.470	0.462	0.462	0.452	0.457
			Greedy attack	0.463	0.447	0.467	0.450	0.433	0.475	0.473	0.457	0.506	0.460
			DICE	0.460	0.441	0.439	0.435	0.432	0.462	0.458	0.458	0.471	0.452
			NEA	0.441	0.434	0.450	0.413	0.437	0.515	0.510	0.512	0.515	0.508
			EDA*	**0.408**	**0.408**	**0.396**	**0.370**	**0.391**	**0.439**	**0.420**	**0.405**	**0.408**	**0.392**
	LPA	NMI	Unattack	0.673	0.673	0.673	0.673	0.673	0.673	0.673	0.673	0.673	0.673
			RA	0.663	0.656	0.652	0.643	0.622	0.651	0.627	0.591	0.560	0.586
			Degree attack	0.621	**0.602**	0.614	0.604	0.596	**0.581**	**0.545**	**0.507**	**0.506**	**0.504**
			Greedy attack	0.646	0.622	0.605	0.599	0.604	0.635	0.617	0.593	0.600	0.605
			DICE	0.620	0.653	0.619	**0.588**	0.582	0.619	0.583	0.541	0.518	0.547
			NEA	0.621	0.613	0.609	0.598	**0.564**	0.620	0.607	0.608	0.604	0.604
			EDA*	**0.606**	0.603	**0.604**	0.599	0.578	0.608	0.565	0.526	0.523	0.513
	EM	NMI	Unattack	0.723	0.723	0.723	0.723	0.723	0.723	0.723	0.723	0.723	0.723
			RA	0.723	0.723	0.724	0.720	0.698	0.701	0.676	0.669	0.655	0.664
			Degree attack	**0.662**	0.680	0.678	0.680	0.693	0.696	0.680	0.670	**0.654**	0.660
			Greedy attack	0.718	0.710	0.716	0.717	0.712	0.718	0.694	0.673	0.665	0.655
			DICE	0.738	0.713	0.710	0.704	0.690	0.710	0.672	0.672	0.671	0.662
			NEA	0.703	0.712	0.716	0.736	0.757	**0.672**	0.749	0.726	0.753	0.758
			EDA*	0.672	**0.673**	**0.668**	**0.661**	**0.659**	0.685	**0.661**	**0.648**	0.657	**0.632**

Dataset	Model	Metric	Baseline	R-50	R-100	R-150	R-200	R-250	A-50	A-100	A-150	A-200	A-250
Cora	HOPE+LR	Micro-F1	Unattack	0.663	0.663	0.663	0.663	0.663	0.663	0.663	0.663	0.663	0.663
			RA	0.663	0.658	0.656	0.657	0.654	0.658	0.657	0.657	0.655	0.654
			Degree attack	0.662	0.658	0.656	0.656	0.658	0.666	0.660	0.648	0.656	0.662
			Greedy attack	0.663	0.648	0.640	0.646	0.638	0.664	0.656	0.651	0.654	0.652
			DICE	0.657	0.659	0.655	0.654	0.649	0.659	0.654	0.654	0.650	0.650
			NEA	0.653	0.650	0.643	0.640	0.635	0.660	0.660	0.657	0.663	0.668
			EDA*	**0.640**	**0.641**	**0.630**	**0.636**	**0.627**	**0.637**	**0.635**	**0.635**	**0.636**	**0.629**
		Macro-F1	Unattack	0.608	0.608	0.608	0.608	0.608	0.608	0.608	0.608	0.608	0.608
			RA	0.607	0.601	0.601	0.601	0.600	0.602	0.598	0.599	0.597	0.598
			Degree attack	0.606	0.603	0.600	0.598	0.604	0.610	0.603	0.595	0.604	0.607
			Greedy attack	0.601	0.589	0.584	0.585	0.582	0.602	0.606	0.595	0.599	0.590
			DICE	0.601	0.604	0.600	0.599	0.591	0.603	0.594	0.595	0.594	0.591
			NEA	0.596	0.596	0.588	0.583	0.574	0.603	0.603	0.602	0.609	0.616
			EDA*	**0.583**	**0.587**	**0.575**	**0.575**	**0.570**	**0.581**	**0.582**	**0.584**	**0.579**	**0.570**
	HOPE+K-Means	NMI	Unattack	0.262	0.262	0.262	0.262	0.262	0.262	0.262	0.262	0.262	0.262
			RA	0.252	0.251	0.249	0.248	0.248	0.253	0.252	0.252	0.251	0.252
			Degree attack	0.251	0.252	0.253	0.252	0.252	0.251	0.252	0.251	0.252	0.252
			Greedy attack	**0.248**	0.251	0.251	0.250	0.249	**0.248**	0.251	0.251	**0.250**	**0.249**
			DICE	0.251	0.250	0.249	0.247	**0.242**	0.251	0.251	0.253	0.252	0.252
			NEA	0.251	0.254	0.251	0.249	0.246	0.251	0.252	0.252	0.252	0.251
			EDA*	**0.248**	**0.247**	**0.243**	**0.245**	0.244	0.250	**0.250**	**0.250**	**0.250**	**0.249**
	LPA	NMI	Unattack	0.488	0.488	0.488	0.488	0.488	0.488	0.488	0.488	0.488	0.488
			RA	0.481	0.481	0.479	0.480	0.480	0.477	0.473	0.468	0.466	0.463
			Degree attack	0.480	0.481	0.480	0.478	0.480	**0.470**	**0.461**	**0.452**	**0.443**	**0.435**
			Greedy attack	**0.478**	0.480	0.481	0.479	0.479	0.473	0.471	0.466	0.459	0.455
			DICE	0.479	0.479	0.477	0.476	0.476	0.475	0.471	0.465	0.462	0.455
			NEA	0.482	0.480	0.478	0.480	0.480	0.483	0.481	0.480	0.481	0.483
			EDA*	**0.478**	**0.474**	**0.476**	**0.472**	**0.473**	0.471	0.464	0.457	0.456	0.455
	EM	NMI	Unattack	0.445	0.445	0.445	0.445	0.445	0.445	0.445	0.445	0.445	0.445
			RA	0.447	0.440	0.438	0.431	0.436	0.445	0.437	0.428	0.415	0.404
			Degree attack	0.443	0.446	0.443	0.439	0.439	0.454	0.455	0.438	0.451	0.429
			Greedy attack	0.446	0.448	0.442	0.444	0.450	0.442	0.429	0.431	0.410	0.414
			DICE	0.443	0.444	0.444	0.440	0.435	0.443	0.430	**0.412**	0.404	0.405
			NEA	**0.418**	0.444	0.464	0.459	0.452	0.457	0.443	0.473	0.465	0.459
			EDA*	0.442	**0.436**	**0.437**	**0.429**	**0.417**	**0.437**	**0.425**	0.414	**0.380**	**0.402**

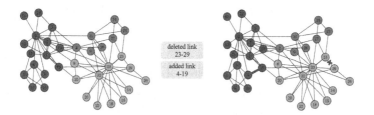

Fig. 9. The network visualization of EDA attack. Left is the original karate network, and the right is the adversarial network generated by EDA, which added a link between nodes 4 and 19, while deleted a link between nodes 23 and 29. Different colors represent different communities. (Color figure online)

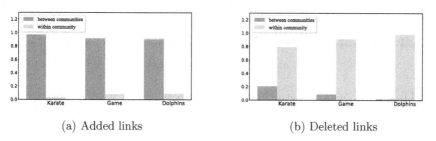

(a) Added links   (b) Deleted links

Fig. 10. The percentages of (a) added links and (b) deleted links within community and between communities.

become inseparable, as shown in Fig. 11(h). This result demonstrates that EDA indeed has a significant effect on network embedding, and can further disturb the subsequent community detection or node classification effectively.

6 Connection with the MDATA Model

MDATA can be regarded as a special knowledge graph which expands spatio-temporal information. Thus representation learning is a common but effective strategy for knowledge construction and knowledge calculation. The network embedding attack algorithm proposed in this chapter can be migrated to MDATA for embedding reliability analysis, which could improve the robustness of MDATA in a targeted way, make the results of knowledge calculation more reliable.

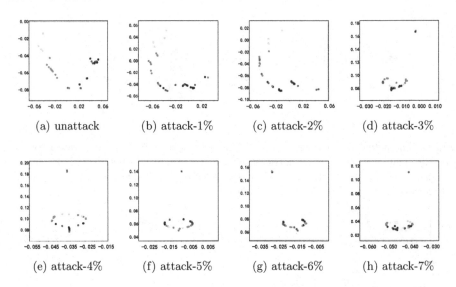

(a) unattack   (b) attack-1%   (c) attack-2%   (d) attack-3%

(e) attack-4%   (f) attack-5%   (g) attack-6%   (h) attack-7%

Fig. 11. The visualization of node vectors in two-dimensional embedding space by attacking certain percentages of links. Different colors represent different communities. As more links are attacked by EDA, it is getting more difficult to distinguish the node vectors of different communities in the embedding space.

7   Chapter Summary

In this chapter, we propose the novel unsupervised attack strategy, namely EDA, on network embedding, with the focus on disturbing the Euclidean distance between nodes in the embedding space as much as possible with minimal changes of the network structure. Since network embedding is becoming the basis of many network algorithms, EDA can be considered as a universal attack strategy that can degenerate many downstream network algorithms.

We take the DeepWalk as the basis to design our EDA, and a number of experiments on real networks validate that EDA is more effective than a set of baseline attack strategies on community detection and node classification, no matter whether these algorithms are based on DeepWalk or other embedding methods, or even not based on embedding. Such results indicate the strong transferability of our strategy. Not that, our EDA is an attack on disturbing global network structure, and we may also focus on disturbing local structure around target nodes and links, to realize target attacks, which belongs to our future work.

Acknowledgments. This work was partially supported by the National Natural Science Foundation of China under Grant No. 61973273 and the Special Scientific Research Fund of Basic Public Welfare Profession of Zhejiang Province under Grant LGF20F020016

References

1. Bengio, Y., Courville, A., Vincent, P.: Representation learning: a review and new perspectives. IEEE Trans. Pattern Anal. Mach. Intell. **35**(8), 1798–1828 (2013)
2. Hong, R. He, Y., Wu, L., Ge, Y., Wu, X.: Deep attributed network embedding by preserving structure and attribute information. IEEE Trans. Syst. Man Cybern.: Syst. (2019)
3. Barabási, A.-L., et al.: Network Science. Cambridge University Press, Cambridge (2016)
4. Liben-Nowell, D., Kleinberg, J.: The link-prediction problem for social networks. J. Am. Soc. Inform. Sci. Technol. **58**(7), 1019–1031 (2007)
5. Andersen, R., Chung, F., Lang, K.: Local graph partitioning using pagerank vectors. In: Null, pp. 475–486. IEEE (2006)
6. Fortunato, S.: Community detection in graphs. Phys. Rep. **486**(3–5), 75–174 (2010)
7. Szegedy, C., et al.: Intriguing properties of neural networks. arXiv preprint arXiv:1312.6199 (2013)
8. Athalye, A., Sutskever, I.: Synthesizing robust adversarial examples. arXiv preprint arXiv:1707.07397 (2017)
9. Papernot, N., McDaniel, P., Jha, S., Fredrikson, M., Celik, Z.B., Swami, A.: The limitations of deep learning in adversarial settings. In: 2016 IEEE European Symposium on Security and Privacy (EuroS&P), pp. 372–387. IEEE (2016)
10. Kurakin, A., Goodfellow, I., Bengio, S.: Adversarial examples in the physical world. arXiv preprint arXiv:1607.02533 (2016)
11. Chen, J., et al.: GA based Q-attack on community detection. arXiv preprint arXiv:1811.00430 (2018)
12. Yu, S., et al.: Target defense against link-prediction-based attacks via evolutionary perturbations. arXiv preprint arXiv:1809.05912 (2018)
13. Zügner, D., Akbarnejad, A., Günnemann, S.: Adversarial attacks on neural networks for graph data. In: Proceedings of the 24th ACM SIGKDD International Conference on Knowledge Discovery & Data Mining, pp. 2847–2856. ACM (2018)
14. Chen, J., Wu, Y., Xu, X., Chen, Y., Zheng, H., Xuan, Q.: Fast gradient attack on network embedding. arXiv preprint arXiv:1809.02797 (2018)
15. Wang, X., Eaton, J., Hsieh, C.-J., Wu, F.: Attack graph convolutional networks by adding fake nodes. arXiv preprint arXiv:1810.10751 (2018)
16. Perozzi, B., Al-Rfou, R., Skiena, S.: DeepWalk: online learning of social representations. In: Proceedings of the 20th ACM SIGKDD International Conference on Knowledge Discovery and Data Mining, pp. 701–710. ACM (2014)
17. Collobert, R., Weston, J.: A unified architecture for natural language processing: deep neural networks with multitask learning. In: Proceedings of the 25th International Conference on Machine Learning, pp. 160–167. ACM (2008)
18. Mikolov, T., Chen, K., Corrado, G., Dean, J.: Efficient estimation of word representations in vector space. arXiv preprint arXiv:1301.3781 (2013)
19. Mikolov, T., Sutskever, I., Chen, K., Corrado, G.S., Dean, J.: Distributed representations of words and phrases and their compositionality. In: Advances in Neural Information Processing Systems, pp. 3111–3119 (2013)
20. Fortunato, S., Hric, D.: Community detection in networks: a user guide. Phys. Rep. **659**, 1–44 (2016)
21. Guerrero, M., Montoya, F.G., Baños, R., Alcayde, A., Gil, C.: Adaptive community detection in complex networks using genetic algorithms. Neurocomputing **266**, 101–113 (2017)

22. Tang, L., Liu, H.: Leveraging social media networks for classification. Data Min. Knowl. Disc. **23**(3), 447–478 (2011)
23. Liu, X., Shen, C., Guan, X., Zhou, Y.: We know who you are: discovering similar groups across multiple social networks. IEEE Trans. Syst. Man Cybern.: Syst. **99**, 1–12 (2018)
24. Tang, J., Aggarwal, C., Liu, H.: Node classification in signed social networks. In: Proceedings of the 2016 SIAM International Conference on Data Mining, pp. 54–62. SIAM (2016)
25. Bhagat, S., Cormode, G., Muthukrishnan, S.: Node classification in social networks. In: Aggarwal, C. (ed.) Social Network Data Analytics, pp. 115–148. Springer, Boston (2011). https://doi.org/10.1007/978-1-4419-8462-3_5
26. Grover, A., Leskovec, J.: node2vec: scalable feature learning for networks. In: Proceedings of the 22nd ACM SIGKDD International Conference on Knowledge Discovery and Data Mining, pp. 855–864. ACM (2016)
27. Tang, J., Qu, M., Wang, M., Zhang, M., Yan, J., Mei, Q.: LINE: large-scale information network embedding. In: Proceedings of the 24th International Conference on World Wide Web, pp. 1067–1077. International World Wide Web Conferences Steering Committee (2015)
28. Pan, S., Hu, R., Long, G., Jiang, J., Yao, L., Zhang, C.: Adversarially regularized graph autoencoder for graph embedding. arXiv preprint arXiv:1802.04407 (2018)
29. Wang, X., Cui, P., Wang, J., Pei, J., Zhu, W., Yang, S.: Community preserving network embedding. In: Thirty-First AAAI Conference on Artificial Intelligence (2017)
30. Lai, Y.-A., Hsu, C.-C., Chen, W.H., Yeh, M.-Y., Lin, S.-D.: Prune: preserving proximity and global ranking for network embedding. In: Guyon, I., et al. (eds.) Advances in Neural Information Processing Systems, vol. 30, pp. 5257–5266, Curran Associates Inc. (2017)
31. Dai, H., et al.: Adversarial attack on graph structured data. arXiv preprint arXiv:1806.02371 (2018)
32. Wu, Z., Pan, S., Chen, F., Long, G., Zhang, C., Yu, P.S.: A comprehensive survey on graph neural networks. arXiv preprint arXiv:1901.00596 (2019)
33. Faramondi, L., et al.: Network structural vulnerability: a multiobjective attacker perspective. IEEE Trans. Syst. Man Cybern.: Syst. **99**, 1–14 (2018)
34. Waniek, M., Michalak, T.P., Wooldridge, M.J., Rahwan, T.: Hiding individuals and communities in a social network. Nat. Hum. Behav. **2**(2), 139 (2018)
35. Bojcheski, A., Günnemann, S.: Adversarial attacks on node embeddings. arXiv preprint arXiv:1809.01093 (2018)
36. Sun, M., et al.: Data poisoning attack against unsupervised node embedding methods. arXiv preprint arXiv:1810.12881 (2018)
37. Qiu, J., Dong, Y., Ma, H.. Li, J., Wang, K., Tang, J.: Network embedding as matrix factorization: unifying DeepWalk, LINE, PTE, and node2vec. In: Proceedings of the Eleventh ACM International Conference on Web Search and Data Mining, pp. 459–467. ACM (2018)
38. Mnih, A., Hinton, G.E.: A scalable hierarchical distributed language model. In: Advances in Neural Information Processing Systems, pp. 1081–1088 (2009)
39. Morin, F., Bengio, Y.: Hierarchical probabilistic neural network language model. In: Aistats, vol. 5, pp. 246–252. Citeseer (2005)
40. Ghosh, R., Lerman, K.: Community detection using a measure of global influence. In: Giles, L., Smith, M., Yen, J., Zhang, H. (eds.) SNAKDD 2008. LNCS, vol. 5498, pp. 20–35. Springer, Heidelberg (2010). https://doi.org/10.1007/978-3-642-14929-0_2

41. Beveridge, A., Shan, J.: Network of thrones. Math Horizons **23**(4), 18–22 (2016)
42. McCallum, A.K., Nigam, K., Rennie, J., Seymore, K.: Automating the construction of internet portals with machine learning. Inf. Retrieval **3**(2), 127–163 (2000)
43. Barabási, A.-L., Albert, R.: Emergence of scaling in random networks. Science **286**(5439), 509–512 (1999)
44. Dreiseitl, S., Ohno-Machado, L.: Logistic regression and artificial neural network classification models: a methodology review. J. Biomed. Inform. **35**(5–6), 352–359 (2002)
45. Ou, M., Cui, P., Pei, J., Zhang, Z., Zhu, W.: Asymmetric transitivity preserving graph embedding. In: Proceedings of the 22nd ACM SIGKDD International Conference on Knowledge Discovery and Data Mining, pp. 1105–1114. ACM (2016)
46. Raghavan, U.N., Albert, R., Kumara, S.: Near linear time algorithm to detect community structures in large-scale networks. Phys. Rev. E **76**(3), 036106 (2007)
47. Newman, M.E.: Modularity and community structure in networks. Proc. Natl. Acad. Sci. **103**(23), 8577–8582 (2006)

Few-Shot Knowledge Reasoning: An Attention Mechanism Based Method

Haocheng Xie[1], Aiping Li[1], and Yan Jia[2(✉)]

[1] National University of Defense Technology, Changsha 410073, China
398005333@qq.com, liaiping@nudt.edu.cn
[2] Harbin Institute of Technology, Shenzhen 518055, China
jiayanjy@vip.sina.com

Abstract. As a core issue of knowledge graph research, knowledge graph reasoning and completion technology have always been a hot topic of current research. Existing knowledge graph reasoning techniques usually require a large amount of training for each relationship; in addition, training each relationship requires a large number of training samples. Inspired by meta-learning [1], this chapter combines the idea of meta-learning and the attention mechanism [2] for knowledge reasoning. We introduce the few-shot reasoning method based on the attention mechanism, which has superior performance. The novel method greatly reduces the number of samples required for each relationship training, which reduces the scale of the reasoning problem. Second, with the attention mechanism, the proposed method could achieve higher accuracy since historical information could be utilized for reasoning. Third, the method could greatly improve the extensibility of knowledge. When dealing with newly added relationship, the method could easily learn the pattern of the relationship and there is no need to retrain the model.

Keywords: MDATA · Knowledge reasoning · Attention mechanism

1   Introduction

The research of knowledge graph can be traced back to the concept of the Semantic Web in 2006, and the RDF model came into being. In 2012, Google officially proposed the concept of knowledge graph [3]. The development of knowledge graph has made significant progress both in data scale and in practical applications. At present, most of the knowledge graph are still expressed based on structured triples. Structural representation of knowledge graph is essential for knowledge extraction, knowledge representation, knowledge fusion, knowledge reasoning, knowledge acquisition and other aspects, especially for data processing of knowledge graph. Although most knowledge graph are large scale, in fact, the data are very sparse and there is a large amount of incomplete information. Therefore, current research on knowledge reasoning technology is very hot. At present, most of the research of knowledge reasoning technology mainly

© Springer Nature Switzerland AG 2021
Y. Jia et al. (Eds.): MDATA: A New Knowledge Representation Model, LNCS 12647, pp. 152–164, 2021.
https://doi.org/10.1007/978-3-030-71590-8_9

establishes the reasoning model according to the organizational characteristics of the knowledge graph, and reasoning the missing triples by the existing triples, including relationship reasoning and tail entity reasoning. Although knowledge reasoning technology develops very rapidly, the reasoning accuracy and training efficiency are not too high, the knowledge reasoning technology still has a lot of room for improvement.

Many achievements have been recorded in the research of knowledge reasoning. However, due to the huge scale of knowledge graph, there are very few methods for knowledge graph reasoning on small samples. At present, most knowledge reasoning techniques are mainly training for each relationship. A definite relationship requires a large amount of sample data. However, large-scale knowledge graph is very sparse, and it is difficult to make sure that each relationship has enough training data. One-Shot Relational Learning for Knowledge graphs [4] applied the idea of meta-learning to knowledge graph reasoning, and it proposed the GMatching model which only needed a small number of samples to complete the model training. The experiments also achieved good results. In this chapter, we introduce two aspects of improving the GMatching model:

1) First, we extended the one-shot model of the few-shot model [5], and added the attention mechanism [2] to improve the accuracy of model reasoning;
2) Second, in the data processing stage, we use the graph convolutional neural network to embed the knowledge graph, and on this basis, the structure of the graph convolutional neural model is improved, the model parameters are cut, the reasoning precision is improved.

The rest of this chapter is organized as follows. The next section mainly introduces the knowledge graph technology and research background that is related to the research of this chapter, as well as the research progress of knowledge reasoning. In Sect. 3, we mainly introduce the knowledge reasoning problem and data preparation. Section 4 focuses on the main improvement model of our work, and compares it with the previous models. In Sect. 5, we mainly conduct experimental analysis and we introduce the data set, designed experiments, and compare the model complexity, training time and accuracy. Finally, we summarize the chapter in Sect. 6.

2   Background

2.1   Related Work

Deep learning has been widely used in the field of knowledge graph, and the representation learning model based on deep learning has developed rapidly. Especially in the aspect of knowledge reasoning, deep learning has gradually became the basis and premise of knowledge reasoning.

At present, there are many knowledge graph representation learning methods. Early studies include neural tensor network model [6]; translation models represented by TransE [7], TransH [8], TransR [9], TransD [10], TransG [11], etc.

Matrix and tensor decomposition model represented by RESCAL decomposition [12]. In recent years, the knowledge graph representation model has also achieved very significant results, including DistMult model [13], ComplEx model [14], and ConvE model [15].

Although these knowledge representation models work well, the training of these models requires sufficient training samples, which are not effective when applied to large-scale sparse knowledge graph. On the other hand, these models do not take into consideration the first order association between entities. However, the neighbor coding in the GMatching model [4] considers the first-order association between entities, but does not consider the association between entities and relations in the coding process.

In this chapter, we improve the coding structure and reduce the parameters of the model. The proposed model improves the reasoning accuracy of the model to a certain extent, and lays the data foundation for the subsequent training process of knowledge reasoning model.

2.2 Knowledge Reasoning Model

With the development of deep neural network in the knowledge graph domain, the knowledge reasoning model based on deep neural network develops rapidly. Especially in the past two years, the knowledge reasoning technology based on reinforcement learning represented by MINERVA [16], DeepPath [17], Multi-Hop [18] model and the variational knowledge reasoning technology represented by DIVA model [19] appeared. Afterwards, the introduction of knowledge reasoning technology into a new field, which provides a new way of thinking for the continuous development of knowledge reasoning.

The main purpose of this chapter is to apply meta-learning ideas to knowledge reasoning, and add attention mechanism. Most of the previous meta-learning work was mostly applied in the visual field until the idea is applied in knowledge reasoning in [4]. The GMatching model is then proposed, which has achieved good results. However, the proposed model still has some drawbacks for improvement. For example, neighbor coding is not taking into consideration the first-order association between the relationship and the entity. The reasoning model does not incorporate the attention mechanism.

In fact, the key to apply few-shot learning to knowledge reasoning lies in the LSTM-based meta-learner [20]. After deduction and calculation, when meta-learning is applied to knowledge reasoning, the training of knowledge reasoning model,s parameters are carried out by training LSTM [21]. Specific contents will be emphatically analyzed in the fourth part of this chapter.

3   Preliminary

3.1 Problem Definition

Knowledge reasoning mainly trains the model through existing known triples, so that the model after training can infer unknown triples, including relational reasoning and tail entity reasoning.

For a knowledge graph, G represents the set of stored triples (e_1, r, e_2), where $e_1, e_2 \in \varepsilon$, $r \in R$ represents the set of all entities, R is the set of all relations. Therefore, the whole knowledge graph can be expressed as $G = \{(e_1, r, e_2)\}$, $e_1, e_2 \in \varepsilon$, $r \in R$.

Knowledge reasoning can be divided into relation reasoning and tail entity reasoning. This chapter focuses on tail entity reasoning. That is, given (e_1, r) as the input of the model after training, reasoning the tail entity e2. In the past, knowledge reasoning models are mainly based on matrix decomposition and reinforcement learning. In order to ensure its accuracy, the training of each relation requires a large number of triple samples, while this chapter mainly focuses on small sample learning. The training of each relation requires only a few samples, and in terms of accuracy is no less than the other existing methods.

3.2   Model Description

Referring to the standard meta-learning model [1,5], we apply the idea of meta-learning to small sample knowledge reasoning in this chapter. According to the number of relations in the knowledge graph, the whole training process is divided into multiple training tasks. Assuming that the knowledge graph has k kinds of relations, k training tasks are set.

We denote the task set corresponding to the m relation as T_m, $T_m \in T$, T represents the collection of all tasks. The task T_m, we set the training set D_{train}^m and testing set D_{test}^m, and $T_m = \{D_{train}^m, D_{test}^m\}$. Suppose the number of training samples is n and the number of test samples is b, that is, the number of elements in the set D_{train}^m is n, $D_{train}^m = \{(e_i^1, r_m, e_i^2) \mid i = 1, 2, 3, \ldots, n\}$. The testing set consists of positive sets and negative sets, that is, $D_{test}^m = D_{test-pos}^m \cap D_{test-neg}^m$ Where the set of positive can be expressed as $D_{test}^m = D_{test-pos}^m \cup D_{test-neg}^m$, The corresponding negative set can be expressed as $D_{test-pos}^m = \{(e_j^1, r_m, e_j^2) \mid j = 1, 2, 3, \ldots, b\}$, The elements in the positive set correspond to the elements in the negative set, but the tail entities are different. The set of all relations in the training task is R_{train}, We represent all training tasks as $T_{meta-train}$, and $T_{meta-train} = \cup_{m=1}^k (T_m)$. The setting of the test task same as the training task except for data, and the set of all relations in the test task is R_{test}, and $R_{train} \cap R_{test} = \phi$, and the test task set is expressed as $T_{meta} - test$. In practice, We train the reasoning model through $T_{meta-train}$ and then whole evaluate the model through $T_{meta-test}$.

The training process of our model is actually similar to the training process of image few-shot model [5], except that the data are RDF triples. We mainly consider using positive and negative samples for training, Score the results obtained from D_{train}^m with the results obtained from $D_{test-pos}^m$ and $D_{test-neg}^m$. The task loss function L_m is designed by using the difference between the positive score and the negative score, after all training tasks are completed, the training model is evaluated globally using the test task set $T_{meta-test}$.

4 Knowledge Reasoning

In this part, we mainly introduce the implementation of the model, including data embedding, model matching, and model training.

4.1 Embedding Model

It is a hot research direction to design the appropriate data embedding method according to the characteristics of the model before knowledge graph reasoning. In fact, although there are many kinds of knowledge graph embedding methods at present, there are very rare embedding models which have high training efficiency,high accuracy and close to the applications.

A simplified version of the graph convolutional network is proposed in the GMatching model [4]. It mainly considers the first-order similarity between entities based on the existing trained embedded data, and further performs representation learning. The implementation is as follows.

We perform representation learning on the entity node e in the knowledge graph, and the set of relation and entity directly connected to the node e can be expressed as N_e, The relation directly connected to the entity node e can be expressed as $r_{e,m}$, The entity directly connected to the entity node e can be represented as e'_m, $emb()$ can be represented as some existing embedding methods of knowledge graph, the neighbor encoder in GMatching model [4] can be expressed as:

$$v_{e'_m} = emb\left(e'_m\right), v_{r_{e,m}} = emb\left(r_{e,m}\right) \tag{1}$$

$$v_{r_{e,m},e'_m} = \mathrm{W}\left(v_{e'_m} \oplus v_{r_{e,m}}\right) + \mathrm{b} \tag{2}$$

where $\oplus$ denotes the vector concatenation.

$$V_e = \sigma\left(\frac{1}{|N_e|} \sum_{\left(r_{e,m},e'_m\right)\in N_e} v_{r_{e,m},e'_m}\right) \tag{3}$$

Finally, the embedded vector V_e of the entity e is obtained.

As can be seen from formula (2), this embedding method does not fully consider the interaction between the entity and relation. In fact, As a matter of fact, there are two shortcomings in combining relation vector and entity vector directly. First, direct splicing increases the vector dimension. On the one hand, if the entity and relation vector dimension are set too small, the embedding vector information may be missing, which may affect the matching accuracy. On the other hand, direct concatenate the entity and relation vectors will double the vector dimensions, resulting in too many parameters in the subsequent training of the reasoning model, thus reducing the training efficiency. Therefore, how to reduce the number of parameters without affecting the accuracy of the model is very important. Second, the concatenation of the entity and relation vector does not fully consider the interaction between the entity and the relation, so that the embedded entity vector does not contain part of the information, which affects the accuracy of the next reasoning model.

We have improved (2) by changing the original formula to:

$$v_{r_{e,m},e'_m} = \left(v_{e'_m} W\right) \oplus \left(v_{r_{e,m}} W\right) + b \tag{4}$$

Considering the accuracy of the next reasoning model, the GMatching model sets the dimension of vector $v_{r_{e,m},e'_m}$ as 2 time of the dimension d of the entity and relation vector. Under the premise of ensuring the accuracy of the reasoning model, we improve the embedding model mainly by improving the (2) formula and changing the formula (2) to (4), and set the dimension of $v_{r_{e,m},e'_m}$ to d, The modified idea refers to the part of attention score function in literature [2]. After the improvement, the number of parameters in the whole model is greatly reduced and the training efficiency is greatly improved. Quantitative and detailed analysis will be carried out next part.

4.2 Reasoning Model

In Sect. 4.1, we mainly introduced the embedding of entities in the knowledge graph based on the similarity between adjacent entities and the interactive correlation between entities and relations.

Now we mainly make further knowledge inference according to the entity embedding vector obtained in Sect. 4.1.

We improved reasoning part of the GMatching model [4] from the one-shot model to the few-shot model and added the attention mechanism. Our reasoning model is similar to the inference process in the GMatching model [3], both of which are based on LSTM. Samples of our reasoning model training are mainly divided into two parts, the support set and the query set. The data in the support set come from the training data in the test task, and the data in the query set come from the test data in the same test task.

The support set is denoted by S, each element in the S set is s_i, $s_i \in S$, $s_i = V_{e_i} \oplus V_{e'_i}$, where $\left[\epsilon_j, r_m, e'_j\right] \in D_{test}^m$, V_e represents the embedding vector of the entity e obtained by the embedding model in Sect. 4.1, $\oplus$ denotes the vector concatenation.

Referring to the part of 3, the number of elements in the support is n. The matrix S_{few} obtained by concatenation these n data in rows.

Similarly, the query set is represented by Q, and each element in the Q set is q_j, and $q_j = V_{e_j} \oplus V_{e'_j}$, where $\left[\epsilon_j, r_m, e'_j\right] \in D_{test}^m$, concatenate the query data in rows to get the matrix Q_{batch}.

GMatching model [4] leverage a LSTM-based recurrent processing block to perform multi-step matching [21]. Compare with GMatching model, our model improved one-shot to few-shot and added attention mechanism [2]. The specific implementation of our model is as follows:

$$h'_{k+1}, c'_{k+1} = LSTM\left(Q_{batch}, [h_k \oplus r, c_k]\right) \tag{5}$$

$$h_{k+1} = h'_{k+1} + Q_b atch \tag{6}$$

$$Attention = softmax\left(h_{k+1} * S'_{few}\right) \tag{7}$$

$$r = Attention * S_f ew \tag{8}$$

$$score = \sum_{few} \frac{h_{k+1} * S'_{few}}{\|h_{k+1}\| \, \|S_{few}\|} \tag{9}$$

where S'_{few} is the transpose of h_{few}, and $LSTM(x, [h, c])$ represents a standard LSTM unit, x is input, h and c are hidden state parameter and cell state parameter in LSTM unit respectively.

The output of our model is h_{k+1}, Calculate the similarity between h_{k+1} and the elements in the support respectively, and then added, get the score of each element in the query set, and the element with the highest score is the final reasoning result of the model.

Suppose the embedding dimension in the data set sample is d, that is, the embedding dimension of the entity and relation is d, the parameters of the two models are shown in Table 1. It can be seen that the number of model parameters can be greatly reduced through the improvement of the model, so that the training efficiency of the model is greatly improved. On the other hand, the large reduction of model parameters may affect the accuracy of the reasoning model. In the fifth part, we mainly analyze the training efficiency of the model and the accuracy of the reasoning model.

Table 1. Model parameters analysis table

Model	GMatching model	Our model
Sample embedding dimension	d	d
Embedding model output dimension	$2d$	$1.5d$
Reasoning model input dimension	$2d$	$1.5d$
Reasoning model output dimension	$2d$	$1.5d$
Embedding model parameters	$18d^2$	$10.5d^2$
Reasoning model parameters	$32d^2 + 8d$	$18d^2 + 6d$
Total parameters	$50d^2 + 8d$	$28.5d^2 + 6d$

4.3   Model Training

In order to improve the accuracy of the model and reduce the training difficulty of the model, we use positive and negative samples to train the reasoning model. In Sects. 4.1 and 4.2, we introduced the embedding model and reasoning model. Now we mainly describe the training process of the model.

Suppose we are currently training for task m, and then, $T_m = \{D_{train}^m, D_{test}^m\}$, where $D_{train}^m = \{(e_i^1, r_m, e_i^2) \mid i = 1, 2, 3, \ldots, n\}$, $D_{test}^m = D_{test-pos}^m \cup D_{test-neg}^m$, $D_{test-pos}^m = \{(e_j^1, r_m, e_j^2) \mid j = 1, 2, 3, \ldots, b\}$, $D_{test-neg}^m = \{(e_j^1, r_m, x_j^2) \mid j = 1, 2, 3, \ldots, b\}$.

First, we use the positive samples as the input of the reasoning model, that is, $T_{m,1} = \{D_{train}^m, D_{test} - pos^m\}$, as the input samples, and get the score S_{pos} of the sample in $D_{test-pos}^m$, and then, put the negative samples into the reasoning model, get the negative score S_{neg}, through the score results of the positive and negative samples, we can get the loss function of the task T_m:

$$l_m = \max\left(r + S_{pos} - S_{neg}\right) \tag{10}$$

Where r can be analogized to the hyperparameter representing the boundary distance in the SVM machine [22].

After the model training is completed, we use $T_{meta-test}$ to evaluate the model as a whole. The specific experimental design and experimental results are described in detail in the next section.

5   Experiment

5.1   DataSet

The existing knowledge graph datasets are numerous and large in number. In order to ensure the efficiency of experiments and the comparability of the models, a simplified subset of the existing large-scale knowledge graph is generally used for experiments.

Currently, commonly used experimental data sets include FB15K, FB2M, FB5M, WN11K, WN15K, etc. Data sets are generally selected according to the characteristics of the models. This chapter mainly studies the knowledge reasoning technology based on small-samples, Therefore, it is suitable for the case that there are few samples of each specific relation in the knowledge graph data set, Based on this feature, we selected NELL-One and WiKi-One data sets in GMatching model [4] for the experiment.

These two data sets are subsets of existing knowledge graph NELL[23] and Wikidata[24], and the data are relatively sparse, which is suitable for the research of small-samples knowledge reasoning technology. The creation process of these two knowledge graph is similar, taking 50 to 500 triples of the same relation as the data set of a task, and randomly dividing the data into training set and test set in each task. The specific statistics of the two datasets are shown in Table 2.

Table 2. Datasets information statistics table

DataSet	Entity	Relatio	Triple	Task
NELL-One	68,545	358	181,109	67
Wiki-One	4,838,244	822	5,859,240	183

5.2   Experiment Design

There are two main aspects in the experimental design part. One is to compare our model with the baseline models in term of efficiency; The second is to compare our model with the baseline model in terms of reasoning accuracy. Based on the experimental results, comprehensively evaluate the characteristics and advantages of our improved model.

Baseline Model Selection. The reasoning model of this chapter is mainly improved on the basis of the GMatching model [4]. Therefore, we chose the GMatching and the current advanced DistMult, Complex, and ConvE as our baseline models.

Operational Efficiency Analysis. We discuss the efficiency of the model by the number of trainable parameters and the running time of the model. Suppose the number of entities is n and the number of relations is r. Since the Wiki-One dataset is much larger than the Nell-One dataset, in order to ensure the progress of the experiment, the NELL-One dataset entity and relation embedding dimension is set to d, and the Wiki-One embedding dimension is 1/2d. The efficiency of the model is shown in Table 3:

Table 3. Model efficiency comprehensive analysis table

Model	Complexity of Trainable parameters	Running time (s)	
		NELL-One	Wiki-One
DistMult	$O(nd + dr)$	45474	85365
Complex	$O(nd + dr)$	59531	106580
ConvE	$O(nd + dr)$	99523	–
GMatching	$O(50d^2 + 8d)$	32394	79650
OursModel (5-shot)	$O(28.5d^2 + 6d)$	29864	65832

From Table 3, we can clearly see that our model has certain advantages both in the number of trainable parameters and in the running time of the model, In particular, compared with the previous model, the number of trainable parameters were significantly reduced, and the efficiency was also greatly improved.

In fact, the number of training parameters of models such as DistMult, Complex, and ConvE is very large. The reason is that these models are based on matrix and tensor decomposition, embedding entities and relations directly, the number of parameters are directly related to the number of entities and relations. Therefore, the number of trainable parameters and running time of these models are very large. The GMatching model and our model are all based on the method of meta-learning. The parameters of the training are not related to the scale of the knowledge graph. The training parameters are greatly reduced compare with the matrix and tensor decomposition methods.

On the other hand, it can be seen from Table 3, comparing with GMatching model, the number of parameters in our model decreases significantly without affecting accuracy, but the running time does not decrease significantly. There are two reasons for the analysis.

First, in the reasoning model, the GMatching model only uses the one-shot structure, and we use the attention-based 5-shot structure model. Second, we have improved the structure of the embedded model; specifically, after we improved the structure of the embedded model, we can compare formulas 3 and 4 and it is clear that the parameters of the model were reduced.

Operational Efficiency Analysis. In this section, we analyze the reasoning accuracy of the inference model, mainly using Hit@1, 5, 10 and the mean reciprocal rank (MRR) as model evaluation indicators to comprehensively compare and analyze our model. The specific situation is shown in Table 4.

Table 4. Comprehensive analysis table of reasoning model accuracy

Model	NELL-One				Wiki-One			
	Hit@1	Hit@5	Hit@10	MRR	Hit@1	Hit@5	Hit@10	MRR
DistMult	6.6	12.6	25.3	15.3	1.9	7.0	10.1	4.8
Complex	8.6	14.6	22.3	15.7	4.0	9.2	12.1	6.9
ConvE	9.8	23.0	29.6	16.8	–	–	–	–
GMatching	11.1	24.8	28.8	17.6	16.4	26.8	31.8	22.3
OursModel (one-shot)	11.3	23.4	28.1	17.1	14.2	24.3	32.7	21.8
OursModel (five-shot)	14.3	26.4	31.1	20.1	18.2	28.3	35.7	24.8

In Table 4, the indicators of the best performance of each model are shown in bold, It can be seen that the accuracy of the meta-learning based GMatching and our model are superior to the existing baseline model, whether on the NELL-One dataset or the Wiki-One dataset. We can see that both the Nell-One dataset and the Wiki-One dataset, based on meta-learning GMatching and our model The accuracy is better than the existing baseline model. Our one-shot model performs slightly worse than the GMatching model, and it mainly analyzes the failure of 1-shot structural attention mechanism, but our five-shot model is obviously better than GMatching model on two datasets, Mainly analysis our model improves the accuracy of the matching model by improving the embedding structure and the reasoning structure.

Analysis of the Results. In the aspect of model running efficiency, the efficiency of the model is evaluated by two indicators: trainable parameters complexity and actual running time. It can be seen from the experimental results that the model based on meta-learning has obvious advantages in the efficiency of knowledge reasoning, and our model training parameters and running time are significantly lower than the GMatching model. Our model performs better in terms of running efficiency. In terms of the accuracy of the inference model, we use Hit@1, 5, 10 and the mean reciprocal rank (MRR) as the evaluation indicators of accuracy. While ensuring the efficiency of the model, our model (5-shot) has a significant improvement in each indicator.

Therefore, our model has obvious advantages over existing reasoning models in terms of efficiency and accuracy.

6   Chapter Summary

In this chapter, we improve the reasoning model in GMatching [4], which mainly includes two aspects. Firstly, the embedding model of graph convolution knowledge graph is used for reference, and the neighbor coding model is improved by considering the correlation between entities and relations. Second, the one-shot model was extended to the few-shot model, and attention mechanism was added.

It can be seen from the experiment that after two improvements of the model, the number of model parameters and training time have been significantly reduced, and the reasoning accuracy has also been improved correspondingly. According to the training time and accuracy of the models, compared with the baseline, our model has three advantages:

- Firstly, it can be seen from the experimental efficiency analysis part that the training parameters of our model is less than other models, and it also has advantages in training time;
- Secondly, it can be seen from the accurate analysis part that our model have advantages over other models in terms of accuracy;
- Third, it can be seen from the nature of the model that the model is highly extensible. After the model training is completed, there is no need to retrain the model when newly relations added.

At the same time, this model can be used for both large-scale knowledge reasoning and sparse small samples knowledge reasoning, and its applicability is more extensive than other models.

References

1. Ren, M., et al.: Meta-learning for semi-supervised few-shot classification. In: 6th International Conference on Learning Representations, ICLR 2018, Vancouver, BC, Canada, 30 April–3 May 2018, Conference Track Proceedings. OpenReview.net (2018)
2. Luong, T., Pham, H., Manning, C.D.: Effective approaches to attention-based neural machine translation. In: Màrquez, L., Callison-Burch, C., Su, J., Pighin, D., Marton, Y. (eds.) Proceedings of the 2015 Conference on Empirical Methods in Natural Language Processing, EMNLP 2015, Lisbon, Portugal, 17–21 September 2015, pp. 1412–1421. The Association for Computational Linguistics (2015)
3. Amit, S.: Introducing the knowledge graph. America: Official Blog of Google (2012)
4. Xiong, W., Yu, M., Chang, S., Guo, X., Wang, W.Y.: One-shot relational learning for knowledge graphs. In: Riloff, E., Chiang, D., Hockenmaier, J., Tsujii, J. (eds.) Proceedings of the 2018 Conference on Empirical Methods in Natural Language Processing, Brussels, Belgium, 31 October–4 November 2018, pp. 1980–1990. Association for Computational Linguistics (2018)
5. Snell, J., Swersky, K., Zemel, R.S.: Prototypical networks for few-shot learning. In: Guyon, I., et al. (eds.) Advances in Neural Information Processing Systems 30: Annual Conference on Neural Information Processing Systems 2017, 4–9 December 2017, Long Beach, CA, USA, pp. 4077–4087 (2017)
6. Socher, R., Chen, D., Manning, C.D., Ng, A.Y.: Reasoning with neural tensor networks for knowledge base completion. In: Burges, C.J.C., Bottou, L., Ghahramani, Z., Weinberger, K.Q. (eds.) Advances in Neural Information Processing Systems 26: 27th Annual Conference on Neural Information Processing Systems 2013. Proceedings of a meeting held December 5–8, 2013, Lake Tahoe, Nevada, United States, pp. 926–934 (2013)
7. Bordes, A., Usunier, N., García-Durán, A., Weston, J., Yakhnenko, O.: Translating embeddings for modeling multi-relational data. In: Burges, C.J.C., Bottou, L., Ghahramani, Z., Weinberger, K.Q. (eds.) Advances in Neural Information Processing Systems 26: 27th Annual Conference on Neural Information Processing Systems 2013. Proceedings of a Meeting Held 5–8 December 2013, Lake Tahoe, Nevada, United States, pp. 2787–2795 (2013)
8. Wang, Z., Zhang, J., Feng, J., Chen, Z.: Knowledge graph embedding by translating on hyperplanes. In: Brodley, C.E., Stone, P. (eds.) Proceedings of the Twenty-Eighth AAAI Conference on Artificial Intelligence, 27–31 July 2014, Québec City, Québec, Canada, pp. 1112–1119. AAAI Press (2014)
9. Lin, Y., Liu, Z., Sun, M., Liu, Y., Zhu, X.: Learning entity and relation embeddings for knowledge graph completion. In: Bonet, B., Koenig, S. (eds.) Proceedings of the Twenty-Ninth AAAI Conference on Artificial Intelligence, 25–30 January 2015, Austin, Texas, USA, pp. 2181–2187. AAAI Press (2015)
10. Ji, G., He, S., Xu, L., Liu, K., Zhao, J.: Knowledge graph embedding via dynamic mapping matrix. In: Proceedings of the 53rd Annual Meeting of the Association for Computational Linguistics and the 7th International Joint Conference on Natural Language Processing of the Asian Federation of Natural Language Processing, ACL 2015, 26–31 July 2015, Beijing, China, Volume 1: Long Papers, pp. 687–696. The Association for Computer Linguistics (2015)
11. Xiao, H., Huang, M., Hao, Y., Zhu, X.: TransG: a generative mixture model for knowledge graph embedding. CoRR, vol. abs/1509.05488 (2015)

12. Nickel, M., Tresp, V., Kriegel, H.: A three-way model for collective learning on multi-relational data. In: Getoor, L., Scheffer, T. (eds.) Proceedings of the 28th International Conference on Machine Learning, ICML 2011, Bellevue, Washington, USA, 28 June–2 July 2011, pp. 809–816. Omnipress (2011)

13. Yang, B., Yih, W., He, X., Gao, J., Deng, L.: Embedding entities and relations for learning and inference in knowledge bases. In: Bengio, Y., LeCun, Y. (eds.) 3rd International Conference on Learning Representations, ICLR 2015, San Diego, CA, USA, 7–9 May 2015, Conference Track Proceedings (2015)

14. Trouillon, T., Dance, C.R., Gaussier, É., Welbl, J., Riedel, S., Bouchard, G.: Knowledge graph completion via complex tensor factorization. J. Mach. Learn. Res. **18**, 130:1–130:38 (2017)

15. Dettmers, T., Minervini, P., Stenetorp, P., Riedel, S.: Convolutional 2D knowledge graph embeddings. In: McIlraith, S.A., Weinberger, K.Q. (eds.) Proceedings of the Thirty-Second AAAI Conference on Artificial Intelligence, (AAAI-18), the 30th innovative Applications of Artificial Intelligence (IAAI-18), and the 8th AAAI Symposium on Educational Advances in Artificial Intelligence (EAAI-18), New Orleans, Louisiana, USA, 2–7 February 2018, pp. 1811–1818. AAAI Press (2018)

16. Das, R., et al.: Go for a walk and arrive at the answer: reasoning over paths in knowledge bases using reinforcement learning. In: 6th International Conference on Learning Representations, ICLR 2018, Vancouver, BC, Canada, 30 April–3 May 2018, Conference Track Proceedings. OpenReview.net (2018)

17. Xiong, W., Hoang, T., Wang, W.Y.: DeepPath: a reinforcement learning method for knowledge graph reasoning. In: Palmer, M., Hwa, R., Riedel, S. (eds.) Proceedings of the 2017 Conference on Empirical Methods in Natural Language Processing, EMNLP 2017, Copenhagen, Denmark, 9–11 September 2017, pp. 564–573. Association for Computational Linguistics (2017)

18. Lin, X.V., Socher, R., Xiong, C.: Multi-hop knowledge graph reasoning with reward shaping. In: Riloff, E., Chiang, D., Hockenmaier, J., Tsujii, J. (eds.) Proceedings of the 2018 Conference on Empirical Methods in Natural Language Processing, Brussels, Belgium, 31 October–4 November 2018, pp. 3243–3253. Association for Computational Linguistics (2018)

19. Chen, W., Xiong, W., Yan, X., Wang, W.Y.: Variational knowledge graph reasoning. CoRR, vol. abs/1803.06581 (2018)

20. Ravi, S., Larochelle, H.: Optimization as a model for few-shot learning. In: 5th International Conference on Learning Representations, ICLR 2017, Toulon, France, 24–26 April 2017, Conference Track Proceedings. OpenReview.net (2017)

21. Vinyals, O., Blundell, C., Lillicrap, T., Kavukcuoglu, K., Wierstra, D.: Matching networks for one shot learning. In: Lee, D.D., Sugiyama, M., von Luxburg, U., Guyon, I., Garnett, R. (eds.) Advances in Neural Information Processing Systems 29: Annual Conference on Neural Information Processing Systems 2016, 5–10 December 2016, Barcelona, Spain, pp. 3630–3638 (2016)

22. Burges, C.J.C.: A tutorial on support vector machines for pattern recognition. Data Min. Knowl. Discov. **2**(2), 121–167 (1998)

23. Mitchell, T.M., et al.: Never-ending learning. Commun. ACM **61**(5), 103–115 (2018)

24. Vrandečić, D., Krötzsch, M.: WikiData: a free collaborative knowledgebase. Commun. ACM **57**(10), 78–85 (2014)

Applications of Knowledge Representation Learning

Chenchen Li, Aiping Li, Ye Wang, and Hongkui Tu[✉]

National University of Defense Technology, Changsha 410073, China
{lichenchen18,liaiping,ye.wang}@nudt.edu.cn, tuhkjet@foxmail.com

Abstract. Knowledge representation learning (KRL) is one of the most important research topics in artificial intelligence, especial in natural language processing (NLP). After extracting entities and relations, some kinds of knowledge, KRL can efficiently calculate the semantics of the entities and the relations in a low-dimensional space, which effectively solve the problem of data sparsity, and can significantly improve the performance of knowledge acquisition, fusion and reasoning. Starting from the three common perspectives of KRL, scoring function, model coding type and additional information, this chapter introduces the overall framework of KRL and the specific model design. In addition, we introduce the corresponding experimental evaluation tasks, including the evaluation metrics and benchmark datasets of each model. Afterwards, we summarize how to apply KRL in various downstream NLP tasks.

Keywords: MDATA · Knowledge representation · Natural language processing

1 Introduction

In recent years, the academic circles at home and abroad have conducted in-depth and extensive research on knowledge representation learning (KRL). Under the large-scale knowledge graph (KG), KRL projects the entities and relations into the low-dimensional continuous real value vector space, which not only preserves the original internal structural information of the KG, but also simplifies the operation and improves the computational efficiency; Moreover, in order to make the entity and relation representation in the KG be further applied to various downstream tasks, it is necessary to continuously explore the methods and techniques of KRL for supporting the high-accuracy representation learning.

Theoretically, KRL is one of the important research topics in the fields of artificial intelligence and natural language processing. The output of KRL can help digital system better understand human intelligence, language and thinking. From the perspective of application, KRL is significant in understanding users' intentions to improve the accuracy of downstream tasks, including question answering system, exploring potential relations and discovering new knowledge, which has great social value and economic benefits.

Y. Jia et al. (Eds.): MDATA: A New Knowledge Representation Model, LNCS 12647, pp. 165–184, 2021.
https://doi.org/10.1007/978-3-030-71590-8_10

In this chapter, we systematically review the latest research progress of KRL. Section 2 reviews some specific model designs and typical methods following the five categories of KG embedding technology. Section 3 summarizes the evaluation tasks, metrics and benchmark datasets that are usually used in the experiments of various embedding technologies. In Sect. 4, the applications of KRL in various downstream NLP tasks, especially in large-scale knowledge base environment, are discussed. We introduce and discuss the relationship between knowledge representation learning and MDATA model in Sect. 5. Finally, we summarize this chapter in Sect. 6.

2   Approaches of Knowledge Representation Learning

In this section, we introduce approaches of knowledge representation learning from five aspects: distance-based models, semantic matching model, bilinear model, neural network model and models with additional information.

2.1   Distance Model

In general, the KRL models judge the reliability of the triplet by the scoring function. Usually, the value of the scoring function of an appropriate triplet is small, otherwise, the value of the score function is large, therefore, it is further used as the criterion to judge the performance of the model. In the distance model, the scoring function measures the rationality of facts by calculating the distance between two entities.

Distance-based models were studied early. In addition to the structured distance model SE [1] and the unstructured distance model UM [2], the most representatives are translation models of Trans series. Bordes et al. [3] was affected by the translation invariance and proposed the TransE. This model uses simple vector form to represent the entities and relations in KG. The relations between entities is regarded as some kind of translation vectors, and it is assumed that the embedding vector of a valid triplet (h,r,t) should satisfy the condition: $\mathbf{h} + \mathbf{r} \approx \mathbf{t}$. Under L_1 or L_2 norm, the scoring function is defined as $f_r(h, t) = \|\mathbf{h} + \mathbf{r} - \mathbf{t}\|_{L_1/L_2}$.

Since TransE can only handle 1-to-1 relations, many extensions of TransE were quickly developed to deal with 1-to-N, N-to-1, N-to-N relations. For example, TransH is proposed in [4], in which the relation is modeled as a hyperplane, and projected the head and tail entity vectors along the normal vector of the relation onto the hyperplane. TransR [5] introduces specific-relation spaces, constructing the embedding of entity and relation in the entity space and the relation space, respectively, and translating in the relation space. Each relation in TransR corresponds to a unique projection matrix, which not only introduces a large number of parameters but also hinders the knowledge sharing.

In order to solve this problem, ITransF is proposed in [6]; through the sparse attention mechanism and the sharing of multiple relations between concepts, the knowledge embedding model of hidden concepts is discovered, as well as the statistical intensity transfer of concept sharing is realized. TransD [7] constructs a dynamic projection matrix for each entity and relation by simultaneously considering the diversity of both entity and relation. In order to solve the problem of the heterogeneity and imbalance of KG that previous embedding models ignored, two versions of TranSparse model with TranSparse (Share) and TranSparse (Separate) are proposed [8]. The former uses the same sparse projection matrix for each relation to get the entity and relation vectors; However, the latter uses two different projection matrices to get the entity and relation vectors.

TransAt [9] introduces an attention mechanism into translation-based embedding, considering the hierarchical structure between entity attributes. TransA is proposed in [10], which replaces the Euclidean distance of traditional scoring function with Mahalanobis distance and learns different weights for each dimension of entities and relations. However, previous models using the scoring function based on distance is too strict to model complex and diverse entities and multi-type relations. Therefore, methods with relatively loose constraints between relations and entities appeared. For example, it relaxes certain degree of rigor and allows flexible transformation between entity and relation vector [11], that is, the embedding vector of a triplet only needs to satisfy $\mathbf{h} + \mathbf{r} \approx \alpha\mathbf{t}$, $\alpha > 0$. TransMS [12] can translate and transmit multi-directional semantics, and can handle complex relations. By adding a bias vector to the relation embedding vector for each triplet, the semantics are transformed from entity to relation.

References [13,14] taked into account entity and relation uncertainties, and model them as random variables. TransG [13] generates a variety of different representations of relations by using the Bayesian non-parametric infinite hybrid embedding model to discover the underlying semantics of relations. KG2E [14] uses the gaussian distribution to represent entities and relations as random vectors. In this model, Kullback-Leibler (KL) divergence and Expected likelihood (EL) are used to construct the scoring function. Where KL divergence is an asymmetric similarity, with scoring function:

$$f_r(h,t) = \int_{x \in R^{k_e}} N(x; \mu_r, \Sigma_r) log \frac{N(x; \mu_e, \Sigma_e)}{N(x; \mu_r, \Sigma_r)} dx \tag{1}$$

and EL is a symmetric similarity, with scoring function:

$$f_r(h,t) = log \int_{x \in R^{k_e}} N(x; \mu_e, \Sigma_e) N(x; \mu_r, \Sigma_r) dx \tag{2}$$

Reference [15] showed that entity and relation can also be represented not only by real-valued space, but also by complex space. Inspired by Euler's identity, Sun et al. proposed RotatE, that projects entity and relation to complex vector space, in which each relation is regarded as a rotation from head entity to tail entity, that is, $\mathbf{t} = \mathbf{h} \circ \mathbf{r}$, where $\circ$ is the product of Hadamard. TorusE [16] is the first model to embed facts outside the real-valued or complex-valued vector space, and selects a torus (compact lie group) as the embedding space.

2.2   Semantic Matching Model

Unlike distance models, semantic matching models mainly use the scoring function based on similarity to measure the credibility by matching the latent semantics of the entity and the similarity of the inclusion relation in the embedded vector space. Therefore, this kind of models can also use the scoring function determining whether the triplets are correct or not.

SME [17] is a multi-relational semantic model, in which the embedding $g_{left}(\mathbf{h}, \mathbf{r})$ and $g_{right}(\mathbf{r}, \mathbf{t})$ of (h, r, t) are calculated separately by combining (h,r) and (r,t) respectively, and the form of scoring function is defined as $f_r(h, t) = g_{left}(\mathbf{h}, \mathbf{r})^\top g_{right}(\mathbf{r}, \mathbf{t})$ representing the semantic combination of multi-relation. The linear and bilinear studies of $g_{left}(\mathbf{h}, \mathbf{r})$ are carried out in this method, which generate two versions of SME.

Tensor decomposition is an important way to obtain the representation of low-dimensional vectors. Reference [18] proposed the model RESACL based on three-way tensor factorization. Later, reference [19] proposed TATEC by improving RESCAL, which can not only model three-way interactions, but also interactions between entities and relations, that is, two-way interactions. It can capture various sequences of data interactions and share sparse potential factors among different relations. DistMult [20] considers using neural tensor to learn the entity and relation representation in the KG. For simplicity, the model restricts the relation matrix to a diagonal matrix, so that it can only deal with symmetric relations.

Inspired by DistMult, ComplEx [21] combines the model with tensor decomposition, and through low-rank decomposition of three-dimensional binary tensors, each row of the matrix is represented as an entity or a relation in the KG. Compared with DistMult, ComplEx can better model asymmetric relations by introducing complex-valued embedding. HolE [22] learns the composition vector representation of the entire KG through holographic embedding. This model combines the expression ability of neural network tensor product with the efficiency and simplicity of TransE [3] and uses the cyclic correlation of vectors to represent entity pairs.

Based on the traditional complex-valued representations, QuatE [23] introduces the super-complex representations to conduct the embedding learning of entity and relation. Differing from RotatE [15], it has two rotation planes and uses quaternions with three virtual components to embed the representation of entity. The relation is also modeled as rotation. ANALOGY [24] extends RESCAL by using the widely existing analogical structure in the KG, and further models the analogical properties of entities and relations by requiring that the linear maps of relations be normal and conform to the property of commutative law. It is proved that the DistMult, HolE and ComplEx introduced above are special versions of the ANALOGY.

2.3   Bilinear Model

This section mainly introduces the models that encode the interaction between entities and relations through bilinear architectures.

Bilinear model represents the relation as a bilinear map by projecting the head entity into the representation space close to the tail entity. The models introduced in Sects. 2.1 and 2.2 contain many typical bilinear models, such as the structural model SE [1], the semantic matching models SME [17], DistMult [20], ComplEx [21], and ANALOGY [24]. Even some methods of the neural network model show the bilinear property. For example, NTN [25] and NAM [26] will be introduced in next subsection encode entities and relations through bilinear operations in the form of $f_r(h, t) = \mathbf{h}^\top \mathbf{M}_r \mathbf{t}$.

LFM [27] represents the learning of relation as matrix decomposition problem, in which the entity is embedded in real-valued space and the relation is encoded as bilinear operation on the entity. DistMult [20] changes the relation matrix into a diagonal matrix based on LFM, which not just simplifies the complexity of calculation, but also significantly improves the experimental results. SimplE [28] also belongs to the bilinear model. The model introduces the inverse of the relations, allowing the model to independently learn the two embedding of each entity. The relation matrix corresponds to the inverse parameter of the relations by adding additional parameters, and its constraint on the relation matrix is similar to DistMult. Finally, Reference [29] studied and compared the expressiveness and correlation among various bilinear models, including RESCAL [18], ComplEx [21], HolE [22] and ANALOGY [24]. Experiments show that the integration of multiple bilinear models can achieve the most advanced link prediction performance.

2.4   Neural Network Model

The models described above use simple operations of addition, subtraction and multiplication to capture the linear relation between entities. In recent studies, more and more scholars have tried to use neural networks in KRL. The model based on neural network has the layering and activation function of neural network, because it contains a large number of parameters, it is the most expressive model. Therefore, they may capture many kinds of relations.

NTN [25] is a kind of neural tensor network model that represents the entity as the average value of its constituent word vectors. It changes the previous idea that the entity is represented as a discrete atomic unit or represented by a single entity vector, which greatly improves the performance of the model. In particular, when the number of layers of the tensor in NTN is set to 0, NTN is reduced to a single layer neural network model (SLM). NAM [26] uses the neural correlation model for semantic matching. It studied two model structures: DNN and RMNN. The former directly connects the embedding vectors of the head and tail entities and feeds them to DNN of L+1 layer, while the latter connects the relation embedding vectors to all hidden layers in the network.

ConvE [30] is a 2D convolutional neural network model with few parameters and high computational efficiency. In this model, the relation between head and tail entity is extracted through convolution operation by transforming the embedding vector stack of them into a 2-dimensional matrix, so as to model the interaction between entities and relations. Notice that ConvE can achieve better experimental results with fewer parameters. Under the same performance, the parameters are 1/8 of DistMult [20] and 1/17 of R-GCN [31]. InteractE [32] increases the expressive ability of ConvE and extends the interaction between entities and relations through three key ideas: feature permutation, checkered reshaping and circular convolution. R-GCN [31] can handles highly multi-relational data features. Its forward propagation is defined as:

$$h_i^{(l+1)} = \sigma(\sum_{r \in \Re} \sum_{j \in N_i^r} \frac{1}{c_{i,r}} W_r^{(l)} h_j^{(l)} + W_0^{(l)} h_i^{(l)}) \tag{3}$$

It can be seen that different types of relations use different weights, but it can easily lead to too many parameters. R-GCN solves this problem by using two regularized weight methods, namely, basis function decomposition and block diagonal decomposition.

ConvKB [33] uses convolutional neural network to encode entities and relations. Differing from ConvE, this model considers not only the relations of different local dimensions, but the relations of the same global dimension as well. In [34], it believed that the low-dimensional representation of triplets in KG was similar to the image to a certain extent, so they proposed CapsE based on ConvKB. ConvKB adds the feature map extracted by convolution to the capsule network [35], and successfully captures the function of deep features mapped by different features on the same dimension.

SACN [36] is composed of two modules, the encoder WGCN and the decoder Conv-TransE, where WGCN can define different weights for different relations, so as to transform a multi-relation graph into multiple single-relation graphs with different strength and weakness; while Conv-TransE uses ConvE without reshaping as a semantic matching metric to train the entire network. GATs [37] is also an end-to-end architecture composed of encoder and decoder, in which the encoder successfully captures the characteristics in the multi-hop neighborhood of a given entity by introducing multi-head attention mechanism to assign different weights to different neighbor nodes. HypER [38] uses the hypernetwork to generate the weight of convolution filter for each relation, and realizes a more complete interaction between entities and relations by simplifying ConvE. HypER is also called tensor decomposition model when the hypernetwork and weight matrix are used as tensors. RSNs [39] is an end-to-end recurrent skip networks that combines recurrent neural network with residual learning. It can capture the long-term dependence relation between and within KG and solve the problem of learning related paths of sequence models.

2.5   Embedding with Additional Information

The models introduced in Sects. 2.1, 2.2, 2.3 and 2.4 are all based on the facts in KG, and there is still a lot of other knowledge-related information that has not been effectively utilized. Therefore, increasing number of researchers consider to combine external information (such as entity types, logical rules, relation paths and time information) with a KG itself to further improve the model and the representation efficiency of tasks.

Entity Types. Entity types refer to the semantic category to which the entity belongs. This kind of information is available in most KGs, which is usually encoded by specific relations and stored as triplets. SSE [40] makes full use of additional semantic information to make the embedding space semantically smoother. By using additional entity category information, SSE can not only capture the semantic correlation between entities but also solve the data sparsity problem prevalent in most KGs, both of which make embedding more accurate. TKRL [41] takes the hierarchical type information as the projection matrix of the entity, models the hierarchical structure with two types of encoders, and defines the scoring function $f_r(h, t) = \|\mathbf{M}_{rh}\mathbf{h} + \mathbf{r} - \mathbf{M}_{rt}\mathbf{t}\|_1$ by regarding the type information as a constraint of the specific relation type. WGCN [36], the encoder part of SACN, takes the attributes of entities as nodes of the KG, acting as a "bridge", and the nodes with the same attributes can share information. In [42], it noticed that the relation type in KG can be divided into attributes or relations. In order to distinguish them, KR-EAR was proposed. The model maximizes the scoring function by defining a common probability between relation triplets and attribute triplets.

Logical Rules. Since logical rules generally contain rich background information, adding logical rules to KRL can improve the performance of embedding models. RPJE [43] is a novel Rule and Path-based Joint Embedding model to learn KG embeddings by integrating triplet facts, Horn rules and paths in a unified framework to enhance the accuracy and the explain ability of representation learning (RL). RUGE [44] iteratively predicts unlabeled triplets using soft rules automatically extracted from KGs, and then generates unlabeled triplets with confidence and adds them to training set to enhance RL. IterE [45] combines traditional representation learning and rule mining together, and iteratively learns embedding and rules through three main parts: embedding learning, axiom induction, and axiom injection, which make up for their shortcomings. KALE [46] is a joint model that emplaces KG facts and logical rules in the same time. It first unifies triplets and rules according to first-order logic, and then minimizes a global loss involving both of them to learn entity and relation embeddings. Finally it achieves the goal of learning embedding compatible with both facts and rules.

Relation Paths. The multi-hop relation paths can also reflect the rich semantic relations between entities in KG, so the researchers added the relation paths to the KG embedding for research and achieved good results. RPE [47] is a relation path embedding model, which utilizes the additional semantics of relation paths to embed each entity into two different potential spaces at the same time. OPTransE [48] projects the head and tail entity of each relation into different spaces to ensure the order of the relation in the path. At the same time, the total energy function of triplets is constructed by using the two-layer pooling strategy to extract the non-linear complex features of different paths. Lin et al. [49] thought the multi-step relations path between entities in the KG also contains rich semantic information, and proposed a path-based representation learning model: PTransE, in which the path involves three types of semantic combination operations: addition, multiplication and recurrent neural network. Reference [50] proposed the first accurate dynamic programming algorithm, which enables all relation paths of bounded lengths to be effectively combined, and removes relation types and intermediate nodes in the representation of the combined paths.

Time Information. The entities and relations in KG will change over time. The previous KRL methods did not consider the time dimension in the KG, and always treated the knowledge graph as static, which is clearly not true. A time-aware embedding model is proposed in [51]. This model uses chronological constraints to establish a transformation model between time-sensitive relations and forces the embedding to be consistent and accurate along the time dimension. However, it only takes time series as a constraint in the embedding process of KG, which does not clearly reflect the characteristics of time. Therefore, HyTE [52] is proposed in order to capture the time-related behavior among entities and relations. The model associates each timestamp with the corresponding hyperplane and explicitly combines time in the embedding space. In a dynamic KG, entities may be connected through multiple identical relations, but these relations are associated with different temporal information. Therefore it uses neural networks to learn the representation of entities at different times in [53], that is each event is represented in the dynamic KG as $m = (e^s, r, e^o, t)$, suggesting that at time t, the relation between the head entity s and the tail entity o is r.

3   Evaluation Tasks and Datasets of Knowledge Representation Learning

In this section, we introduce the widely adopted evaluation tasks, evaluation metrics and common benchmark datasets used in the experiment of KRL models.

3.1   Evaluation Tasks and Metrics

In this section, we introduce the two most common evaluation tasks used by the KG embedding techniques discussed above: link prediction and triplet classification, and their corresponding evaluation metrics.

Link Prediction. Link prediction is the most commonly used evaluation task in KRL [3,30]. The purpose of link prediction is to predict new tail/head entities based on existing head/tail entities and relations in the KG, or predict the relation through entities to complete the missing knowledge in the KG. This evaluation task uses the scoring function to measure the possibility of links, then sorts all candidate answers in the KG, calculates the score of each candidate triplet, and selects the one with the highest score as the final predicted triplet, so as to realize the evaluation of the model. In general, the link prediction task uses the following evaluation metrics:

1) Mean Rank (MR), the evaluation metric ranks a series of scores calculated by the scoring function in ascending order, and then averages the ranking of the correct answers in each test triplet;
2) Mean Reciprocal Rank (MRR), this evaluation metric takes the inverse of the rank where the correct answer is obtained as its accuracy, and then averages all the reciprocal orders;
3) Hits@N(%), which also sorts the scores, and calculates the proportion of the correct answer in top N of each test triplet.

Triplet Classification. Triplet classification is another most commonly used evaluation task in KRL [4,25], whose purpose is to distinguish whether a given triplet is correct or not. It calculates the score of each triplet through KG embedding model, and set a threshold, if the triplet's score greater than or equal to the threshold, then this triplet is right, otherwise it is wrong. The accuracy of the final model depends on the number of triplets classified correctly, so that the quality of each model is evaluated. Generally, the triplet classification task uses the average precision of micro and macro as the evaluation metric, which takes the area enclosed by the P-R (precision-recall) curve as the average precision. The better the model performance, the higher the average precision and the lower recall rate.

3.2   Benchmark Datasets

In this section, we introduce the KG open source benchmark datasets used in KRL, including the general datasets, domain-specific datasets, and datasets for specific evaluation tasks of knowledge graph embedding technology.

General Datasets. At present, the most representative large-scale open knowledge graphs are WordNet [54], Wikidata [55], YAGO [56], Freebase [57], NELL [58] and so on. The statistics of their initial release time, build manner and category are shown in Table 1. WordNet is the most famous manually constructed lexical knowledge graph, first published in 1995 by Plimpton university's cognitive science laboratory, containing 155,000 words. Launched by Wikipedia in 2012, Wikidata is a collaborative, multi-language encyclopedic knowledge graph that supports more than 350 languages and has nearly 25 million entities. YAGO is a large-scale ontology that integrates Wikipedia, GeoNames and WordNet. It integrates WordNet's word definition with Wikipedia's classification to have a richer entity classification system. At present, YAGO has about 4.59 million entities and 24 million facts in 10 languages. Freebase is an open and large-scale linked database coming from a semantic web project launched by a Silicon Valley startup in 2005 with more than 40 million entities and 2.4 billion fact triplets. NELL is a text extraction knowledge base developed by Carnegie Mellon university. So far, NELL has extracted more than 3 million triplets of knowledge.

Table 1. Statistics of general knowledge graph datasets

Dataset	Source	Year	Language	Category	Building manner
WordNet	Plimpton university	1995	English	language KG	Artificial building
Wikidata	Wikipedia	2012	Multi-language	Language KG	Machine and Artificial building
YAGO	Max Planck institute	2007	Multi-language	Factual KG	Wikipedia-based building
Freebase	Metaweb	2008	Multi-language	Factual KG	Wikipedia-based building
NELL	Carnegie Mellon University	2009	Multi-language	Text extraction KG	Machine building

Domain-Specific Datasets. The semantic matching models [17,18] and the bilinear models [27] used UMLS [59], Kinships [60] and Cora [61] datasets for experiments. The common points of these three datasets is that they belong to specific domain knowledge base, as shown in Table 2. UMLS is a semantic network belonging to the medical field, which describes the relations between medical concepts, including 135 entities, 49 relations and 6,800 triplets. Kinships describes the kinship relations among people, including 104 entities, 26 relations and 10,800 triplets. Cora is a large real-world dataset that is commonly used to evaluate the performance of relation learning methods in tasks such as classification or entity resolution. It contains 2497 entities, 7 relations and 39,255 triplets.

Specific Evaluation Task Datasets. Most of the datasets used in the experiment of KRL are specific datasets adopted according to their own evaluation tasks. In general, these specific datasets are subsets of the large-scale open source datasets mentioned above. As shown in Table 2, the subsets of large-scale knowledge graph datasets frequently used in KRL include:

1) The subsets of WordNet are WN11, WN18, and WN18RR, with WN11 containing 11 relations and WN18 containing 18 relations. The relation type

contains symmetric/antisymmetric and inverse relations, while WN18RR is a subset of WN18 that removes the inverse relations;

2) The subsets of Freebase include FB15k, FB15k-401, FB15k-237, FB13 and FB40k. Among them FB15k contains symmetric/antisymmetric and inverse relations types. FB15k-401 is a subset of FB15k that only contains frequent relations. FB15k-237 is a subset of FB15k with inverse relations deleted. FB13 is a relation triplet extracted from the People field in Freebase, which contains 13 relations. FB40k is a smaller dataset, which contains all the entities in The New York Times and 1,336 relations;

3) The subset of YAGO has YAGO37, which is extracted from the core facts of YAGO3.5. In the process of extraction, less than 10 times of the entity is discarded;

4) The subset of NELL has NELL-995, which contains 75,492 entities and 200 different relations;

5) A subset of Wikidata is Wikidata12k, which contains the 24 most frequent time relations and produces 40k triplets containing 12.5k entities.

Table 2. The statistics of datasets for domain-specific and specific tasks

Dataset	#Relation	#Entity	#Train	#Valid	#Test
UMLS	46	135	2516	652	661
Kinships	25	104	8544	1068	1074
WN18	18	40943	141442	5000	5000
WN18RR	11	40943	86835	3034	3134
FB15k	1345	14951	483142	50000	59071
FB15k-237	237	14541	272115	17535	20466
FB13	13	75043	316232	5908	23733
FB40k	1336	39528	370648	67946	96678
YAGO37	37	123189	989132	50000	50000
NELL-995	200	75492	149678	543	3992
Wikidata12k	24	12554	32500	4000	4000

4   Applications in Downstream Tasks

The vector representation learned in KRL can be used to efficiently complete various downstream tasks, such as KG based recommendation system, relations extraction and question answering system. This section introduces how to apply the learned embedding of entities and relations to these domains.

4.1   Recommendation System

CKE [62] is a hybrid recommendation system that introduces structural information to automatically extract semantic representation from the structure, text and visual knowledge in KG. Among them, structural information uses TransR [5] to learn the representation of entities. DKN is proposed in [63], which combines KG embedding and CNN for news recommendation, which combines semantic representation of news with knowledge representation to form a new embedding representation. RippleNet [64] solves the limitations of the existing embedded and path-based KG perception recommendation methods, simulates the propagation process of user interest in KG, and naturally integrates KG into the recommendation system. MKR [65] is a multi-task feature learning method for KG recommendation. This model uses KG embedding to assist recommendation tasks, and trains the entire model through alternate learning of KG embedding and recommendation methods. KPRN [66] constructs the relation between user and item pairs through KG, which provides interpretability for user behavior.

4.2   Relation Extraction

In [67], it proposes a method for relation extraction from unstructured text, which is mainly based on weak supervision for relation extraction from knowledge graph. The method learns two models: one is to correspond the relation mentioned in the text to the relation in the KG; the other is the embedding of entities and relations in the KG. Plain text and knowledge graphs are embedded jointly [68] to achieve relations extraction. By using collaborative filtering technology, text and KGs are represented in the same matrix, and then the matrix is decomposed to learn the vector embedding and KG relations of entity pairs. Inspired by the rich semantic correlation between the long-tail data and the data at the top of the distribution, it proposed a model for learning relational knowledge by combining KG embedding and graph convolution networks in [69].

4.3   Question Answering

Reference [70, 71] introduced a system for learning to answer question through open KGs, which requires only a few manually designed rules. The correct answer is selected by calculating the correlation between the embedding of questions and candidate answers. BAMnet [72] introduces a new bidirectional attention memory network, which can successfully capture the interaction between the problem and the underlying knowledge base, aiming to enhance the problem and KG representation by further utilizing bidirectional attention. KEQA [73] only focuses on simple question answering type. It answers the questions by representation of entities and predicates in the embedding space of the KG, especially in order to make up for the differences between predicates in the questions and the KG. In this work, the author uses the Bi-LSTM model based on attention to learn predicate representation.

5   Association with MDATA

At present, Big Search is faced with the problem of unified representation of multi-domain knowledge, that is, the knowledge formed in different fields is different, and the representation of knowledge is different. Even if the same knowledge is summarized in different fields, it may be expressed in different ways. At the same time, because of the inconsistency of knowledge representation learning, it also leads to the difficult problem of knowledge correlation and fusion analysis in different fields and dimensions.

In order to solve the above problems, MDATA model comes into being. Knowledge representation learning, as the basic work of constructing knowledge graph, is particularly important in the unified representation of multi-domain knowledge. The MDATA model contains two different methods to represent learning. One is to represent the relations between the head and tail entities with an edge. The relation of the edge is treated as a relational set, and then other methods are used to process the relational set. However, this method is difficult to express the unidirectional and bidirectional nature of the relations, which requires additional processing methods. The other is to represent each relation as an edge, which can effectively represent the unidirectional and bidirectional characteristics of the relations. In addition, MDATA contains temporal and spatial features that capture knowledge more accurately. Therefore, it is worth studying to use knowledge representation learning methods to model MDATA.

6   Chapter Summary

KRL is a frontier issue in the research of artificial intelligence. By embedding entities and relations into continuous low-dimensional vector space, it can significantly improve the computational efficiency and alleviate the data sparseness problem. This survey systematically reviewed the latest research progress of KRL. Firstly, it introduces the characteristics of different types of embedding models in KRL, then summarizes the evaluation tasks, metrics and datasets used in experiments of these models, and finally discusses the application of KRL in downstream tasks.

The future research of KRL will further expand the landscape of KGs in many fields, such as Intelligent Search in Cyberspace and Natural Language Processing related applications. KRL will greatly promote the construction of domain KG in more future applications as well as the following KG completion and reasoning tasks, bring huge social and economic benefits.

References

1. Bordes, A., Weston, J., Collobert, R., Bengio, Y.: Learning structured embeddings of knowledge bases. In: Burgard, W., Roth, D. (eds.) Proceedings of the Twenty-Fifth AAAI Conference on Artificial Intelligence, AAAI 2011, San Francisco, California, USA, 7–11 August 2011. AAAI Press (2011)

2. Bordes, A., Glorot, X., Weston, J., Bengio, Y.: Joint learning of words and meaning representations for open-text semantic parsing. In: Proceedings of the Fifteenth International Conference on Artificial Intelligence and Statistics, AISTATS 2012, La Palma, Canary Islands, Spain, 21–23 April 2012, vol. 22 of JMLR Proceedings, pp. 127–135. JMLR.org (2012)
3. Bordes, A., Usunier, N., García-Durán, A., Weston, J., Yakhnenko, O.: Translating embeddings for modeling multi-relational data. In: Burges, C.J.C., Bottou, L., Ghahramani, Z., Weinberger, K.Q. (eds.) Advances in Neural Information Processing Systems 26: 27th Annual Conference on Neural Information Processing Systems 2013. Proceedings of a Meeting Held 5–8 December 2013, Lake Tahoe, Nevada, United States, pp. 2787–2795 (2013)
4. Wang, Z., Zhang, J., Feng, J., Chen, Z.: Knowledge graph embedding by translating on hyperplanes. In: Brodley, C.E., Stone, P. (eds.) Proceedings of the Twenty-Eighth AAAI Conference on Artificial Intelligence, 27–31 July 2014, Québec City, Québec, Canada, pp. 1112–1119. AAAI Press (2014)
5. Lin, Y., Liu, Z., Sun, M., Liu, Y., Zhu, X.: Learning entity and relation embeddings for knowledge graph completion. In: Bonet, B., Koenig, S. (eds.) Proceedings of the Twenty-Ninth AAAI Conference on Artificial Intelligence, 25–30 January 2015, Austin, Texas, USA, pp. 2181–2187. AAAI Press (2015)
6. Xie, Q., Ma, X., Dai, Z., Hovy, E.H.: An interpretable knowledge transfer model for knowledge base completion. In: Barzilay, R., Kan, M. (eds.) Proceedings of the 55th Annual Meeting of the Association for Computational Linguistics, ACL 2017, Vancouver, Canada, 30 July–4 August 2017, Volume 1: Long Papers, pp. 950–962. Association for Computational Linguistics (2017)
7. Ji, G., He, S., Xu, L., Liu, K., Zhao, J.: Knowledge graph embedding via dynamic mapping matrix. In: Proceedings of the 53rd Annual Meeting of the Association for Computational Linguistics and the 7th International Joint Conference on Natural Language Processing of the Asian Federation of Natural Language Processing, ACL 2015, 26–31 July 2015, Beijing, China, Volume 1: Long Papers, pp. 687–696. The Association for Computer Linguistics (2015)
8. Ji, G., Liu, K., He, S., Zhao, J.: Knowledge graph completion with adaptive sparse transfer matrix. In: Schuurmans, D., Wellman, M.P. (eds.) Proceedings of the Thirtieth AAAI Conference on Artificial Intelligence, 12–17 February 2016, Phoenix, Arizona, USA, pp. 985–991. AAAI Press (2016)
9. Qian, W., Fu, C., Zhu, Y., Cai, D., He, X.: Translating embeddings for knowledge graph completion with relation attention mechanism. In: Lang, J. (ed.) Proceedings of the Twenty-Seventh International Joint Conference on Artificial Intelligence, IJCAI 2018, 13–19 July 2018, Stockholm, Sweden, pp. 4286–4292. Ijcai.org (2018)
10. Xiao, H., Huang, M., Hao, Y., Zhu, X.: TransA: an adaptive approach for knowledge graph embedding. CoRR, vol. abs/1509.05490 (2015)
11. Feng, J., Huang, M., Wang, M., Zhou, M., Hao, Y., Zhu, X.: Knowledge graph embedding by flexible translation. In: Baral, C., Delgrande, J.P., Wolter, F. (eds.) Principles of Knowledge Representation and Reasoning: Proceedings of the Fifteenth International Conference, KR 2016, Cape Town, South Africa, 25–29 April 2016, pp. 557–560. AAAI Press (2016)
12. Yang, S., Tian, J., Zhang, H., Yan, J., He, H., Jin, Y.: TransMS: knowledge graph embedding for complex relations by multidirectional semantics. In: Kraus, S. (ed.) Proceedings of the Twenty-Eighth International Joint Conference on Artificial Intelligence, IJCAI 2019, Macao, China, 10–16 August 2019, pp. 1935–1942. Ijcai.org (2019)

13. Xiao, H., Huang, M., Hao, Y., Zhu, X.: TransG: a generative mixture model for knowledge graph embedding. CoRR, vol. abs/1509.05488 (2015)
14. He, S., Liu, K., Ji, G., Zhao, J.: Learning to represent knowledge graphs with Gaussian embedding. In: Bailey, J., et al. (eds.) Proceedings of the 24th ACM International Conference on Information and Knowledge Management, CIKM 2015, Melbourne, VIC, Australia, 19–23 October 2015, pp. 623–632. ACM (2015)
15. Sun, Z., Deng, Z., Nie, J., Tang, J.: RotatE: knowledge graph embedding by relational rotation in complex space. In: 7th International Conference on Learning Representations, ICLR 2019, New Orleans, LA, USA, 6–9 May 2019. OpenReview.net (2019)
16. Ebisu, T., Ichise, R.: TorusE: knowledge graph embedding on a lie group. In: McIlraith, S.A., Weinberger, K.Q. (eds.) Proceedings of the Thirty-Second AAAI Conference on Artificial Intelligence, (AAAI-18), the 30th Innovative Applications of Artificial Intelligence (IAAI-18), and the 8th AAAI Symposium on Educational Advances in Artificial Intelligence (EAAI-18), New Orleans, Louisiana, USA, 2–7 February 2018, pp. 1819–1826. AAAI Press (2018)
17. Glorot, X., Bordes, A., Weston, J., Bengio, Y.: A semantic matching energy function for learning with multi-relational data. In: Bengio, Y., LeCun, Y. (eds.) 1st International Conference on Learning Representations, ICLR 2013, Scottsdale, Arizona, USA, 2–4 May 2013, Workshop Track Proceedings (2013)
18. Nickel, M., Tresp, V., Kriegel, H.: A three-way model for collective learning on multi-relational data. In: Getoor, L., Scheffer, T. (eds.) Proceedings of the 28th International Conference on Machine Learning, ICML 2011, Bellevue, Washington, USA, 28 June - 2 July 2011, pp. 809–816. Omnipress (2011)
19. García-Durán, A., Bordes, A., Usunier, N.: Effective blending of two and three-way interactions for modeling multi-relational data. In: Calders, T., Esposito, F., Hüllermeier, E., Meo, R. (eds.) ECML PKDD 2014. LNCS (LNAI), vol. 8724, pp. 434–449. Springer, Heidelberg (2014). https://doi.org/10.1007/978-3-662-44848-9_28
20. Yang, B., Yih, W., He, X., Gao, J., Deng, L.: Embedding entities and relations for learning and inference in knowledge bases. In: Bengio, Y., LeCun, Y. (eds.) 3rd International Conference on Learning Representations, ICLR 2015, San Diego, CA, USA, 7–9 May 2015, Conference Track Proceedings (2015)
21. Trouillon, T., Welbl, J., Riedel, S., Gaussier, É., Bouchard, G.: Complex embeddings for simple link prediction. In: Balcan, M., Weinberger, K.Q. (eds.) Proceedings of the 33nd International Conference on Machine Learning, ICML 2016, New York City, NY, USA, 19–24 June 2016, vol. 48 of JMLR Workshop and Conference Proceedings, pp. 2071–2080. JMLR.org (2016)
22. Nickel, M. Rosasco, L., Poggio, T.A.: Holographic embeddings of knowledge graphs. In: Schuurmans, D., Wellman, M.P. (eds.) Proceedings of the Thirtieth AAAI Conference on Artificial Intelligence, 12–17 February 2016, Phoenix, Arizona, USA, pp. 1955–1961. AAAI Press (2016)
23. Zhang, S., Tay, Y., Yao, L., Liu, Q.: Quaternion knowledge graph embeddings. In: Wallach, H.M., Larochelle, H., Beygelzimer, A., d'Alché-Buc, F., Fox, E.B., Garnett, R. (eds.) Advances in Neural Information Processing Systems 32: Annual Conference on Neural Information Processing Systems 2019, NeurIPS 2019, 8–14 December 2019, Vancouver, BC, Canada, pp. 2731–2741 (2019)
24. Liu, H., Wu, Y., Yang, Y.: Analogical inference for multi-relational embeddings. In: Precup, D., Teh, Y.W. (eds.) Proceedings of the 34th International Conference on Machine Learning, ICML 2017, Sydney, NSW, Australia, 6–11 August 2017, vol. 70 of Proceedings of Machine Learning Research, pp. 2168–2178. PMLR (2017)

25. Socher, R., Chen, D., Manning, C.D., Ng, A.Y.: Reasoning with neural tensor networks for knowledge base completion. In: Burges, C.J.C., Bottou, L., Ghahramani, Z., Weinberger, K.Q. (eds.)Advances in Neural Information Processing Systems 26: 27th Annual Conference on Neural Information Processing Systems 2013. Proceedings of a Meeting Held 5–8 December 2013, Lake Tahoe, Nevada, United States, pp. 926–934 (2013)

26. Liu, Q., Jiang, H., Ling, Z., Wei, S., Hu, Y.: Probabilistic reasoning via deep learning: Neural association models. CoRR, vol. abs/1603.07704 (2016)

27. Jenatton, R., Roux, N.L., Bordes, A., Obozinski, G.: A latent factor model for highly multi-relational data. In: Bartlett, P.L., Pereira, F.C.N., Burges, C.J.C., Bottou, L., Weinberger, K.Q. (eds.) Advances in Neural Information Processing Systems 25: 26th Annual Conference on Neural Information Processing Systems 2012. Proceedings of a Meeting Held 3–6 December 2012, Lake Tahoe, Nevada, United States, pp. 3176–3184 (2012)

28. Kazemi, S.M., Poole, D.: Simple embedding for link prediction in knowledge graphs. In: Bengio, S., Wallach, H.M., Larochelle, H., Grauman, K., Cesa-Bianchi, N., Garnett, R. (eds.)Advances in Neural Information Processing Systems 31: Annual Conference on Neural Information Processing Systems 2018, NeurIPS 2018, 3–8 December 2018, Montréal, Canada, pp. 4289–4300 (2018)

29. Wang, Y., Gemulla, R., Li, H.: On multi-relational link prediction with bilinear models. In: McIlraith, S.A., Weinberger, K.Q. (eds.) Proceedings of the Thirty-Second AAAI Conference on Artificial Intelligence, (AAAI-18), the 30th innovative Applications of Artificial Intelligence (IAAI-18), and the 8th AAAI Symposium on Educational Advances in Artificial Intelligence (EAAI-18), New Orleans, Louisiana, USA, 2–7 February 2018, pp. 4227–4234. AAAI Press (2018)

30. Dettmers, T., Minervini, P., Stenetorp, P., Riedel, S.: Convolutional 2D knowledge graph embeddings. In: McIlraith, S.A., Weinberger, K.Q. (eds.) Proceedings of the Thirty-Second AAAI Conference on Artificial Intelligence, (AAAI-18), the 30th innovative Applications of Artificial Intelligence (IAAI-18), and the 8th AAAI Symposium on Educational Advances in Artificial Intelligence (EAAI-18), New Orleans, Louisiana, USA, 2–7 February 2018, pp. 1811–1818. AAAI Press (2018)

31. Schlichtkrull, M., Kipf, T.N., Bloem, P., van den Berg, R., Titov, I., Welling, M.: Modeling relational data with graph convolutional networks. In: Gangemi, A., et al. (eds.) ESWC 2018. LNCS, vol. 10843, pp. 593–607. Springer, Cham (2018). https://doi.org/10.1007/978-3-319-93417-4_38

32. Vashishth, S., Sanyal, S., Nitin, V. Agrawal, N., Talukdar, P.P.: InteractE: improving convolution-based knowledge graph embeddings by increasing feature interactions. In The Thirty-Fourth AAAI Conference on Artificial Intelligence, AAAI 2020, The Thirty-Second Innovative Applications of Artificial Intelligence Conference, IAAI 2020, The Tenth AAAI Symposium on Educational Advances in Artificial Intelligence, EAAI 2020, New York, NY, USA, 7–12 February 2020, pp. 3009–3016. AAAI Press (2020)

33. Nguyen, D.Q., Nguyen, T.D., Nguyen, D.Q., Phung, D.Q.: A novel embedding model for knowledge base completion based on convolutional neural network. In: Walker, M.A., Ji, H., Stent, A. (eds.) Proceedings of the 2018 Conference of the North American Chapter of the Association for Computational Linguistics: Human Language Technologies, NAACL-HLT, New Orleans, Louisiana, USA, 1–6 June 2018, Volume 2 (Short Papers), pp. 327–333. Association for Computational Linguistics (2018)

34. Nguyen, D.Q., Vu, T., Nguyen, T.D., Nguyen, D.Q., Phung, D.Q.: A capsule network-based embedding model for knowledge graph completion and search personalization. In: Burstein, J., Doran, C., Solorio, T. (eds.) Proceedings of the 2019 Conference of the North American Chapter of the Association for Computational Linguistics: Human Language Technologies, NAACL-HLT 2019, Minneapolis, MN, USA, 2–7 June 2019, Volume 1 (Long and Short Papers), pp. 2180–2189. Association for Computational Linguistics (2019)

35. Sabour, S., Frosst, N., Hinton, G.E.: Dynamic routing between capsules. In: Guyon, I., et al. (eds.) Advances in Neural Information Processing Systems 30: Annual Conference on Neural Information Processing Systems 2017, 4–9 December 2017, Long Beach, CA, USA, pp. 3856–3866 (2017)

36. Shang, C., Tang, Y., Huang, J., Bi, J., He, X., Zhou, B.: End-to-end structure-aware convolutional networks for knowledge base completion. In: The Thirty-Third AAAI Conference on Artificial Intelligence, AAAI 2019, The Thirty-First Innovative Applications of Artificial Intelligence Conference, IAAI 2019, The Ninth AAAI Symposium on Educational Advances in Artificial Intelligence, EAAI 2019, Honolulu, Hawaii, USA, 27 January–1 February 2019, pp. 3060–3067. AAAI Press (2019)

37. Nathani, D., Chauhan, J., Sharma, C., Kaul, M.: Learning attention-based embeddings for relation prediction in knowledge graphs. In: Korhonen, A., Traum, D.R., Màrquez, L. (eds.) Proceedings of the 57th Conference of the Association for Computational Linguistics, ACL 2019, Florence, Italy, 28 July–2 August 2019, Volume 1: Long Papers, pp. 4710–4723. Association for Computational Linguistics (2019)

38. Balažević, I., Allen, C., Hospedales, T.M.: Hypernetwork knowledge graph embeddings. In: Tetko, I.V., Kůrková, V., Karpov, P., Theis, F. (eds.) ICANN 2019. LNCS, vol. 11731, pp. 553–565. Springer, Cham (2019). https://doi.org/10.1007/978-3-030-30493-5_52

39. Guo, L., Sun, Z., Hu, W.: Learning to exploit long-term relational dependencies in knowledge graphs. In: Chaudhuri, K., Salakhutdinov, R. (eds.) Proceedings of the 36th International Conference on Machine Learning, ICML 2019, 9–15 June 2019, Long Beach, California, USA, vol. 97 of Proceedings of Machine Learning Research, pp. 2505–2514. PMLR (2019)

40. Guo, S., Wang, Q., Wang, B., Wang, L., Guo, L.: SSE: semantically smooth embedding for knowledge graphs. IEEE Trans. Knowl. Data Eng. **29**(4), 884–897 (2017)

41. Xie, R., Liu, Z., Sun, M.: Representation learning of knowledge graphs with hierarchical types. In: Kambhampati, S. (ed.) Proceedings of the Twenty-Fifth International Joint Conference on Artificial Intelligence, IJCAI 2016, New York, NY, USA, 9–15 July 2016, pp. 2965–2971. IJCAI/AAAI Press (2016)

42. Lin, Y., Liu, Z., Sun, M.: Knowledge representation learning with entities, attributes and relations. In: Kambhampati, S. (ed.) Proceedings of the Twenty-Fifth International Joint Conference on Artificial Intelligence, IJCAI 2016, New York, NY, USA, 9–15 July 2016, pp. 2866–2872. IJCAI/AAAI Press (2016)

43. Niu, G., et al.: Rule-guided compositional representation learning on knowledge graphs. In: The Thirty-Fourth AAAI Conference on Artificial Intelligence, AAAI 2020, The Thirty-Second Innovative Applications of Artificial Intelligence Conference, IAAI 2020, The Tenth AAAI Symposium on Educational Advances in Artificial Intelligence, EAAI 2020, New York, NY, USA, 7–12 February 2020, pp. 2950–2958. AAAI Press (2020)

44. Guo, S., Wang, Q., Wang, L., Wang, B., Guo, L.: Knowledge graph embedding with iterative guidance from soft rules. In: McIlraith, S.A., Weinberger, K.Q. (eds.) Proceedings of the Thirty-Second AAAI Conference on Artificial Intelligence, (AAAI-18), the 30th innovative Applications of Artificial Intelligence (IAAI-18), and the 8th AAAI Symposium on Educational Advances in Artificial Intelligence (EAAI-18), New Orleans, Louisiana, USA, 2–7 February 2018, pp. 4816–4823. AAAI Press (2018)

45. Zhang, W., et al.: Iteratively learning embeddings and rules for knowledge graph reasoning. CoRR, vol. abs/1903.08948 (2019)

46. Guo, S., Wang, Q., Wang, L., Wang, B., Guo, L.: Jointly embedding knowledge graphs and logical rules. In: Su, J., Carreras, X., Duh, K. (eds.) Proceedings of the 2016 Conference on Empirical Methods in Natural Language Processing, EMNLP 2016, Austin, Texas, USA, 1–4 November 2016, pp. 192–202. The Association for Computational Linguistics (2016)

47. Lin, X., Liang, Y., Giunchiglia, F., Feng, X., Guan, R.: Relation path embedding in knowledge graphs. Neural Comput. Appl. **31**(9), 5629–5639 (2019)

48. Zhu, Y., Liu, H., Wu, Z., Song, Y., Zhang, T.: Representation learning with ordered relation paths for knowledge graph completion. In: Inui, K., Jiang, J., Ng, V., Wan, X. (eds.) Proceedings of the 2019 Conference on Empirical Methods in Natural Language Processing and the 9th International Joint Conference on Natural Language Processing, EMNLP-IJCNLP 2019, Hong Kong, China, 3–7 November 2019, pp. 2662–2671. Association for Computational Linguistics (2019)

49. Lin, Y., Liu, Z., Luan, H., Sun, M., Rao, S., Liu, S.: Modeling relation paths for representation learning of knowledge bases. In: Màrquez, L., Callison-Burch, C., Su, J., Pighin, D., Marton, Y. (eds.) Proceedings of the 2015 Conference on Empirical Methods in Natural Language Processing, EMNLP 2015, Lisbon, Portugal, 17–21 September 2015, pp. 705–714. The Association for Computational Linguistics (2015)

50. Toutanova, K., Lin, X.V., Yih, W., Poon, H., Quirk, C.: Compositional learning of embeddings for relation paths in knowledge base and text. In: Proceedings of the 54th Annual Meeting of the Association for Computational Linguistics, ACL 2016, 7–12 August 2016, Berlin, Germany, Volume 1: Long Papers. The Association for Computer Linguistics (2016)

51. Jiang, T., et al.: Encoding temporal information for time-aware link prediction. In: Su, J., Carreras, X., Duh, K. (eds.) Proceedings of the 2016 Conference on Empirical Methods in Natural Language Processing, EMNLP 2016, Austin, Texas, USA, 1–4 November 2016, pp. 2350–2354. The Association for Computational Linguistics (2016)

52. Dasgupta, S.S., Ray, S.N., Talukdar, P.P.: HyTE: hyperplane-based temporally aware knowledge graph embedding. In: Riloff, E., Chiang, D., Hockenmaier, J., Tsujii, J. (eds.) Proceedings of the 2018 Conference on Empirical Methods in Natural Language Processing, Brussels, Belgium, 31 October–4 November 2018, pp. 2001–2011. Association for Computational Linguistics (2018)

53. Trivedi, R., Dai, H., Wang, Y., Song, L.: Know-evolve: deep temporal reasoning for dynamic knowledge graphs. In: Precup, D., Teh, Y.W. (eds.) Proceedings of the 34th International Conference on Machine Learning, ICML 2017, Sydney, NSW, Australia, 6–11 August 2017. Proceedings of Machine Learning Research, vol. 70, pp. 3462–3471. PMLR (2017)

54. Miller, G.A.: WordNet: a lexical database for English. Commun. ACM **38**(11), 39–41 (1995)

55. Vrandecic, D., Krötzsch, M.: WikiData: a free collaborative knowledgebase. Commun. ACM **57**(10), 78–85 (2014)
56. Fabian, M., Gjergji, K., Gerhard, W., et al.: Yago: a core of semantic knowledge unifying WordNet and Wikipedia. In: 16th International World Wide Web Conference, WWW, pp. 697–706 (2007)
57. Bollacker, K.D., Evans, C., Paritosh, P., Sturge, T., Taylor, J.: Freebase: a collaboratively created graph database for structuring human knowledge. In: Wang, J.T. (ed.) Proceedings of the ACM SIGMOD International Conference on Management of Data, SIGMOD 2008, Vancouver, BC, Canada, 10–12 June 2008, pp. 1247–1250. ACM (2008)
58. Carlson, A., Betteridge, J., Kisiel, B., Settles, B., Hruschka Jr., E.R., Mitchell, T.M.: Toward an architecture for never-ending language learning. In: Fox, M., Poole, D. (eds.) Proceedings of the Twenty-Fourth AAAI Conference on Artificial Intelligence, AAAI 2010, Atlanta, Georgia, USA, 11–15 July 2010. AAAI Press (2010)
59. Bodenreider, O.: The unified medical language system (UMLS): integrating biomedical terminology. Nucleic Acids Res. **32**(Database–Issue), 267–270 (2004)
60. Kemp, C., Tenenbaum, J.B., Griffiths, T.L., Yamada, T., Ueda, N.: Learning systems of concepts with an infinite relational model. In: AAAI, vol. 3, p. 5 (2006)
61. Kemp, C., Tenenbaum, J.B., Griffiths, T.L., Yamada, T., Ueda, N.: Learning systems of concepts with an infinite relational model. In: Proceedings, The Twenty-First National Conference on Artificial Intelligence and the Eighteenth Innovative Applications of Artificial Intelligence Conference, 16–20 July 2006, Boston, Massachusetts, USA, pp. 381–388. AAAI Press (2006)
62. Zhang, F., Yuan, N.J., Lian, D., Xie, X., Ma, W.: Collaborative knowledge base embedding for recommender systems. In: Krishnapuram, B., Shah, M., Smola, A.J., Aggarwal, C. C., Shen, D., Rastogi, R. (eds.) Proceedings of the 22nd ACM SIGKDD International Conference on Knowledge Discovery and Data Mining, San Francisco, CA, USA, 13–17 August 2016, pp. 353–362. ACM (2016)
63. Wang, H., Zhang, F., Xie, X., Guo, M.: DKN: deep knowledge-aware network for news recommendation. In: Champin, P., Gandon, F.L., Lalmas, M., Ipeirotis, P.G. (eds.) Proceedings of the 2018 World Wide Web Conference on World Wide Web, WWW 2018, Lyon, France, 23–27 April 2018, pp. 1835–1844. ACM (2018)
64. Wang, H., et al.: RippleNet: propagating user preferences on the knowledge graph for recommender systems. In: Cuzzocrea, A., et al. (eds.) Proceedings of the 27th ACM International Conference on Information and Knowledge Management, CIKM 2018, Torino, Italy, 22–26 October 2018, pp. 417–426. ACM (2018)
65. Wang, H., Zhang, F., Zhao, M., Li, W., Xie, X., Guo, M.: Multi-task feature learning for knowledge graph enhanced recommendation. In: Liu, L., et al. (eds.) The World Wide Web Conference, WWW 2019, San Francisco, CA, USA, 13–17 May 2019, pp. 2000–2010. ACM (2019)
66. Wang, X., Wang, D., Xu, C., He, X., Cao, Y., Chua, T.: Explainable reasoning over knowledge graphs for recommendation. In: The Thirty-Third AAAI Conference on Artificial Intelligence, AAAI 2019, The Thirty-First Innovative Applications of Artificial Intelligence Conference, IAAI 2019, The Ninth AAAI Symposium on Educational Advances in Artificial Intelligence, EAAI 2019, Honolulu, Hawaii, USA, 27 January - 1 February 2019, pp. 5329–5336. AAAI Press (2019)

67. Weston, J., Bordes, A., Yakhnenko, O., Usunier, N.: Connecting language and knowledge bases with embedding models for relation extraction. In: Proceedings of the 2013 Conference on Empirical Methods in Natural Language Processing, EMNLP 2013, 18–21 October 2013, Grand Hyatt Seattle, Seattle, Washington, USA, A meeting of SIGDAT, a Special Interest Group of the ACL, pp. 1366–1371. ACL (2013)

68. Riedel, S., Yao, L., McCallum, A., Marlin, B.M.: Relation extraction with matrix factorization and universal schemas. In: Vanderwende, L., D. III, H., Kirchhoff, K. (eds.) Human Language Technologies: Conference of the North American Chapter of the Association of Computational Linguistics, Proceedings, 9–14 June 2013, Westin Peachtree Plaza Hotel, Atlanta, Georgia, USA, pp. 74–84. The Association for Computational Linguistics (2013)

69. Zhang, N., et al.: Long-tail relation extraction via knowledge graph embeddings and graph convolution networks. In: Burstein, J., Doran, C., Solorio, T. (eds.) Proceedings of the 2019 Conference of the North American Chapter of the Association for Computational Linguistics: Human Language Technologies, NAACL-HLT 2019, Minneapolis, MN, USA, 2–7 June 2019, Volume 1 (Long and Short Papers), pp. 3016–3025. Association for Computational Linguistics (2019)

70. Bordes, A., Weston, J., Usunier, N.: Open question answering with weakly supervised embedding models. In: Calders, T., Esposito, F., Hüllermeier, E., Meo, R. (eds.) ECML PKDD 2014. LNCS (LNAI), vol. 8724, pp. 165–180. Springer, Heidelberg (2014). https://doi.org/10.1007/978-3-662-44848-9_11

71. Bordes, A., Chopra, S., Weston ,J.: Question answering with subgraph embeddings. In: Moschitti, A., Pang, B., Daelemans, W. (eds.) Proceedings of the 2014 Conference on Empirical Methods in Natural Language Processing, EMNLP 2014, 25–29 October 2014, Doha, Qatar, A meeting of SIGDAT, a Special Interest Group of the ACL, pp. 615–620. ACL (2014)

72. Chen, Y., Wu, L., Zaki, M.J.: Bidirectional attentive memory networks for question answering over knowledge bases. In: Burstein, J., Doran, C., Solorio, T. (eds.) Proceedings of the 2019 Conference of the North American Chapter of the Association for Computational Linguistics: Human Language Technologies, NAACL-HLT 2019, Minneapolis, MN, USA, 2–7 June 2019, Volume 1 (Long and Short Papers), pp. 2913–2923. Association for Computational Linguistics (2019)

73. Huang, X., Zhang, J., Li, D., Li, P.: Knowledge graph embedding based question answering. In: Culpepper, J.S., Moffat, A., Bennett, P.N., Lerman, K. (eds.) Proceedings of the Twelfth ACM International Conference on Web Search and Data Mining, WSDM 2019, Melbourne, VIC, Australia, 11–15 February 2019, pp. 105–113. ACM (2019)

Detection and Defense Methods of Cyber Attacks

Kai Xing[1], Aiping Li[1(✉)], Rong Jiang[1], and Yan Jia[2]

[1] National University of Defense Technology, Changsha 410073, China
{xingkai18,liaiping,jiangrong}@nudt.edu.cn
[2] Harbin Institute of Technology, Shenzhen 518055, China
jiayanjy@vip.sina.com

Abstract. Cyberspace has been threatened by attacks ever since its birth. With the development of the information technologies, especially big data and artificial intelligence, many kinds of cyber attacks are emerging every day, causing severe consequences to society. Meanwhile, intelligent defense methods are proposed to detect these attacks. Such attack and defense methods are constantly being renovated. In particular, advanced persistent threats are intensifying. How to effectively prevent this type of attack has become the a vital problem in recent years. The detection and defense technologies have made great progress. This chapter mainly discusses the research progress of APT attack detection and defense strategies at home and abroad, and focuses on the practice of using machine learning methods to perform attack detection while elaborating on traditional attack detection methods. We also introduce game theory based defense strategy to find the best defense strategy in limited resources, dynamic information flow tracking and cloud platform. With the development of knowledge representation, how to use the MDATA model to characterize the APT attacks is also be discussed in this chapter.

Keywords: MDATA · Cyber security · APT attack · Cyber defense

1 Introduction

Cyberspace has been hailed as the fifth battlefield, and governments are paying increasingly attention to the rights and interests of cyberspace [1]. With the development of the Internet and artificial intelligence (AI), people are enjoying the great convenience of the Internet, however the internet has been constantly threatened by cyber-attacks at the same time. In addition, the smart grid and the industrial Internet are also threatened by various attacks in recent years.

According to the statistics of the National Internet Emergency Center (CNCERT), merely in February 2020, China received a total of 9266 cyber-security incidents reported at home and abroad. The forms of cyberattacks are endless, and technical means are constantly being renovated, especially the rapid

© Springer Nature Switzerland AG 2021
Y. Jia et al. (Eds.): MDATA: A New Knowledge Representation Model, LNCS 12647, pp. 185–198, 2021.
https://doi.org/10.1007/978-3-030-71590-8_11

development of intelligent technology has spawned intelligent and efficient network attack methods. Advanced Persistent Threat (APT) attacks, such as Duqu [2], Ocean Lotus [3], Flame [4], have been active since 2010, when the "Stuxnet" virus attack on Iran's nuclear facilities. Unlike earlier cyberattacks, APT attacks are often funded by organizations behind them, with a complex background or purpose.

At the beginning of 2020, the 360 Security Brain disclosures a cyberattack organization named APT-C-39, which is conducted a 11-year-long cyberattack infiltration, mainly involving aerospace, oil, scientific research institutions and large Internet units. Because of its serious destructiveness, APT attacks are highly valued by many governments, international agencies and security companies. The academic community has also made many useful explorations of APT-related research and many innovative methods are proposed by efficient data fusion and data extraction. We proposed a network security knowledge base and inference rules based on the 5-tuple model in [5]. In [6], it deeply summarized the related research and progress of knowledge fusion in recent years.

On this basis, this chapter discusses the method of APT attack and defense strategies based on game theory. The rest of the chapter is organized as follows. The next section briefly introduces the background knowledge of APT, and Sect. 3 states the detection method of APT attack. In Sect. 4, we summarize and discuss the defense strategy against APT attacks. We discuss about how MDATA model could improve the detection in Sect. 5, and we finally summarize this chapter in Sect. 6.

2   APT Background Knowledge

The term Advanced Persistent Threat (APT) originated from the warning of abandoning Trojan horses to leak sensitive information. Although the name "APT" was not used at that time, "Advanced Persistent Threat" was used until 2006, when it was formally introduced by Colonel Greg Rattray of the US Air Force. APT attacks are well known in the field of information security due to the "Stuxnet" virus attack on Iran's nuclear facilities in 2010 and the serious hacking attack on Google Inc. With the rapid popularization of network technology, such attacks are continuing to emerge and always threatening the security of cyberspace.

2.1   Definition of APT Attacks

Advanced Persistent Threat [7] attacks are a form of attack that uses advanced attack methods to carry out long-term persistent cyber-attacks on specific targets. In March 2011, the National Institute of Standards and Technology (NIST) finalized SP 800-39, a framework guide for information security risk management. In this guide, a lot of space is devoted to one of the hottest risks of the moment: APT attacks. In this document, the NIST definition of APT is given [8]: an adversary with a wealth of expertise and resources that can create opportunities to achieve its goals by using multiple attack methods (e.g., cyber, physical, and deception). These objectives typically include establishing and expanding a foothold within the target organization's information technology infrastructure in order to sift (transfer from the internal network to external servers) information that disrupts or hinders critical aspects of the mission, process or organization; or positioning itself to achieve these objectives in the future. Advanced persistent threat attacks repeatedly pursue its objectives over a long period of time; adapt to the efforts of the defenders to resist it; and are determined to maintain the level of interaction necessary to implement its objectives.

2.2 Basic Characteristics of APT Attacks

With the development of emerging technologies, APT attack activities are becoming more and more frequent. Although the attack methods and attack targets are different, through the specific cases in recent years, as shown in Table 1, three obvious characteristics of APT attacks can be analyzed and summarized.

Table 1. Summary of Classic APT Attack Cases

Time	Organization	Target
2009	APT-C-39	China
2012	Ocean Lotus	South-East Asian, China
2012	APT33 (Suspected)	Middle-East,Europe
2014	APT38	Global,SWIFT
2016	APT28 (Suspected)	Ukraine
2017	Hades	Korea
2018	APT28	North America, Europe
2018	Blue Mushroom	China
2018	BITTER	China, Pakistan
2018	Dark Hotel	China

First, APT attacks are a kind of advanced means of attacks. Attackers often have all-round support. They always use social engineering, zero-day vulnerabilities, covert communication and machine learning to achieve their goals. But it does not mean that one attack is a single attack, it often on the behalf of a combination of multiple methods.

Second, APT attacks usually have long duration. The attacker seeks long-term access control to the target, which is highly concealed and will not be easily exposed until the goal is achieved. The time can be as long as several years. For example, the APT-C-39 organization disclosed by 360 Security Brain conducted a 11-year-long cyberattack infiltration in key areas.

Third, APT attacks are often High level of threat. APT attacks mainly target high-value government departments, infrastructure, and large enterprises. Once these targets are captured, the losses are often in the hundreds of millions.

2.3 Trends in APT Attacks

With the accumulation of massive data, the development of computing power, and the continuous innovation and evolution of machine learning methods and systems, artificial intelligence has entered a period of rapid development, such as image recognition, speech recognition, natural language translation and other artificial intelligence technologies are widely deployed and widely used. It is predicted that by 2025, 100 billion people will be connected globally, covering 77% of the population; 85% of enterprise applications will be deployed to the cloud; and smart home robots will enter 12% of homes, creating a $100 billion market.

APT attacks are committed to the long-term lurking of high-value targets. With the help of AI technology, attackers can create intelligent attack methods. After the neural network is trained with data, it can construct a more reliable social engineering attack; using Hivenets and Swarmbots, large-scale intelligent network attacks can be launched; by using the "raise noise floor" technology attackers can generate a large number of false positive training models and lose their effectiveness, resulting in loss of control of threat intelligence; with the advantage of Generative Adversarial Networks (GAN), malware can circumvent the detection of antivirus software. Although AI technology is also used in network security defense technology, the difficulty of finding and defending against APT attacks will become more difficult.

3 Detection Methods of APT Attacks

There is heterogeneity in APT attacks, and different scholars have proposed different detection and defense approaches for different scenarios. Although the forms are kaleidoscopic, they all follow certain laws, especially the rapid development of game theory [9] and machine learning that provides more innovative and convenient methods.

3.1 Social Engineering Based Detection Methods

The main key step in an APT attack is to gain access. Before an intrusion begins, attackers often use open source intelligence and social engineering to conduct a lengthy information gathering exercise. This stage generally stays at the initial stage of the APT, so detection alerts are conducted at this stage with minimal harm. In response to this feature, the main method often used is network event association analysis. Network event correlation analysis is mainly through the network crawler to collect the content information on the network, mine the data embodied in the network user behavior patterns, understand its social attributes, and then provide guidance and basis for attack detection. For hybrid and low-level attacks, it proposed a detection scheme in [10], which correlates OS events with network events using low-level listening and based on semantic relationships defined between entities in the system ontology, the main framework is shown in Fig. 1.

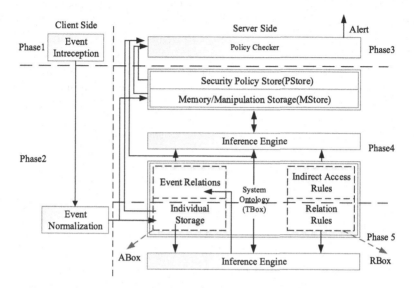

Fig. 1. Basic framework structure for hybrid and early attack detection

In this method, malicious events are deduced and detected based on event relationships and defined security policies, especially implicit violations of security policies. And this method can track the flow of information between existing subjects to reconstruct distributed attack vectors. Social engineering-based detection methods rely heavily on social information and open source intelligence to detect early attacks to some extent. As attackers are able to use such information to deceive, diversify and falsify their methods, the chances of an attack increase significantly.

3.2   Anomalous Flow Based Detection Methods

Abnormality detection comes in contrast to normal behavior and focuses on finding abnormalities. The core idea of network traffic anomaly detection is to identify anomalous behavior through network traffic analysis modeling. The traffic anomalies are often present in APT attacks. In [11], it reduces the workload of expert analysis by analyzing the weak signals of traffic transmission anomalies during data theft and outputting the ranking of suspiciousness of internal hosts. Anomalies are detected by machine learning method in [12], which utilizes time transformation by comparing normal load and traffic containing malicious load for APT malicious code incoming process. In [13], it classifies APT-based anomalous traffic patterns by processing feature vectors obtained from TCP/IP session information and propose a new algorithm based on correlated fractal dimensions. By transforming the event list into an information stream, a theory of real-time detection of APT attacks based on stealth Markov is proposed in [14]. In [15], it proposed a new method for detecting APT attacks using OODA loop and Black Swan theory, considering the current detection problem and how to improve the detection rate of early unknown attacks. Based on this theoretical approach a novel deep learning stack [16] is proposed for detecting APT attacks. In this approach, APT is considered a continuous multi-vector, multi-phase attack. In order to capture these attacks, the entire network stream, especially the raw data, must be used as input to the detection process, and certain types of anomalies and behaviors can be captured by combining different types of customized deep learning methods, as shown in Fig. 2.

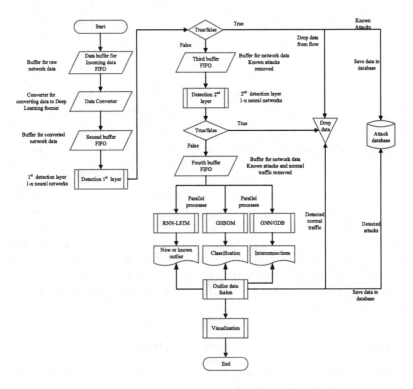

Fig. 2. Data flow in detection processing

However, APT attackers often use covert methods to disguise their own network traffic or hide in legitimate normal network data streams, which cannot solve the detection of encrypted channels well. At the same time, the massive nature of data sources limits the use of traffic anomaly detection.

3.3   Machine Learning Based Detection Methods

The detection of APT attacks has always faced a huge amount of data, and machine learning plays a big role in APT attack detection. Machine learning-based detection methods mainly use the computational power of machine learning to categorically store threats and behavioral patterns to achieve early warning of unknown threats, without human intervention in the process. Traditional APT attack detection methods mainly target a single attack mode, the advantage is obvious in dealing with attacks with a short time span, but some attacks have a long time span, traditional attacks cannot well reflect the problem of the timing of APT attacks, in the case of attack data samples are small, the attack duration is long, the accuracy becomes very low. In response to this problem, an APT attack detection method is creatively proposed in [17], combining Generative Adversarial Networks (GAN) and Long Short-Term Memory (LSTM), as shown in Fig. 3.

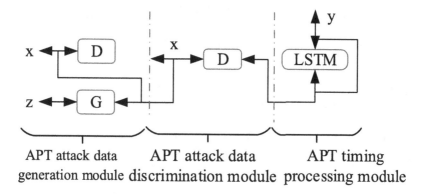

Fig. 3. Basic architecture of the GAN-LSTM model

By generating simulated attack data and optimizing the discriminant model, the accuracy of the original discriminant model was improved by 2.84% points. For early detection and early warning of threats, it proposed a new MLAPT system in [18], as shown in Fig. 4.

Due to the dynamic nature of the APT attack process, security products deployed on traditional defense-based enterprise networks are often unable to detect APT infections, resulting in a significant waste of resources, and the sensitive issue of how to identify or narrow the scope of infected hosts. To overcome the limitations of attack network dynamics faced by current APT research, an innovative APT attack detection model based on semi-supervised learning methods and complex network features is proposed in [19], as shown in Fig. 5.

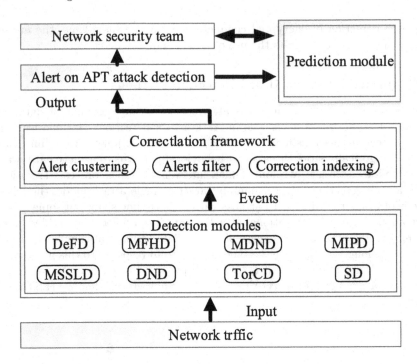

Fig. 4. MLAPT system architecture

Experiments show that the model can effectively detect suspicious hosts at different stages of the APT attack process. Machine learning-based detection methods often use a combination of algorithms to process large amounts of data and find traces of APT attacks, but such methods have high hardware requirements, so how to handle the overhead in computing engineering is of concern. At the same time, the lack of adequate marker samples has limited its development.

4   Defense Strategies Against APT Attacks

APT attack and defense is a long and continuous process of confrontation, and many scholars are dedicated to the study of defense strategies for APT attack, and game theory provides a good reference in APT defense. In APT attack detection, the attacking and defending sides are analogized to the game sides, and the knowledge of game theory is fully used to find the optimal solution. This section focuses on the defense strategy for APT attacks based on game theory.

4.1   APT Attack Defense Strategy Based on Limited Resources

In an APT attack, the attacker relies on his resources to create an asymmetry in relation to the attacker. In the case of those attacked, the knowledge and

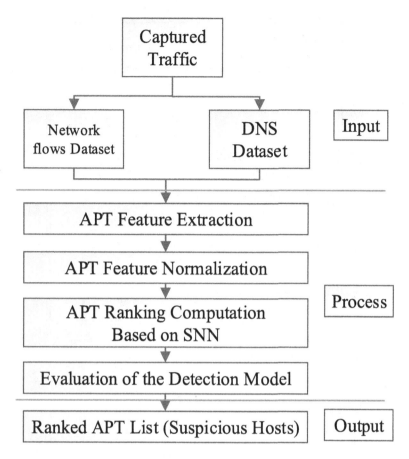

Fig. 5. APT detection architecture based on semi-supervised learning methods and complex network features

means available to them are limited. Resource-based APT attack defense strategy mainly considers the utilization of resources during APT attack and seeks the best strategy for defense. In [20], it proposes a dynamic planning-based APT detection algorithm based on the study of a game theory model to protect multi-node systems from covert attacks, which provides a solution for APT attacks in limited resource situations. Considering the repair resources, a potential system for computing the APT repair game is derived in [21], by establishing an evolutionary model for organizations with time-varying communication relationships and suggest respective repair strategies for organizations. It divides the APT attacks into three phases in [22], and it proposes a general framework using matrix and sequential games, as shown in Fig. 6.

The overall best defense strategy was obtained based on the best defense derived at each stage. Honeypot is an active defense technique [23] through which certain hosts, network services or information can be laid out as decoys

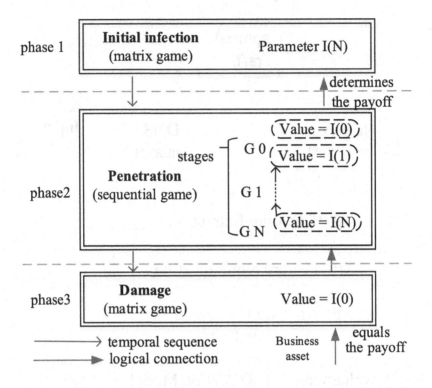

Fig. 6. Cross-system multi-stage game model

so that attack behavior can be detected and analyzed [24]. Unlike other security tools, most honeypots can only generate logs due to their low level of automation. The honeypot game theory model of low-interaction mode and high-interaction mode is adopted in [25] to investigate offensive and defensive interactions and optimize defensive strategies against APT, considering that manual analysis and honeypot distribution costs are limited resources.

4.2 APT Attack Defense Strategy Based on Information Flow Tracking

The DIFT defenses contaminate and track suspicious information flows throughout the network in order to identify possible attacks at the cost of additional memory overhead for tracking non-adversarial information flows [26]. An analytical model is proposed in [27], which includes a multi-stage game and derives an efficient algorithm for computing attack and defense strategies. In [28], a dynamic information flow tracking game is proposed, which is based on information flow diagrams considering the game has an asymmetric information structure. The game model provides efficient detection of APT attacks through a multi-stage dynamic game, which in turn provides the best defense strategy for defenders.

The underlying design of DIFT enables better tracking of information flows, and tracking latency and memory overhead affect the development of DIFT tools.

4.3   Defense Strategy for Cloud-Based APT Attacks

At this stage, the development of the cloud platform is hot, and the security of the cloud platform has always been a concern, and the probability of APT attacks is also rising. The core of the defense strategy for APT attacks based on cloud platform is to consider the effectiveness of the defense against APT attacks on the "cloud". In [29], it studies the framing effect of the main attacker in a pure strategy game and show how the value distortion of the attacker under an uncertain scan interval affects the APT defense performance, and then apply it to a mobile cloud computing system to study the detection performance of the main APT attacker in a dynamic game by studying the cumulative foreground theory-based PHC hot-start APT detection scheme. In response to the problem of detecting unknown threats hidden in APT attacks, a technical framework is proposed in [30], which is based on "cloud, transport layer, endpoint and human response" collaboration theory based on real-world experience, as shown in Fig. 7.

For cloud storage systems, a CPU allocation scheme based on "hot-start" strategy crawl is proposed [31], which uses experience in similar scenarios to initialize quality values for faster learning, so that defenders can get the best APT defense performance without having to play in a dynamic game. It formulates two APT games with discrete strategies based on the study of the dynamic stability of cloud storage systems, and analyze APT attack and defense strategies for cloud storage using evolutionary game theory [32].

5   Relations with MDATA Model

APT attacks are often complex attacks. Studying on APT attacks often needs to associate knowledge in different fields, but it is difficult to associate and analyze knowledge in different fields and different dimensions. The MDATA model provides a good solution to detecting such APT attacks, since it can be describe the characteristics of APT attacks very well, especially the temporal and spatial attributes. In the process of APT attacks, since the latency time is generally long, it is easy to ignore the relevance of attack events in previous representation models. Combining spatio-temporal representation in the MDATA model, we can enhance the relevance of events and associate incidents that seem to occur accidentally. The stored dynamic knowledge in the MDATA model could help identify these events that are highly related, even though the duration of the events is long. Mining out the relevance of the attack event, the complicated cyber attacks including the APT attacks can be described in more detail. Not only that, the real-time detection of APT attacks is an important issue. Realizing the MDATA model in a distributed way could reduce the detection time, which provides real-time detection of such complicated cyber attacks.

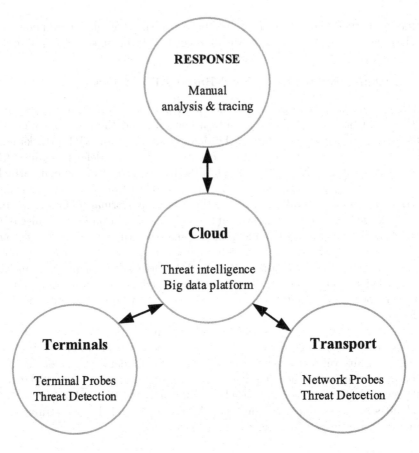

Fig. 7. Cross-system multi-stage game model

6   Chapter Summary

In terms of APT detection and defense methods, many existing research uses different approaches from different perspectives, from technical and mathematical models to model their combined use. Considering the diversity, stealth and latent nature of APT attacks, traditional protection methods, traditional network detection and traditional monitoring and detection mechanisms cannot effectively identify intrusive APT attacks. This chapter looks at both detection and defense strategies against such complicated cyber attacks. The attack detection approaches focus on more mainstream detection methods and the practice of using machine learning for detection. Defensive strategies are about how to use game theory to find the best defensive strategy in resource-limited, DIFI and cloud platforms. Machine learning and game theory present many opportunities for the detection and defense of APT attacks, but there are also some unprecedented challenges to solve the problems of computational overhead, small samples, and time spans. In the future, how to apply the MDATA model specifically to APT attack detection is still an important research field.

References

1. Chen, R.-D., Zhang, X.-S., Niu, W.-N., Lan, H.-Y.: A research on architecture of apt attack detection and countering technology. J. Univ. Electron. Sci. Technol. China **48**, 870–879 (2019)
2. Langner, R.: StuxNet: dissecting a cyberwarfare weapon. IEEE Secur. Priv. **9**(3), 49–51 (2011)
3. Tankard, C.: Advanced persistent threats and how to monitor and deter them. Netw. Secur. **2011**(8), 16–19 (2011)
4. Auty, M.: Anatomy of an advanced persistent threat. Netw. Secur. **2015**(4), 13–16 (2015)
5. Jia, Y., Qi, Y., Shang, H., Jiang, R., Li, A.: A practical approach to constructing a knowledge graph for cybersecurity. Engineering **4**(1), 1–164 (2018)
6. Zhao, X., Jia, Y., Li, A., Jiang, R., Song, Y.: Multi-source knowledge fusion: a survey. World Wide Web **23**(4), 2567–2592 (2020). https://doi.org/10.1007/s11280-020-00811-0
7. Lee, C.Y., Lee, T.J., Park, H.R.: The characteristics of APT attacks and strategies of countermeasure. In: International Conference on Information Engineering (2014)
8. Radack, S.: Managing information security risk: organization, mission and information system view. Technical report, National Institute of Standards and Technology (2011)
9. Xiao, L., Xu, D., Mandayam, N.B., Poor, H.V.: Attacker-centric view of a detection game against advanced persistent threats. IEEE Trans. Mob. Comput. **17**(11), 2512–2523 (2018)
10. Lajevardi, A.M., Amini, M.: A semantic-based correlation approach for detecting hybrid and low-level APTs. Future Gener. Comput. Syst. **96**, 64–88 (2019)
11. Marchetti, M., Pierazzi, F., Colajanni, M., Guido, A.: Analysis of high volumes of network traffic for advanced persistent threat detection. Comput. Netw. **109**, 127–141 (2016)
12. Lu, J., Zhang, X., Junfeng, W., Lingyun, Y.: APT traffic detection based on time transform. In: International Conference on Intelligent Transportation (2017)
13. Siddiqui, S., Khan, M.S., Ferens, K., Kinsner, W.: Detecting advanced persistent threats using fractal dimension based machine learning classification. In: Verma, R.M. Rusinowitch, M. (eds.) Proceedings of the 2016 ACM on International Workshop on Security And Privacy Analytics, IWSPA@CODASPY 2016, New Orleans, LA, USA, 11 March 2016, pp. 64–69. ACM (2016)
14. Brogi, G.: Real-time detection of advanced persistent threats using information flow tracking and hidden Markov models. (Détection temps réel de Menaces Persistantes Avancées par Suivi de Flux d'Information et Modèles de Markov Cachés). Ph.D. thesis, Conservatoire national des arts et métiers, Paris, France (2018)
15. Bodström, T., Hämäläinen, T.: A novel method for detecting APT attacks by using OODA loop and black swan theory. In: Chen, X., Sen, A., Li, W.W., Thai, M.T. (eds.) CSoNet 2018. LNCS, vol. 11280, pp. 498–509. Springer, Cham (2018). https://doi.org/10.1007/978-3-030-04648-4_42
16. Bodstrm, T., Hmlinen, T.: A novel deep learning stack for apt detection. Appl. Sci. **9**(6), 1055 (2019)
17. Liu, H., Wu, T., Shen, J., Shi, C.: Advanced persistent threat detection based on generative adversarial networks and long short-term memory. Comput. Sci. **47**(1), 281–286 (2020)

18. Ghafir, I., et al.: Detection of advanced persistent threat using machine-learning correlation analysis. Future Gener. Comput. Syst. **89**, 349–359 (2018)
19. Zimba, A., Chen, H., Wang, Z.: Bayesian network based weighted APT attack paths modeling in cloud computing. Future Gener. Comput. Syst. **96**, 525–537 (2019)
20. Zhang, M., Zheng, Z., Shroff, N.B.: A game theoretic model for defending against stealthy attacks with limited resources. In: Khouzani, M.H.R., Panaousis, E., Theodorakopoulos, G. (eds.) GameSec 2015. LNCS, vol. 9406, pp. 93–112. Springer, Cham (2015). https://doi.org/10.1007/978-3-319-25594-1_6
21. Yang, L., Li, P., Zhang, Y., Yang, X., Xiang, Y., Zhou, W.: Effective repair strategy against advanced persistent threat: a differential game approach. IEEE Trans. Inf. Forensics Secur. **14**(7), 1713–1728 (2019)
22. Zhu, Q., Rass, S.: On multi-phase and multi-stage game-theoretic modeling of advanced persistent threats. IEEE Access **6**, 13958–13971 (2018)
23. Wang, K., Du, M., Yang, D., Zhu, C., Shen, J., Zhang, Y.: Game-theory-based active defense for intrusion detection in cyber-physical embedded systems. ACM Trans. Embed. Comput. Syst. **16**(1), 18:1–18:21 (2016)
24. Aijuan, C., Baoxu, L., Rongsheng, X.U.: Summary of the honeynet and entrapment defense technology. Comput. Eng. **9**, 1–3 (2004)
25. Tian, W., XiaoPeng, J., Liu, W., Zhai, J., Huang, S.: Honeypot game-theoretical model for defending against apt attacks with limited resources in cyber-physical systems. ETRI J. **41**(1), 585–598 (2019)
26. Zhen, F.: Design of security monitor module at runtime based on dynamic information flow tracking. Comput. Appl. Softw. (2012)
27. Sahabandu, D., Xiao, B., Clark, A., Lee, S., Lee, W., Poovendran, R.: DIFT games: dynamic information flow tracking games for advanced persistent threats. In: 57th IEEE Conference on Decision and Control, CDC 2018, Miami, FL, USA, 17–19 December 2018, pp. 1136–1143. IEEE (2018)
28. Moothedath, S., et al.: A game theoretic approach for dynamic information flow tracking to detect multi-stage advanced persistent threats. CoRR, vol. abs/1811.05622 (2018)
29. Xu, D., Xiao, L., Mandayam, N.B., Poor, H.V.: Cumulative prospect theoretic study of a cloud storage defense game against advanced persistent threats. In: 2017 IEEE Conference on Computer Communications Workshops, INFOCOM Workshops, Atlanta, GA, USA, 1–4 May 2017, pp. 541–546. IEEE (2017)
30. Li, Y., Zhang, T., Li, X., Li, T.: A model of APT attack defense based on cyber threat detection. In: Yun, X., et al. (eds.) CNCERT 2018. CCIS, vol. 970, pp. 122–135. Springer, Singapore (2019). https://doi.org/10.1007/978-981-13-6621-5_10
31. Min, M., Xiao, L., Xie, C., Hajimirsadeghi, M., Mandayam, N.B.: Defense against advanced persistent threats in dynamic cloud storage: a colonel blotto game approach. IEEE Internet Things J. **5**(6), 4250–4261 (2018)
32. Abass, A.A.A., Xiao, L., Mandayam, N.B., Gajic, Z.: Evolutionary game theoretic analysis of advanced persistent threats against cloud storage. IEEE Access **5**, 8482–8491 (2017)

A Distributed Framework for APT Attack Analysis

Yulu Qi[1], Rong Jiang[1(✉)], Aiping Li[1], Zhaoquan Gu[2], and Yan Jia[3]

[1] National University of Defense Technology, Changsha, China
qiyulu1103@163.com, {jiangrong,liaiping}@nudt.edu.cn
[2] Guangzhou University, Guangzhou, China
zqgu@gzhu.edu.cn
[3] Harbin Institute of Technology, Shenzhen, China
jiayanjy@vip.sina.com

Abstract. Information security is an important part of Internet security. As more and more industries rely on the Internet, it has become urgent to protect information security of these industries, spawned local area networks (LANs), intranets and so on. With the development of information sensor technology, the Internet of Things (IoT) that interconnects physical devices has emerged. As a unity of computing process and physical process, the Cyber-physical systems (CPS) is the next generation intelligent system which integrates computing, communication and controlling capabilities. CPS covers a wide range of applications and critical infrastructures, including intelligent transportation systems, telemedicine, smart grids, aerospace, and many other fields. The APT attacks are typically conducted directly against these critical infrastructures around the world, which would incur severe consequences. It is meaningful to protect these information by detecting the APT attacks timely and accurately, and effective defensive measures could be adopted. Although the APT attacks seem destructive, the attack process are complex and changeable. In essence, the attack process usually follows certain rules. In this chapter, we introduce a distributed framework for detecting the APT attacks. Cyber security knowledge graph stores existing knowledge and the attack rules, which plays an important role in analyzing the attacks. We first analyze potential attack events by the proposed distributed framework on Spark, then we mine the attack chains from massive data with the spatial and temporal characteristics. These steps could help identify complicated attacks. We also conduct extensive experiments, the results show that the analysis accuracy depends on the completeness of the cyber security knowledge graph and the precision of the detection results from security equipments. With the rational expectation about more exposure of attacks and faster upgrade of security equipments, it is sufficient and necessary to improve the cyber security knowledge graph constantly for better performance.

Keywords: MDATA · APT attack · Cyberspace security · Distributed framework

© Springer Nature Switzerland AG 2021
Y. Jia et al. (Eds.): MDATA: A New Knowledge Representation Model, LNCS 12647, pp. 199–219, 2021.
https://doi.org/10.1007/978-3-030-71590-8_12

1   Introduction

There are a growing number of Advanced Persistent Threat (APT) attacks on critical infrastructure. For example, the notably Ukrainian blackout happened on December 23, 2015 1.4 million residents in parts of the Ukrainian capital Kiev and western Ukraine suddenly found themselves without power in their homes. The power outage was not due to a shortage of electricity, but an attack by hackers. On the same day, hackers attacked about 60 substations. The hackers used deception to get power company employees to download a malware called "Black Energy". The malware disconnected the power company's main computer from the substation, and then planted a virus in the system that disabled the entire computer. At the same time, the hackers also jammed the power company's phone communications, preventing residents affected by the outage from contacting the power company.

In addition to the Ukrainian blackout, there are some well-known APT attacks, such as famous the Google Aurora attack and the Ocean Lotus attack, etc. After extensive analysis and research, we found that threat intelligence can be used to describe the attack process of the complicated APT attacks. Generally, the attack information can be described by the threat intelligence as the following components:

1) The attack source, that is, the attacker's identity IP, DNS, and URL, belonging to a group or organization, geographic location, etc.;
2) The attack mode, arsenal used, attack strategy, etc.;
3) The attack object, type of operating system attacked, application software, cyber service, etc.;
4) The vulnerability information, exploited operating system vulnerabilities, software vulnerabilities, or configuration vulnerabilities.

Actually, there also exist some unknown attacks the might not be described accurately. When the unknown attacks happen, the threat intelligence can also quickly form the corresponding security knowledge by analyzing the components of the attacks.

APT attacks are usually multi-step attacks, and each step can be described separately or comprehensively by the above description models, but there are some special relationships among the attack steps. For example, the temporal relationship, spatial relationship, quantitative relationship, dependency relationship, and so on. It can be assumed that a complete attack includes four steps that occur in chronological order: target reconnaissance, host infiltration, privilege, and stealing information. Each step includes several events, and the relationship between the steps is the temporal relationship; if an attack process requires a springboard, for example, the attacker is IP_A, the springboard is IP_B, and IP_A controls IP_C and IP_D by IP_B and finally attacks IP_D. The relationship between the attack steps is the spatial relationship; one example of quantitative relationship is brute force attack; if an attack is triggered by multiple events according to certain rules, the relationship between them is the dependency relationship.

The main contribution of this chapter is to propose a framework to analysis APT attack. The framework consists of four modules: the cyber security knowledge graph module, data processing module, self-define rules module, association analysis and attack judgment module.

Firstly, an automatic reasoning program is added to the cyber security knowledge graph module. The automatic reasoning program uses a rule-based reasoning method to mine hidden relationships between entities, thereby expanding the cyber security knowledge graph. Secondly, the data processing module mainly fuses multi-source heterogeneous data, extracts threat information, and processes it into a unified format. Then, in the self-define rules module, we can set the rules for generating threat elements by alarms in the traffic data and the rules among threat elements related to attacks. Finally, in the association analysis and attack judgment module, the execution program iteratively matches the collected data with the cyber security knowledge graph, using custom rules as constraints, associates the relevant steps of the APT attack from a large number of threat elements, and outputs the analysis results at certain time intervals.

The knowledge graph was proposed by Google in 2012 and successfully applied to search engines afterwards [1]. The advantage of applying the knowledge graph in the field of intelligent searching is to exchange space for time. In recent years, the knowledge graph has also been used to analyze the relationships between entities to discover and analyze problems in certain areas, such as finance and intelligence. In the field of network security, computer networks naturally have the characteristics of knowledge graphs. A computer network is composed of multiple computing nodes, and there are network connection relationships among these computing nodes, so a computer network can form a knowledge graph.

A knowledge graph constructed based on a computer network is called a cyber security knowledge graph (CSKG), and the CSKG includes two parts: a security knowledge graph (SeKG) and a scene knowledge graph (ScKG). The SeKG includes known information about vulnerabilities, attacks, assets and the relationships among them. The above information can be obtained from various vulnerability and attack analysis websites and can be updated gradually. The ScKG includes network node information and network connectivity information involved in specific attacks. Generally, the SeKG is the core graph and the ScKG is the extended graph. The data source of the CSKG is known as cyber security knowledge, which can be transformed into different types of attack information, such as attack source, attack mode, attack object and vulnerability information. The data source of the scene knowledge graph depends on all the information about the current attack.

In the field of cyber security, the mainstream research direction is the anomaly detection technology based on machine learning. However, the result of exception detection can only tell us whether it is normal or abnormal, without the specific state of the current network or node, which can only be presented by situational awareness. Situational awareness is a way to improve the ability to discover, identify, understand, analyze and respond to security threats from a global perspective based on security big data, and is usually classified into detection, analysis, prediction and defense. This chapter focuses on the analysis part, while prediction and defense are not in the scope of discussion here. The premise of the attack analysis in this chapter is the understanding of the general steps of testing cyber-attacks, and the experience of security analysis at the same time, with the help of the security device detection results and the characteristics of attacks. It involves a lot of human work, and since the experience is different among different people, the time and accuracy of the analysis will also be different. Therefore, the prior knowledge of security analysts can be stored in a computer according to certain rules, and the cyber-attacks then can be analyzed automatically with the help of computer algorithms and programs.

Based on the above ideas, this chapter proposes a distributed framework for analyzing cyber-attack and defense. First, we build a CSKG, including SeKG and ScKG, set up a threat element association base and a composite attack rule base. Second, we fuse the multi-source heterogeneous input data and extract threat elements. The extracted threat elements are sequentially matched with the threat element knowledge base. If the match is successful, we carry out the association statistics of the threat elements and then match with the CSKG. If the match is unsuccessful, the threat elements are directly matched with the CSKG. Furthermore, we judge if the threat elements could match with the CSKG successfully, the framework returns single-step attacks if they are matched. Otherwise, we add the threat elements to the CSKG. Due to the occurrence of false positives, the ScKG is used to determine whether the single-attack is effective, and we delete the invalid single-attack event. Finally, after association analysis (composite attack rule base and space-time attribute constraints) of these effective single-step attacks, the single-step attacks related to the same composite attack are respectively associated and analyzed in the form of attack chains.

The rest of the chapter is organized as follows. The next section introduces the background of ATP attack analysis. In Sect. 3, we present the distributed framework and the experimental results are analyzed in Sect. 4. Finally, we summarize the chapter in Sect. 5.

2   Background

The concept of ontology [2] was first applied in the field of philosophy. The German scholar Studer gave the definition of ontology in 1998: ontology is a formal specification of shared conceptual models [3]. Ontology is a conceptual model that abstracts objective facts from the objective world. There are many construction methods of ontology, such as the IDEF-5 (IntegratedComputerAidedManufacturing DEFinition-5) method, TOVE (TOronto Virtual Enterprise) modeling method, Methontology method, Skeletal Methodology method, seven-step method and construction of a domain ontology based on a thesaurus. Most of the current ontology construction is manual, and ontologies cannot be automatically constructed yet. A classification method is proposed in [4] to organize ontologies and express the ontology model by using concepts, relationships, functions, axioms and examples. Guarino et al. It subdivided an ontology into top-level, domain, task, method and application ontologies according to the degree of domain dependency [5]. An attack ontology model is established in [6] according to the classification of attacks, and strictly defined the logic relationship and hierarchical structure of the ontology in the ontology model, thereby achieving effective reuse of attack knowledge. A threat intelligence ontology model is proposed in [6], which could not only realize the extraction of entities and entity relations, but also provide the function of visual display. An ontology construction model is proposed in [7], which used servers, network devices and security devices as nodes, business data flow as the relationship connecting two nodes, and the direction of business data flow as the direction of the relationship. A network security knowledge graph is constructed in [8], which parallelized the association analysis algorithm and realized a distributed association analysis system.

The comprehensive analysis of cyber-attacks makes cyber security event association analysis technology a high concern. In recent years, many authors have summarized the cyber security event association analysis methods. It summarized the different technical methods of security event association analysis based on attribute characteristics, logic reasoning, probability statistics and machine learning [9]. Attribute-based security event association analysis technology commonly uses methods including the finite state machine and rule-based association analysis methods. The association analysis model is proposed based on the state machine in [10]; while the RETE algorithm is proposed in [11], which has been the most effective algorithm based on forward chain reasoning. The principle of the Rule Engine is proposed in [12], which improved the RETE algorithm. The common methods of security event association analysis based on logical reasoning include case inference and model inference. An association technology is proposed in [13] based on case inference, and an association technology based on model inference is presented in [14]. The common methods of security event association technology based on probability and statistics include dependency graph-based association analysis technology, the Bayesian network model and the Markov model. A dependency graph-based association analysis technology is introduced in [15]. The common methods of security event association analysis based on machine learning include the neural network (ANN), the support vector machine (SVM), and so on. In addition, open source association analysis tools mainly include Swatch [16], SEC [17], OSSEC [18], OSSIM [19], Drools [20], Esper [21], and so on. In terms of attack scenario restoration, an alert correlation method based on the causality of attacks is proposed in [22], and a real-time alert correlation analysis method is also proposed in [23], which is based on an attack plan graph, which improved the attack scenario.

The products for APT attack detection tend to be mature, and have been strongly supported by the governments. The representative products are: Fire-Eye malicious code defense system, which mainly uses intelligent sandbox technology and static analysis technology to detect 0day vulnerabilities, unknown attacks and Trojan horse programs; Fortinet's detection products, which mainly use sandbox technology and network traffic analysis technology to detect 0 day vulnerabilities, Rootkit, Trojan Horse program, DDOS and other attacks; Bit9 Trusted Security Platform, which mainly uses software trusted technology, real-time detection audit technology and security cloud technology, which can detect and resist various advanced threats and malicious code; Trend Micro Deep Discovery, which mainly uses intrusion detection technology, malicious code detection sandbox technology and association rule technology to detect 0day vulnerabilities, bots, worms and other attacks; RSA NetWitness, which has three components: Spectrum, Panorama and Live, mainly for detection and defense of APT attacks; Kelai Network Full Flow Security Analysis System, which mainly uses large data security analysis technology and full flow storage analysis technology to detect unknown attacks such as 0day vulnerabilities and advanced Trojan.

3   Attack Analysis Framework

At present, the mainstream research of cyber-attacks is carried out in the form of simulations. Thus, we introduce the proposed cyber-attack and defense test platform. It integrates all kinds of common equipments in the field of cyber security attack and defense, and uses professional attack and defense methods to provide simulation scenarios. The cyber-attack and defense test platform provides attack and defense drills, and a variety of collection and detection systems. The collection systems can implement terminal collection, traffic collection, honeypot collection, log collection, IDS alert collection, vulnerability scanning, virus scanning, and so on. The detection systems mainly perform preliminary detection on the collected data. The attack analysis framework for the cyber-attack and defense test platform proposed in this chapter is based on the above modules. The preliminary detection result is the input of the framework; with the help of the CSKG, the association analysis method is applied to analyze the current cyber status. The workflow schematic diagram of the framework is shown in Fig. 1.

3.1   Cyber Security Knowledge Graph Construction

The steps to construct the cyber security knowledge graph are divided into ontology construction, ontology data model construction, self-defined reasoning rules determination and entity extraction. We introduce these steps in detail.

Cyber Security Knowledge Graph Construction

1. Security Knowledge Ontology Model

We uses the five-tuple model proposed in [24] to construct a security knowledge graph. The five-tuple model includes entities, attributes of entities, relationships

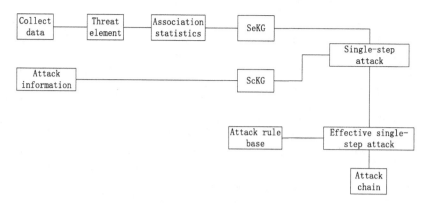

Fig. 1. The workflow schematic diagram of the framework

between entities, and reasoning rules. We use SeKG (security knowledge graph) to represent the security knowledge graph, SO (security ontology) to represent the security knowledge ontology, SI (security instance) to represent the security instance, SOP (security object properties) to represent the relationships between the security ontologies, SDP (security data properties) to represent the properties of the security instance and SRR (security reasoning rule) to represent the reasoning rules of security knowledge. The formal expression is as follows:

$$SKG = <SO, SI, SOP, SDP, SRR>; \qquad (1)$$

- $SO = SO_i|i = 1, ..., n$. Security knowledge ontology is a concept summarized and abstracted from security knowledge, and usually divided into multi-level ontologies. For example, asset is a first-level ontology, and can be divided into second-level ontologies: software and hardware. The software is divided into a three-level ontology, including operating system, application software, etc. The hardware is divided into a three-level ontology, including PC, server, switch, etc. The operating system is divided into a four-level ontology, including the Windows operating system and the Linux operating system. The Linux operating system is divided into a five-level ontology, including Ubuntu, SUSE, Debian, Redhat and CentOS operating systems. Again, for instance, vulnerability is a first-level ontology, and can be divided into a second-level ontology, including ddos vulnerability, privilege escalation vulnerability, buffer overflow vulnerability, etc. The same applies to the ontology division of attacks, Trojans, worms, snort alerts and security events.
- $SI = SI_i|i = 1, ..., m$. The security instance is the specific security knowledge corresponding to the last level of an ontology, such as, examples of asset software operating system are: Windows 7, Windows 10, and so on; examples of vulnerability-buffer overflow vulnerability are: CVE-2019-1010309, CVE-2019-1010306, CVE-2019-1010298, CVE-2019-1010238, CVE-2019-1010208, and so on.

- $SDP = <SI_i, Pro_{ij}, value_j>$. The data attributes of the security instance, such as the version number of the operating system, the discovery time, update time, hazard level of the vulnerability, and so on.

- $SOP = <SO_i, Rcc, SO_j> \mid <SO_i, Rc_i, SI_i> \mid <SI_i, Rcc, SI_j>$. The object property of the security instance is the relationship between the security instances. For example, the relationship between multi-level ontologies is sub-ClassOf, such as (asset, subClassOf, hardware), (asset, subClassOf, software); the relationship between different ontologies includes hasExit and exploit, such as (Windows operating system, hasExit, buffer overflow vulnerability), (buffer overflow attack, exploit, buffer overflow vulnerability). After adding instances to the ontology, the relationship between ontology and instance is instanceOf, such as (CVE-2019-1010298, instanceOf, buffer overflow vulnerability), and so on.

- $SRR = \{SRR|SRR = <SI_i, newR_{ij}, SI_j> \mid <SO_i, newRij, SI_j> \mid < SI_i, Proij, newValue_j>\}$. Based on SKG, reasoning rules can be used to reason out new attributes of the security instance and new relationships between security instances.

2. Ontology-Instance Data Model

The security knowledge used in this chapter mainly comes from six aspects: vulnerability database, virus database, snort alert, preliminary detection results, log information and attack classification. This chapter is mainly concerned with the relationships between vulnerabilities, viruses, snort alerts, preliminary detection results, log information and attacks. We classify the relationships into three types: 1:1, n:1 and 1:n.

In particular, log information can be incorporated into security events. Instances of security event and snort alert are directly stored in the corresponding model based on prior knowledge. For certain instances of vulnerability, Trojan and worm, the entity-relationship needs to be extracted directly, and for other instances, the entity needs to be extracted and then added to the corresponding model. Although Trojans and worms are both viruses, they have specific classifications and different relationships with attacks, so they are respectively taken as ontologies.

- 1:1 data model

Construct attack ontology, security event ontology, vulnerability ontology, Trojan ontology, worm ontology, snort alert ontology and secondary ontology, determine the relationships between secondary ontologies, and then add instances to secondary ontologies respectively. Take vulnerability as an example. If all instances in each category of the vulnerability are associated with the same attack, then construct the ontology model between vulnerability and attack. The schematic diagram ontology relationship is shown in Fig. 2.

- n:1 data model

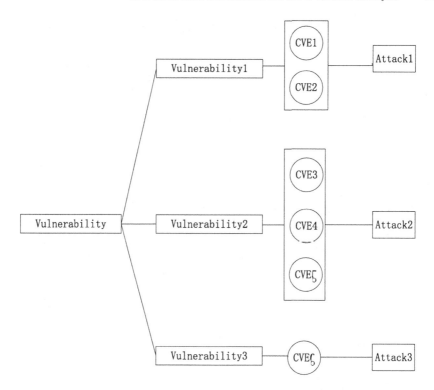

Fig. 2. The schematic diagram ontology relationship 1 vs 1

Construct attack ontology, vulnerability ontology, Trojan ontology, worm ontology and secondary ontology, determine the relationships between secondary ontologies, and then add instances to secondary ontologies respectively. Take vulnerability as an example. If all instances in each category of the vulnerability are associated with the same multiple attacks, then construct the ontology model between vulnerability and attack. The schematic diagram ontology relationship is shown in Fig. 3.

– 1:n data model

Construct attack ontology, security event ontology, vulnerability ontology, Trojan ontology, worm ontology, snort alert ontology and secondary ontology, determine the relationships between secondary ontologies, and then add instances to secondary ontologies respectively. Take vulnerability, Trojan and worm as examples. If all instances of vulnerability, Trojan and worm are associated with the same attack, then construct the ontology model between vulnerability, Trojan, worm and attack. The schematic diagram ontology relationship is shown in Fig. 4.

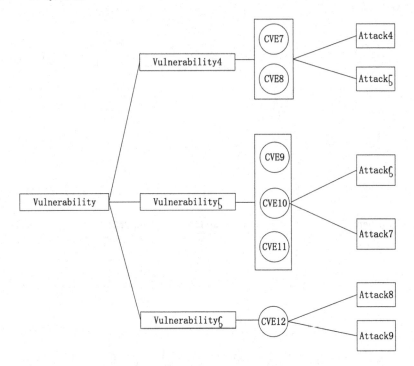

Fig. 3. The schematic diagram ontology relatiomship n vs 1

Self-defined Reasoning Rules

1. Fixed reasoning rules

The entities of machine learning and manual recognition are added to the 1:1 data model, 1:n data model and n:1 data model according to the entity classification and relationship classification, applied with reasoning rules (instance 1, belongs to, ontology1), (instance 2, belongs to, ontology 2), (ontology 1, relationship 1, ontology 2) → (instance 1, relationship 1, instance 2). Instances of vulnerability, Trojan, worm, snort alert and security event are then associated with types of attack, and stored in the cyber security knowledge graph as cyber security knowledge. For convenience, we convert the 1:n and n:1 data models into the 1:1 model for reasoning. Examples of reasoning rules are shown in Table 1.

2. Specific reasoning rules

When new knowledge emerges, it is necessary to associate the new knowledge with the existing knowledge to enrich the cyber security knowledge graph. Applied with reasoning rules (instance 1, relationship 1, instance 2), (instance 2,

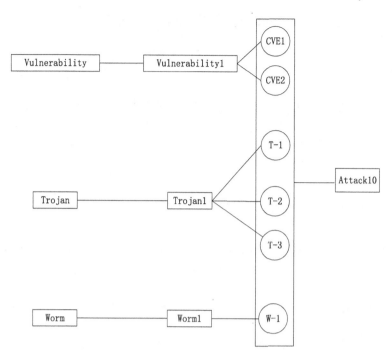

Fig. 4. The schematic diagram ontology relatiomship 1 vs n

belongs to, Ontology 2), (instance 3, belongs to, ontology 3), (ontology 2, relationship 2, ontology 3) → (instance 1, relationship 2, instance 3), then instances of new vulnerabilities, new Trojans or new worms can be associated with types of attack, and stored in the cyber security knowledge graph. Examples of reasoning rules are shown in Table 2.

Scene Knowledge Graph. The scene knowledge graph is composed of the details of multiple simulation attacks of the scene, including node IP, software and hardware, existing vulnerabilities, backdoors, standby status, network status, open services and ports, and so on.

Table 1. Fixed reasoning rules

rule: (?m NamedIndividualof ?n), (?p NamedIndividualof ?q), (?n r1 ?q) → (?m r1?p)
rule: (?m NamedIndividualof ?n), (?p NamedIndividualof ?q), (?n r2 ?q) → (?m r2?p)

Table 2. Specific reasoning rules.

rule1: (?m NamedIndividualof ?n), (?p NamedIndividualof ?q), (?n r2 ?q) → (?m r2?p)
rule2: (?l equal ?m), (?m r2 ?p) → (?l r2 ?p)
rule1: (?m NamedIndividualof ?n), (?p NamedIndividualof ?q), (?n r2 ?q) → (?m r2?p)
rule2: (?l SameCategory ?m), (?m r2 ?p) → (?l r2 ?p)

An ontology model is also needed to construct a scene knowledge graph, and the focus of scene knowledge is data attributes. Construct the node ontology, software ontology, hardware ontology, backdoor ontology, standby state ontology, network state ontology, port ontology, service ontology and vulnerability ontology. Determine the data attributes for the ontologies, and then add instances and data attributes of the instances according to the ontology model.

3.2   Threat Element Association Statistics

After data fusion and threat element extraction, we can extract vulnerabilities, Trojans, worms, snort alerts and security events from input data. Vulnerabilities, Trojans, worms, certain snort alerts and security events can be directly matched with the security knowledge graph, but there are two special cases of certain snort alerts and security events. (i) For the same IP, within a certain time interval, count the same snort alert time. If it exceeds the set threshold, the attack corresponding to the snort alert can be considered to have occurred, and the same is true for security events. (ii) For the same IP, within a certain time interval, multiple different snort alerts are reported in turn. Count the number of alerts, and if it exceeds the set threshold, the attack corresponding to the multiple different snort alerts can be considered to have occurred, and the same is true for security events.

Set Frequency Threshold. If the counted time of an alert is greater than or equal to the set threshold, match the alert information with the knowledge graph and return the attack associated with the alert information. If the counted time of the alert is less than the set threshold, the statistical results are cached and participate in the calculation of the next time window. The same is true for security events. The calculation formula of the alert information is shown below.

$$sum_{ik} = \sum_{t=t_0}^{t_1} \sum_{i=1}^{i} (key_i, alert_k) \tag{2}$$

where key_i stands for different IP and alertk stands for different alert information of the same IP in a (t_0, t_1) time period. The calculation formula of the security event is shown below.

$$sum_{ik} = \sum_{t=t_0}^{t_1} \sum_{i=1}^{i} (key_i, se_k) \qquad (3)$$

where key_i stands for different IP and sek stands for different security events of the same IP in a (t_0, t_1) time period.

Set Number Threshold. If the counted number of alerts is greater than or equal to the set threshold, match the last alert information with the knowledge graph and return the attack associated with the alert information. If the counted number of alerts is less than the set threshold, the statistical results are cached and participate in the calculation of the next time window. The same is true for security events.

The calculation formula of the alert information is shown below.

$$sum_{ik} = count \left(\sum_{t=t_0}^{t_1} \sum_{i=1}^{i} (key_i, [alert_1, alert_2, \cdots alert_k]) \right) \qquad (4)$$

where key_i stands for different IP and alert1, alert2 alertk represents multiple alert messages corresponding to the same IP in a (t_0, t_1) time period.

The calculation formula of the security event is shown below.

$$sum_{ik} = count \left(\sum_{t=t_0}^{t_1} \sum_{i=1}^{i} (key_i, [se_1, se_z, \cdots se_k]) \right) \qquad (5)$$

where key_i stands for different IP and $se_1, se_2 se_k$ represents multiple alert messages corresponding to the same IP in a (t_0, t_1) time period.

3.3   Threat Element Association Statistics

Attack Rule Base. Any action that attempts to breach resource integrity, confidentiality and availability is called an attack. When an attack has an independent and undecomposed purpose, it is a single-step attack. However, a successful attack process often contains multiple single-step attacks, which is called a composite attack.

We know that cyber-attacks can be divided into single-step attacks and composite attacks. Composite attacks can be regarded as a combination of multiple single-step attacks. Only by following certain rules can single-step attacks be composed of composite attacks. For example, if many attacks occurred on the same node, as shown in Fig. 5, how could we determine what attacks are targeted on the node B? This chapter solves this problem by establishing an attack rule base.

The framework models to describe attacks mainly include Kill Chain, the ATT&CK model and the NSA/CSS technical threat framework. These framework models summarize the steps for composite attacks. Based on the above models, this paper summarizes the general rules of composite attacks, some of

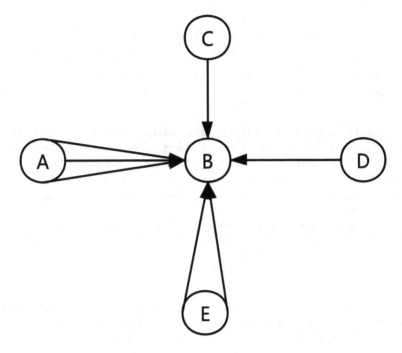

Fig. 5. The example of different attacks on the same node

```
[
    {
        "arID": 1,
            "arNameList": ["scan_attack", "delivery_attack", "execution_code_attack", "gain_information_attack"],
            "attrChain":"scan_attack->delivery_attack->execution_code_attack->gain_information_attack"

    },
    {
        "arID": 2,
            "arNameList": ["phishing_attack", "delivery_attack", "execution_code_attack", "directory_traversal_attack",
    "remote_control_attack"],
            "attrChain":"phishing_attack->delivery_attack->execution_code_attack->directory_traversal_attack->remote_control_attack"

    },

]
```

Fig. 6. The examples of attack rule

which are shown in Fig. 6. An attack rule base can be added or modified as analysis progresses.

Even if multiple single-step attacks against the same node conform to the attack rules, they cannot be judged as composite attacks, as shown in Fig. 7. Attacks on node B exactly conform to attack rule 2, but they actually belong to five different composite attacks. Obviously, composite attacks cannot be accurately analyzed just by setting up the attack rule base. This chapter solves this problem by setting spatiotemporal constraints.

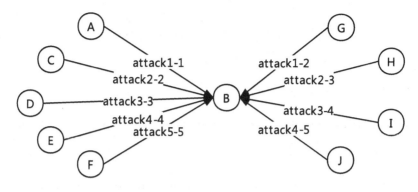

Fig. 7. The examples of special attack

Spatiotemporal Constraints. The duration of each composite attack is different. We cannot know the duration of each composite attack in advance, and it is impossible to set the analysis interval for each composite attack separately. If the duration of the attack is less than the time of analysis, an attack has occurred and caused the damage, but the analysis has not been completed. If the duration of the attack is greater than the time of analysis, the attack has not finished yet, but the analysis has finished, which means we cannot obtain the full attack chain. For these two situations, we set the analysis time interval and time interval offset on Spark, and iteratively output the results of each analysis to ensure the accuracy of the composite attack analysis.

Spark [25] is good at processing stream data. The basic principle is to divide stream data into small pieces of time (a few seconds) and process these small pieces of data in a way similar to batch processing. The attack analysis framework uses the Spark framework to process data in parallel, and uses time windows and time-increasing offsets to iteratively output the analysis results, thereby greatly reducing the false negative and false positive rates of the analysis results, and the analysis response time is close to a real-time response. The process of composite attack analysis is described as follows:

- set the analysis time window and offset on the Spark framework, and respectively set the alert base and security event base that need to be associated statistically;
- in a time window, after data fusion and threat element extraction, the input data is first matched with the alert base and security event base set in the first step. If the matching fails, it can be directly matched with the security knowledge graph. If the match is successful, then it is matched with the security knowledge graph after statistical association;
- the result returned in the previous step is for single-step attacks after using the scene knowledge graph to filter out invalid attacks;
- match effective single-step attacks with attack rule bases, while constraining time and IP propagation;

– after the analysis of the input data within a time window is completed, the analysis results are cached and output as intermediate results. With the offset of the time window, the results of each analysis are iteratively output. When the attack ends, the complete attack chain will be output. Intermediate results and final results are output in the form of an attack chain.

Evaluation Mechanism. The effective attack analysis framework for the cyber-attack and defense test platform proposed in this chapter is based on the cyber security knowledge graph. The core of the analysis is to first match a threat element with the cyber security knowledge graph and return a single-attack result, and then generate possible composite attack chains within the constraints of an attack rule base and spatiotemporal properties. We know that some vulnerabilities, Trojans and worms can correspond to multiple attacks, but in actual simulations, they can only correspond to one attack at a time. Therefore, based on the analysis results of the cyber security knowledge graph, the number of analysis results will be equal to or greater than the number of simulated attacks. In order to verify the effectiveness of this method, we save the simulated attack information in advance, match the analysis results with it, and use the matched results as the basis of the verification method. At present, there is no general evaluation mechanism to verify the effectiveness of this method. There may be four cases that affect the results of attack analysis:

1) Simulated attacks are all successful, and detection results are all correct;
2) Simulated attacks are partially successful, and detection results are all correct;
3) Simulated attacks are all successful, and detection results are partially correct;
4) Simulated attacks are partially successful, and detection results are partially correct.

The results of the theoretical attack analyses in these four cases are shown in Table 3.

In order to quantify the above indicators, this chapter proposes a concept: efficiency of attack analysis. The number of simulated attacks is denoted as F1, the number of single-step attacks obtained by matching with the security knowledge graph is denoted as F2, the number of effective single-step attacks obtained by matching with the scene knowledge graph is denoted as F3, the number of invalid attacks is denoted as F4, the number of attacks obtained by association analysis is denoted as F5, matching of the analyzed attack with the simulated attack and the number of successful matches is recorded as F6 and the efficiency of the attack analysis is recorded as R. The formula is as follows:

$$R = \begin{cases} \frac{F6}{F1}, & if \ \ simulated \ attacks \ are \ all \ effective \\ \frac{F6}{F1-F4}, & if \ \ simulated \ attacks \ are \ partially \ effective \end{cases} \tag{6}$$

Table 3. Attack analysis

	Simulated attacks are all successful	Simulated attacks are partially successful
Detection results are all correct	100%	100%
Detection results are partially correct	<100%	<100%

4   Experimental Results

The simulation of the composite attacks is completed on the cyber-attack and defense test platform by running the attack script. The attack script sets the path of the attack. The cyber-attack and defense test platform provides test node mirrors. In the node mirror, software and hardware can be arbitrarily installed, network state and standby can be set arbitrarily and the open state of the port and service can be set arbitrarily. Deploy the attack script, then generate a virtual machine mirror, start the virtual machine, execute the attack script, run a command to complete the attack simulation, and at the same time, the cyber-attack and defense test platform will provide collection and detection systems, such as vulnerability scanning, virus detection, terminal collection, mail collection, honeypot collection, computing node data collection, file detection, sandbox detection analysis, network detection and honeypot terminal behavior detection.

The experiment is divided into two parts. The first part is to verify the validity of self-defined reasoning during the expanding of the knowledge graph. The second part is to verify the feasibility of the analysis framework and the evaluation mechanism. The first part uses the comparison of analysis results of known and unknown vulnerabilities to verify the validity of the self-defined reasoning. The second part simulates all possibilities in the occurrence of attacks and detections, and uses the analysis results to verify the feasibility of the evaluation mechanism. The test deployment is shown in Fig. 8. In this test, 3 attacks are simulated, the duration of these attacks is 15 min and the analysis time window is set to 5 min.

4.1   Verify the Validity of Self-defined Reasoning Rules

It is known that CVE-2019-1010153 is not stored in the safety knowledge graph, and the relationship between CVE-2019-1010153 and CVE-2013–3525 is known. It is assumed that all simulation attacks are successful and the detection results are all correct. The original knowledge graph and the expanded knowledge graph are used to compare the results, and the results are shown in Table 4 (see the previous sections for detailed analysis).

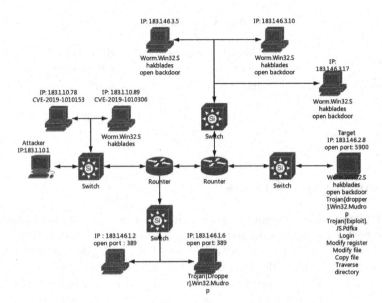

Fig. 8. Test deployment

Table 4. Analysis results of different knowledge graphs.

	F1	F2	F3	F4	F5	F6	R
Original SKG	3	24	24	0	3	2	66.7%
Expanded SKG	3	26	26	0	3	3	100%

4.2 Verify the Feasibility of the Analysis Framework

Divide the test into four cases, each of which uses the extended security knowledge graph. In the first case, the simulated attacks are all successful and the detection results are all correct; in the second case, the simulated attacks are partially successful, the standby state of the node with IP 183.146.1.6 is set to shut down to simulate a failed attack, and the detection results are all correct; in the third case, the simulated attacks are all successful and the detection results are partially correct, and the Trojan information of the node with IP 183.146.2.8 is lost; in the fourth case, the simulated attacks are partially successful, the standby state of the node with IP 183.146.1.6 is set to shut down to simulate a failed attack, the detection results are partially correct, and the Trojan information of the node with IP 183.146.2.8 is lost. The effective results of the attack analysis under different cases are shown in Table 5 (see the previous sections for detailed analysis).

Table 5. The effective results of attack analysis under different cases.

	Simulated attacks are all successful	Simulated attacks are partially successful
Detection results are all correct	1000%	100%
Detection results are partially correct	66.7%	33.4%

The test results show that the richer the security knowledge graph, the higher the efficiency of the attack analysis; the fewer false positives and false negatives in the detection result, the higher the efficiency of the attack analysis. When new knowledge appears and has not been added to the cyber security knowledge graph and attack rule base, even if it is detected, a complete attack chain cannot be analyzed. In the simulation environment, the analysis framework proposed in this chapter is feasible. However, when the detection results are wrong, the complete attack chain cannot be analyzed. Future work will mainly focus on how to comprehensively develop self-defined reasoning rules, and how to complete the attack chain with the help of a scene knowledge graph and an attack rule base.

5   Chapter Summary

The core of this chapter is to apply a cyber security knowledge graph to attack analysis, which is divided into a security knowledge graph and a scene knowledge graph. The security knowledge graph is constructed and expanded semi-automatically, and the scene knowledge graph is constructed manually. Using the cyber security knowledge graph, attack rule base and spatiotemporal property constraints, composite attack chains are mined from multiple single-attacks. At present, the construction of the cyber security knowledge graph and attack rule bases also requires a lot of manual operations, and the flexibility is poor. The goal of future work is to achieve semi-automatic or automated construction. Since the results of the analysis may not generate a complete attack chain, this chapter proposes the effectiveness of attack analysis. The effectiveness of attack analysis is proportional to the accuracy of the detection results. The focus of future work is how to improve the effectiveness of attack analysis. The framework proposed in this chapter is only applicable to the analysis of attacks with prior knowledge that can be stated in a cyber security knowledge graph and an attack rule base, and is not designed for the discovery of unknown attacks.

References

1. Grey, D.F.: Knowledge mapping: a practical overview. SWS J., March 1999
2. Shan, L.: Overview of researches on ontology. J. Comput. Res. Dev. **7**, 1041–1052 (2004)

3. Studer, R., Benjamins, V.R., Fensel, D.: Knowledge engineering: principles and methods. Data Knowl. Eng. **25**(1–2), 161–197 (1998)
4. Pérez, A.G., Benjamins, V.R.: Overview of knowledge sharing and reuse components: ontologies and problem-solving methods. In: Proceedings of the IJCAI-99 workshop on Ontologies and Problem-Solving methods (KRR5), pp. 1–15. Stockholm, Sweden (1999)
5. Guarino, N.: Semantic matching: formal ontological distinctions for information organization, extraction, and integration. In: Pazienza, M.T. (ed.) SCIE 1997. LNCS, vol. 1299, pp. 139–170. Springer, Heidelberg (1997). https://doi.org/10. 1007/3-540-63438-X_8
6. Tong, W., Zhong-Liang, A.I., Xian-Guo, S.: Knowledge graph construction of threat intelligence based on deep learning. Comput. Mod. **12**, 21 (2018)
7. Feng, N., Wang, H.J., Li, M.: A security risk analysis model for information systems: causal relationships of risk factors and vulnerability propagation analysis. Inf. Sci. **256**, 57–73 (2014)
8. Wang, W., Jiang, R., Jia, Y., Li, A., Chen, Y.: KGBIAC: knowledge graph based intelligent alert correlation framework. In: Wen, S., Wu, W., Castiglione, A. (eds.) CSS 2017. LNCS, vol. 10581, pp. 523–530. Springer, Cham (2017). https://doi. org/10.1007/978-3-319-69471-9_41
9. An-Kang, U., Yuan-Bo, G., Tai-Ming, Z., Tong, W.: Survey on network security event correlation analysis methods and tools. Computer Science (2017)
10. Mastani, S.A.: Reduced merge_fsm pattern matching algorithm for network intrusion detection. Int. J. Recent Trends Eng. Technol. **10**(2), 117 (2014)
11. Forgy, C.: Rete: a fast algorithm for the many patterns/many objects match problem. Artif. Intell. **19**(1), 17–37 (1982)
12. Liu, D., Gu, T., Xue, J.-P.: Rule engine based on improvement rete algorithm. In: The 2010 International Conference on Apperceiving Computing and Intelligence Analysis Proceeding, pp. 346–349 IEEE (2010)
13. Esmaili, M., Balachandran, B., Safavi-Naini, R., Pieprzyk, J.: Case-based reasoning for intrusion detection. In: 12th Annual Computer Security Applications Conference (ACSAC 1996), 9–13 December 1996, San Diego, CA, USA, pp. 214–223. IEEE Computer Society (1996)
14. Bo, C., Ling, Y.U., Jun-Mo, X.: An application of simulated annealing algorithm in model-based reasoning intrusion detection. J. Univ. Electron. Sci. Technol. China **34**(1), 36–39 (2005)
15. Rubin, D.E., Mital, V., Beckman, B.C., Katzenberger, G.S.: Dependency graph in data-driven model, 8 January 2013. US Patent 8,352,397
16. Hansen, S.E., Atkins, E.T.: Automated system monitoring and notification with swatch. In: Proceedings of the 7th Conference on Systems Administration (LISA 1993), Monterey, California, USA, 1–5 November 1993. USENIX (1993)
17. Rouillard, J.P.: Real-time log file analysis using the simple event correlator (SEC). In: Damon, L. (ed.) Proceedings of the 18th Conference on Systems Administration (LISA 2004), Atlanta, USA, 14–19 November 2004, pp. 133–150. USENIX (2004
18. Timofte, J., et al.: Intrusion detection using open source tools. Inform. Economica J. ISSN **14531305**, 75–79 (2008)
19. Nguyen, G., Fischer, M., Strufe, T.: Ossim: a generic simulation framework for overlay streaming. In: Bruzzone, A.G., Kropf, P.G., Riley, L.A., Davoudpour, M., Solis, A.O. (eds.) 2013 Summer Simulation Multiconference, SummerSim 2013, Toronto, Canada, 07–10 July 2013, p. 30. Society for Computer Simulation International/ACM DL (2013)

20. Proctor, M.: Drools: a rule engine for complex event processing. In: Schürr, A., Varró, D., Varró, G. (eds.) AGTIVE 2011. LNCS, vol. 7233, p. 2. Springer, Heidelberg (2012). https://doi.org/10.1007/978-3-642-34176-2_2
21. EsperTech. Esper. http://www.espertech.com
22. Ning, P., Cui, Y., Reeves, D.S.: Constructing attack scenarios through correlation of intrusion alerts. In: Atluri, V. (ed.) Proceedings of the 9th ACM Conference on Computer and Communications Security, CCS 2002, Washington, DC, USA, 18–22 November 2002, pp. 245–254. ACM (2002)
23. Zhang, J., Li, X., Wang, H.: Real-time alert correlation approach based on attack planning graph. J Comput. Appl. **36**(6), 1538–1543 (2016)
24. Jia, Y., Qi, Y., Shang, H., Jiang, R., Li, A.: A practical approach to constructing a knowledge graph for cybersecurity. Engineering **4**(1), 53–60 (2018). Cybersecurity
25. Gupta, S., Dutt, N., Gupta, R., Nicolau, A.: Spark: a high-level synthesis framework for applying parallelizing compiler transformations. In: 2003 16th International Conference on VLSI Design, Proceedings, pp. 461–466 (2003)

Social Unrest Events Prediction by Contextual Gated Graph Convolutional Networks

Haiyang Wang[1], Bin Zhou[1], Zhipin Gu[1], and Yan Jia[2(✉)]

[1] National University of Defense Technology, Changsha 410073, China
{wanghaiyang19,binzhou,guzhipin19}@nudt.edu.cn
[2] Harbin Institute of Technology, Shenzhen 518055, China
jiayanjy@vip.sina.com

Abstract. In a wide range of social unrest events prediction, the dynamic graph convolutional network (DGCN) has been successfully leveraged to achieve reliable performance. The innovation of DGCN mainly focuses on capturing the temporal features of unrest events. Inspired by the DGCN, we propose a new graph convolutional network model called Contextual Gated Graph Convolutional Network (CGGCN), which is adopted to predict and analyze social unrest events. The CGGCN uses the contextual gated layer, which improves the layer-wise propagation rules of graph convolutional networks. The contextual gated layer can re-learn the keyword representation to capture the contextual semantic features of unrest events by using squeeze and excitation module. The principle of the squeeze and excitation module is to increase the weight of meaningful words for event prediction and to suppress weaker ones. In our work, we obtain historical texts including published news and short tweets related to social unrest events. Based on these historical texts data, the CGGCN can predict the occurrence of social unrest events efficiently. In addition, we propose a method for establishing the evolution graph of unrest events. In this way, we can use several core words to summarize the evolution of the event. Finally, we conduct extensive experiments on the unrest events data sets. The experimental results show that the CGGCN leads by about 5%–7% in the performance of prediction compared with other mainstream methods.

Keywords: MDATA · Social unrest events · Graph convolutional network

1 Introduction

Social unrest can be defined as a group behavior of protesters using force to destroy public order. The occurrence of social unrest events will seriously affect the stability of the state power, social harmony and even the safety of people. In order to reduce the negative impacts of social unrest events or curb its occurrence, many countries and non-governmental organizations often adopt various

© Springer Nature Switzerland AG 2021
Y. Jia et al. (Eds.): MDATA: A New Knowledge Representation Model, LNCS 12647, pp. 220–233, 2021.
https://doi.org/10.1007/978-3-030-71590-8_13

measures to predict the time and location of social unrest events. In recent years, many researchers have predicted social unrest events based on public news texts. For example, a method was proposed in [1] to predict the risk of social unrest in a particular country by analyzing the emotional tendencies in the news. However, in the previous research on social unrest events prediction, there are mainly the following limitations:

- Public news texts are often used as the data source for unrest prediction models. However, the news texts will cause the occurrence of social unrest events which cannot be predicted in time. Besides, it is well known that the dynamics of public social opinion are the core factors influencing unrest events. Nevertheless, taking the news texts as data source makes the prediction model unable to capture the dynamics of public social opinion in time;
- Most traditional event prediction models use various machine learning (ML) algorithms. The characteristic of those algorithms is to extract the features with high discrimination. However, with the increasing data size and the faster data update rate, the prediction accuracy of such methods is low and the time complexity is very high;
- As we all know, the theme of most social unrest events can be summarized by a few keywords. However, in the extant event prediction models, these keywords have not been fully utilized;
- Many extant prediction models use global features over a long period, the impacts of data changes between short time slices of the events are ignored. At the same time, many existing methods cannot analyze the evolution of social unrest events.

To address these problem, we propose the Contextual Gated Graph Convolutional Networks (CGGCN) model to overcome the above limitations. Contextual Gated Graph convolutional network can use tweets as the data source. Moreover, we revise the propagation formula of the graph convolutional network layer so that the CGGCN can capture the contextual semantic information of the data. In this chapter, we introduce how to build an evolution graph that can reflect the dynamics of social unrest events. The contributions of this chapter are summarized as follows:

- We improve the traditional graph convolution networks model and propose the CGGCN to predict social unrest events. Our model can use social media texts such as tweets as the data source, which can enable our model to capture the dynamic changes in public opinion promptly;
- We propose a contextual gated layer based on squeeze & excitation module creatively. The contextual gated layer can not only fully obtain the temporal features of data, but also make full use of the contextual semantic information of data;
- We use an innovative method to construct social unrest evolution graphs. Benefit from the evolution graph of unrest events, we can understand the development process of an unrest event intuitively. Besides, The staff of government departments can use the evolution graph to analyze and replay the social unrest events.

The proposed CGGCN model is evaluated on the data sets of Hong Kong and Thailand unrest events, and we tested the performance of it through quantitative and sensitivity analysis experiments.

The rest of the chapter is organized as follows: the next section introduces the related work about social unrest events prediction. Then we introduce the proposed model framework and details of the CGGCN in Sect. 3. We conduct extensive experiments and the results are depicted in Sect. 4. We introduce the challenges brought by the dynamic knowledge in Sect. 5 and we finally summarize the chapter in Sect. 6.

2 Related Work

In this section, we review the development and application of graph convolution network and summarize some related research work on events prediction models using Twitter or GDELT datasets. In addition, we describe the previous research work of the Squeeze & Excitation (SE) module.

2.1 Graph Convolution Network

Graph convolution network (GCN) first introduced by Kipf and Welling [2]. The graph convolution network model can directly process graph data without conversion. There are two different ways to construct GCN: Spatial Construction and Spectral Construction.

The GCN can describe the structure of a graph and capture spatial features between the nodes by using the adjacency matrix or the Laplacian matrix. Based on GCN, dynamic graph convolution network (DGCN) is proposed for event forecasting with the goal of modeling contextual information [3]. In this chapter, we draw the experience of some ideas from the DGCN model and improve the model.

The GCN model has many variants and application areas. Relational Graph Convolutional Networks (R-GCNs) are developed specifically to deal with the highly multi-relational data characteristic of realistic knowledge bases, and R-GCNs can be applied to link prediction and entity classification [4]. A substantial improvement by stacking both GCN and LSTM layers on the standard benchmark (CoNLL-2009) is proposed for both Chinese and English in [5]. Text Graph Convolutional Network (T-GCN) is applied to text classification, and the model is very robust when there are few training data [6]. In addition, the GCN model can also be applied in event detection [7], discovering the geographic location of social media users [8], and recognizing human movements [9].

2.2 Event Prediction Based on Twitter or GDELT Datasets

Event prediction base on Twitter data is an important and challenging problem. A generative model for prediction of Spatiotemporal events based on tweet data is proposed in [10]. The model characterizes the underlying development of future events by jointly modeling the structural contexts and spatiotemporal burstiness. In other fields, twitter data is used to predict elections [11], crime [12], stock prices[13], popularity of topics [14], the occurrence of influenza virus in the population [15] and many other meaningful things [16,17]. Furthermore, Twitter data also plays an indispensable role in predicting social unrest. An automatically encoded data set GDELT is used in [18] to construct a framework based on hidden Markov models, which could predict the occurrence of social unrest events. Their experiments have shown that the framework is valid for data from five countries in Southeast Asia. Moreover, tweets can also be used to analyze the process of mobilization before the social protest. In [19], it uses Random Forests, Boosting, and Neural Networks to complete the task of identifying, explaining, and predicting when social unrest will occur based on the GDELT data. In this chapter, we use Twitter data as historical texts and the GDELT dataset as the data source for social unrest events.

2.3   Squeeze and Excitation (SE) Module

Squeeze-and-Excitation networks are proposed in [20]. It is a lightweight gating mechanism, which is designed to enhance the representational power of basic modules throughout the network. After that, three variants of SE modules are introduced in [21]. They are squeezing spatially and exciting channelwise, squeezing channel-wise and exciting spatially, and joint spatial and channel squeeze & excitation. Three variants of SE modules are devoted to Fully Convolutional Neural Networks (F-CNNs) to increase segmentation accuracy in three medical image datasets. Besides, squeeze-and-excitation module is used in [22] to re-weight different historical observations and get the contextual information of images and. In our module, we also use the SE module to recalculate the weights of words to capture contextual semantic features.

3   Methods

In this section, we mainly describe the main components of the Contextual Gated graph convolutional network (CGGCN), which is proposed to predict social unrest events. In general, the CGGCN model has three functions:

1) The CGGCN model can predict the occurrence of social unrest based on historical texts data such as tweets;
2) The CGGCN model can make full use of the contextual semantic information in the texts data and maximize the effect of them on prediction;
3) The CGGCN model can construct evolution graphs which allow researchers to learn the development trend of social unrest events intuitively.

The framework of the CGGCN model is shown in Fig. 1. Firstly, for a social unrest event, we collect historical texts for k consecutive days, which is from public news or tweets. Then historical texts data are represented in the form of graph after data processing. After that, the graphs are imported into the model in

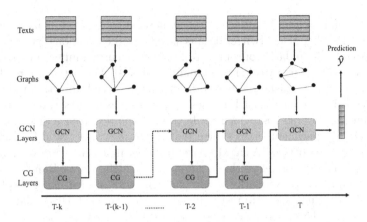

Fig. 1. System framework of the Contextual Gated Graph Convolutional Network

chronological order and they are calculated by the graph convolutional network layer and the contextual gated layer. After all the graphs are calculated, the model can return the predicted value of the unrest events which is represented by 0 or 1 respectively. As for the label of unrest events, we define whether an event will happen (1 means will happen, while 0 means not) according to the correlation between the events and historical texts.

3.1   Graph Construction

As shown in Fig. 2, the goal of graph construction is to extract keywords from texts and calculate Pointwise Mutual Information (PMI) between keywords.

For an unrest event, given its collection of past historical texts, we extract n keywords after removing stop words as nodes of a graph and use the PMI [23] method to calculate the weight between nodes. After that, we set up the adjacency matrix to represent graphs based on nodes and edge weights. A series of adjacency matrices can be obtained based on past historical texts. The edge weights of the word i and j at t day can be defined as:

$$A_t[i,j] = \begin{cases} PMI_t(i,j), PMI_t(i,j) > 0 \\ 0 \quad , PMI_t(i,j) \leq 0 \end{cases} \tag{1}$$

The PMI on day t can be calculated using the following formula:

$$PMI_t(i,j) = \ln \frac{D_t * d_t(i,j)}{d_t(i) * d_t(j)} \tag{2}$$

D_t is the total number of texts in the collection on day t; $d_t(i,j)$ is the total number of texts where both word i and word j appeared at current time t; $d_t(i)$ and $d_t(j)$ is the number of texts that word i and j appeared. Regarding the

Twitter data, they can be counted by the number of tweets. When calculating A_t, we only consider the case where $PMI_t(i,j) > 0$ and this implies word i appears at least once.

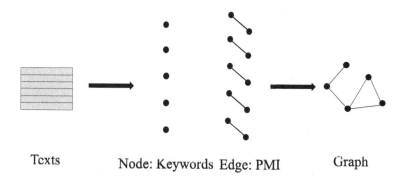

Texts   Node: Keywords Edge: PMI   Graph

Fig. 2. Graph construction process

3.2 Graph Convolutional Network Layer

The layer-wise propagation rule of the graph convolution network is proposed in [2]. And it is defined as the following formula:

$$H_{l+1} = \delta\left(\widetilde{D}^{-\frac{1}{2}}\tilde{A}\widetilde{D}^{-\frac{1}{2}}H^{(l)}W^{(l)}\right) \tag{3}$$

The GCN model can capture the spatial features by stacking multiple convolutional layers. However, in order to enable the model capture temporal features and semantic information between nodes, we modified the layer-wise propagation rules as follows:

$$H_{t+1} = \delta\left(\widetilde{D}^{-\frac{1}{2}}\tilde{A}_t\widetilde{D}^{-\frac{1}{2}}\widetilde{H}_tW^{(t)} + b^{(t)}\right) \tag{4}$$

Given the adjacency matrix $A_t \in R^{n \times n}$, we can get $\tilde{A}_t$ by $\tilde{A}_t = A_t + I_N$. I_N is an n-dimensional identity matrix. $\widetilde{D}$ is the degree matrix and it can be calculated by $\widetilde{D}_{ii} = \sum_j \tilde{A}_{t_i}$. $\delta(\cdot)$ denotes an activation function which is $ReLU(\cdot) = \max(0, \cdot)$. $\widetilde{H}_t \in R^{n \times m(t)}$ is the matrix of activations at day t. In particular, $H_0 \in R^{n \times m}$ is a matrix containing word embedding vectors of all n words, $W^{(t)} \in R^{m(t) \times m(t+1)}$, b^{t+1} depict the model where $m(t)$ is the input feature dimensions and $m(t+1)$ is the output feature dimensions. By stacking GCN layers, the nodes can get information from further neighbor nodes. The layer-wise propagation rule is shown in Fig. 3.

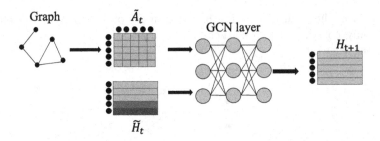

Fig. 3. Layer-wise propagation rule

3.3   Contextual Gated Layer

We propose the Contextual Gated Layer to capture the contextual semantic features of graphs. Inspired by the gating mechanism, we concatenate the initial word embedding vector and the output of the GCN layer. Then we use the squeeze & excitation module to re-weight different words. The workflow of the contextual gated layer is shown in Fig. 4.

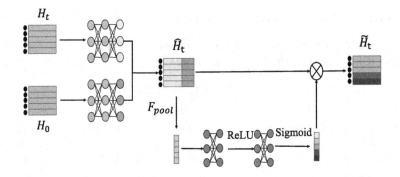

Fig. 4. The workflow of contextual gated layer

In order to learn semantic information and the learned GCN features of each node, we apply linear transformations to the initial embedding vector matrix H_0 and the learned vector matrix H_t by the GCN model. After that, we get H_e^t and H_p^t; then we apply concatenation on H_e^t, H_p^t and take the result to the tanh function [3]. This process is defined as follows:

$$H_e^{(t)} = H_0 W_e^{(t)} + b_e^{(t)} \tag{5}$$

$$H_p^{(t)} = H_t W_p^{(t)} + b_p^{(t)} \tag{6}$$

$$\widehat{H}_t = \gamma \left(\left[H_P^{(t)} \| H_e^{(t)} \right] \right) \tag{7}$$

where $W_p^{(t)} \in R^{m^{(t)} \times \beta}$, $W_e^{(t)} \in R^{m \times \left(m^{(t)} - \beta\right)}$, $0 \le \beta \le m^{(t)}$, and $\gamma(\cdot)$ is the tanh function.

In order to find the vital words and emphasize the importance of these words by giving higher weights, we use the global average pooling F_{pool} over all vectors to produce the summary of each word and get z_i. Then, a gated mechanism with a sigmoid activation is applied to z_t and it transforms Z_t to S_t. Finally, S_t is applied to the scale each word vector. This process is defined as follows:

$$z_{t_i} = F_{pool}\left(\hat{h}_t\right) = \frac{1}{m} \sum_{j=0}^{m} \hat{h}_{t_i} \, for \, i = 1, 2, 3 \cdots n \tag{8}$$

$$s_t = \sigma\left(W_1 \delta\left(W_2 z_t\right)\right) \tag{9}$$

$$\tilde{H}_t = \widehat{H}_t \circ s_t \tag{10}$$

where W_1 and W_2 are the corresponding weights, $\delta(\cdot)$ is the ReLU function, and $\sigma(\cdot)$ is the sigmoid function.

3.4   Output Layer

In our model, k graphs are calculated through the stacked GCN layer and CG layer sequentially. After passing the last GCN layer, we can get $H_T \in R^{n \times 1}$, which can be regarded as an n output layer. We conduct a nonlinear transformation on H_T. The process is shown in Fig. 5 and we define them formally as follows:

$$\hat{y} = \sigma\left(H_T W_T + b_T\right), \tag{11}$$

where $W_T \in R^{1 \times n}$, $b_T \in R$. W_T and b_T are parameters that can be learned. σ is the sigmoid function. In the end, we choose the cross-entropy loss function after comparing the effect of existing loss functions and use the back-propagation algorithm for training.

3.5   Construction of the Evolution Graph

In our model, the input data is a graph with n nodes; these constructed graphs contain information that is related to the event to be predicted. However, these graphs have a lot of nodes and complex structure. For these reasons, these graphs cannot be used directly to analyze the development of events. In order to generate intuitive and straightforward evolution graphs, we use the weight sequence of nodes to extract core words from everyday news. For any event, we can conclude $s = [s_{T-k}, s_{T-2}, \cdots s_{T-1}]$ and $s_t \in R^n$. We sort S_t according to the weights and then select the words whose weights are in the top. After selecting the core words, we extract the isomorphic subgraph of the corresponding node in the initial graph.

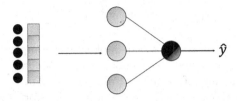

Fig. 5. The workflow of output layer

4   Experiment

In this section, we evaluate the proposed Contextual Gated Graph Convolutional Networks model. We compared the CGGCN model with DGCN model in predictingsocial unrest events. Furthermore, we also make use of the evolution graph to analyze an unrest event which was happened in Hong Kong.

4.1   Datasets

GDELT. We design the experiment based on the GDELT (Global Database of Events, Language, and Tone) event database. The dataset records more than 300 human activities worldwide, from social unrest events to friendly exchanges. GDELT project captures a lot of attributes for each event, including the location, time, theme and organization. In this chapter, we focus on social unrest events which were happened in Hong Kong.

Twitter. From September to October of 2019, many social unrests broke out in Hong Kong. Therefore, we collected tweets related to Hong Kong from 2019-09-24 to 2019-10-31 for research purpose. These tweets are used as historical texts data required by the prediction model. In addition, we also use the Thailand data provided in some related works [3] to compare the performance of models.

4.2   Data Preprocessing

GDELT. After getting the GDELT data, we first remove the duplicate events, then retain the time, title, keywords and content of the event. After that, we separate the events according to time, and count the number of events that occur every day, which is shown in Table 1.

Twitter. Given the Twitter data, we first separate all tweets by time and we only retain tweets that has been forwarded greater than 10 times. Table 2 shows the number of retained tweets every day. For the retained tweets, we preprocess them by cleaning and tokenizing words. After that, as for the samples of every unrest event, we select 1000 tweets every day which are related to the event title or the keywords from the retained tweets. Furthermore, at the same time, the date of tweets is selected within 7 days before the event date. Then we extract 500 keywords from 7000 tweets for every event using the TF-IDF method. These keywords are the foundation of constructing the adjacency matrix and the evolution graph of unrest events.

Table 1. The number of unrest events

Date	0924	0925	0926	0927	0928	0929	0930	1001	1002	1003	1004	1005	1006	1007
Amount	541	401	519	497	529	670	825	1498	1024	991	1079	714	689	829

Table 2. The number of related tweets

Date	0924	0925	0926	0927	0928	0929	0930	1001	1002	1003	1004	1005	1006	1007
Amount	2829	2708	2956	3250	3746	6001	4978	7565	5796	4346	6720	6511	6141	7479

4.3 Prediction Performance

We compare the prediction performance of methods on the two datasets (Hong Kong and Thailand) and the experiment results are shown in Table 3. $Pre_{HK}, Rec_{HK}, F1_{HK}$ are the performance results of Hong Kong datasets. $Pre_{TH}, Rec_{TH}, F1_{TH}$ are the performance results of Thailand datasets. From the results, the CGGCN method has better performance in the events happened in Hong Kong and Thailand, compared to the DGCN method. The experimental results also show that the F1 value is increased by about 5%, and the Rec is increased by about 7%. We found that the model does not perform as well as the Thailand dataset on the Hong Kong dataset. We think this is because the Hong Kong dataset is based on Twitter data, which contains a lot of noisy tweets. It is challenging to match tweets and unrest events correctly. Overall, the CGGCN model is ahead of the DGCN model in the prediction performance.

4.4 The Evolution Graph

In order to visually show the role of the evolution graph, we select a case of unrest event that broke out in Hong Kong on October 1, 2019. Figure 6 shows the evolution graph of the event. In the figure, the red nodes represent words with higher weights. The title of the news reporting for this event was Hong Kong police fire water cannon, tear gas as protests spread. In this unrest event, it can be seen from the selected core words that the opposing parties to the unrest are the police and the protesters. In order to maintain a stable social order and curb violence, the police used water cannon and tear gas. In particular, the two words of "tear" and "gas" appeared very frequently in these two days before the unrest event. This phenomenon presages the occurrence of this event to a certain

Table 3. Performance comparison

Method	$Prec_{HK}$	Rec_{HK}	$F1_{HK}$	$Prec_{TH}$	Rec_{TH}	$F1_{TH}$
DGCN	0.7627	0.7258	0.7438	0.7941	0.7788	0.7864
CGGCN	0.7647	0.7879	0.7761	0.8056	0.8365	0.8208

extent. However, there are still some positive words in the core words such as love, which shows the beautiful expectations of the people for Hong Kong. In summary, our model can summarize the evolution of unrest events and capture the vital information of them.

5   Challenges

There are many challenges when we make a prediction for social events by using dynamic time or spatial feature.

For dynamic time features, relationship extraction for entities at a different time is very important. Entity interactions and relationship change have an impact on event development. Accurate entity relation extraction will be helpful for generating events evolution graph lines. Besides, long-term event dependency is also vital for events prediction. In many cases, social events are related to some activities in the past or future.

As for dynamic spatial features, social events are usually not independent of each other. It is important to consider multiple geolocations simultaneously and study the influence of neighbor locations. Moreover, the prediction of the spread of social events in different regions is also a challenge by using dynamic spatial features.

6   Chapter Summary

The prediction of social unrest events is vital for national security and social stability. In this chapter, we propose the Contextual Gated Graph Convolutional Networks model for social unrest prediction creatively by combining the squeeze & excitation module with graph convolutional networks. We verified the validity and accuracy of the model on the unrest events data set based on the Twitter and GDELT data. In the future, our research direction will mainly focus on the following aspects. First, we will combine news text data with Twitter text data in an effective way. The combination of two types of data can not only guarantee the authority but also capture the dynamics of public opinion fully. In our opinion, this will help improve the effectiveness of the prediction model. Second, multi-events correlation is also very important. The reasons for the outbreak of social

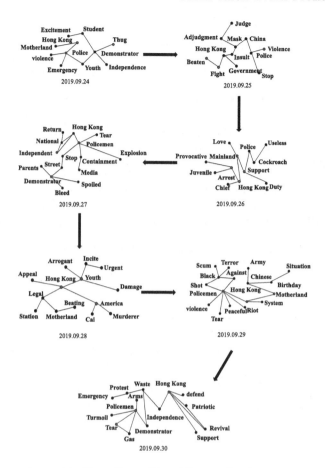

Fig. 6. An unrest event in Hong Kong: Hong Kong police fire water cannon, tear gas as protests spread.

unrest events are complex; some seemingly unrelated events might cause a large part of them. Therefore, the establishment of a multi-events correlation chain is significant for the prediction of social unrest events.

References

1. Alikhani, E.: Computational social analysis: social unrest prediction using textual analysis of news. Dissertations & Theses (2014)
2. Jia, N., Tian, X., Zhang, Y., Wang, F.: Semi-supervised node classification with discriminable squeeze excitation graph convolutional networks. IEEE Access **8**, 148226–148236 (2020)

3. Deng, S., Rangwala, H., Ning, Y.: Learning dynamic context graphs for predicting social events. In: Teredesai, A., Kumar, V., Li, Y., Rosales, R., Terzi, E., Karypis, G. (eds.) Proceedings of the 25th ACM SIGKDD International Conference on Knowledge Discovery & Data Mining. KDD 2019, Anchorage, AK, USA, 4–8 August 2019, pp. 1007–1016. ACM (2019)

4. Schlichtkrull, M., Kipf, T.N., Bloem, P., van den Berg, R., Titov, I., Welling, M.: Modeling relational data with graph convolutional networks. In: Gangemi, A., et al. (eds.) ESWC 2018. LNCS, vol. 10843, pp. 593–607. Springer, Cham (2018). https://doi.org/10.1007/978-3-319-93417-4_38

5. Marcheggiani, D., Bastings, J., Titov, I.: Exploiting semantics in neural machine translation with graph convolutional networks. In: Walker, M.A., Ji, H., Stent, A. (eds.) Proceedings of the 2018 Conference of the North American Chapter of the Association for Computational Linguistics: Human Language Technologies, NAACL-HLT, New Orleans, Louisiana, USA, 1–6 June 2018, Volume 2 (Short Papers), pp. 486–492. Association for Computational Linguistics (2018)

6. Nguyen, T.H., Grishman, R.: Graph convolutional networks with argument-aware pooling for event detection. In: McIlraith, S.A., Weinberger, K.Q. (eds.) Proceedings of the Thirty-Second AAAI Conference on Artificial Intelligence, (AAAI-18), the 30th Innovative Applications of Artificial Intelligence (IAAI-18), and the 8th AAAI Symposium on Educational Advances in Artificial Intelligence (EAAI-18), New Orleans, Louisiana, USA, 2–7 February 2018, pp. 5900–5907. AAAI Press (2018)

7. Liu, X., You, X., Zhang, X., Wu, J., Lv, P.: Tensor graph convolutional networks for text classification. In: The Thirty-Fourth AAAI Conference on Artificial Intelligence, AAAI 2020, The Thirty-Second Innovative Applications of Artificial Intelligence Conference, IAAI 2020, The Tenth AAAI Symposium on Educational Advances in Artificial Intelligence, EAAI 2020, New York, NY, USA, 7–12 February 2020, pp. 8409–8416. AAAI Press (2020)

8. Rahimi, A., Cohn, T., Baldwin, T.: Semi-supervised user geolocation via graph convolutional networks. In: Gurevych, I., Miyao, Y. (eds.) Proceedings of the 56th Annual Meeting of the Association for Computational Linguistics, ACL 2018, Melbourne, Australia, 15–20 July 2018, Volume 1: Long Papers, pp. 2009–2019. Association for Computational Linguistics (2018)

9. Li, Y., He, Z., Ye, X., He, Z., Han, K.: Spatial temporal graph convolutional networks for skeleton-based dynamic hand gesture recognition. EURASIP J. Image Video Process. **2019**(1), 1–7 (2019). https://doi.org/10.1186/s13640-019-0476-x

10. Zhao, L., Chen, F., Lu, C., Ramakrishnan, N.: Spatiotemporal event forecasting in social media. In: Venkatasubramanian, S., Ye, J. (eds.) Proceedings of the 2015 SIAM International Conference on Data Mining, Vancouver, BC, Canada, 30 April–2 May 2015, pp. 963–971. SIAM (2015)

11. Tumasjan, A., Sprenger, T.O., Sandner, P.G., Welpe, I.M.: Predicting elections with twitter: what 140 characters reveal about political sentiment. In: Cohen, W.W., Gosling, S. (eds.) Proceedings of the Fourth International Conference on Weblogs and Social Media. ICWSM 2010, Washington, DC, USA, 23–26 May 2010. The AAAI Press (2010)

12. Gerber, M.S.: Predicting crime using Twitter and kernel density estimation. Decis. Support Syst. **61**, 115–125 (2014)

13. Pagolu, V.S., Challa, K.N.R., Panda, G., Majhi, B.: Sentiment analysis of Twitter data for predicting stock market movements, CoRR, vol. abs/1610.09225 (2016)

14. Wang, X., Wang, C., Ding, Z., Zhu, M., Huang, J.: Predicting the popularity of topics based on user sentiment in microblogging websites. J. Intell. Inf. Syst. **51**(1), 97–114 (2017). https://doi.org/10.1007/s10844-017-0486-z

15. Achrekar, H., Gandhe, A., Lazarus, R., Yu, S., Liu, B.: Predicting flu trends using Twitter data, pp. 702–707 (2011)

16. Deng, L., Jia, Y., Zhou, B., Huang, J., Han, Y.: User interest mining via tags and bidirectional interactions on Sina Weibo. World Wide Web **21**(2), 515–536 (2018). https://doi.org/10.1007/s11280-017-0469-6

17. Quan, Y., Jia, Y., Zhou, B., Han, W., Li, S.: Repost prediction incorporating time-sensitive mutual influence in social networks. J. Comput. Sci. **28**, 217–227 (2018)

18. Qiao, F., Li, P., Zhang, X., Ding, Z., Cheng, J., Wang, H.: Predicting social unrest events with hidden Markov models using GDELT. Discrete Dyn. Nat. Soc. **2017**, 1–13 (2017)

19. Galla, D., Burke, J.: Predicting social unrest using GDELT. In: Perner, P. (ed.) MLDM 2018. LNCS (LNAI), vol. 10935, pp. 103–116. Springer, Cham (2018). https://doi.org/10.1007/978-3-319-96133-0_8

20. Hu, J., Shen, L., Albanie, S., Sun, G., Wu, E.: Squeeze-and-excitation networks. IEEE Trans. Pattern Anal. Mach. Intell. **42**(8), 2011–2023 (2020)

21. Roy, A.G., Navab, N., Wachinger, C.: Recalibrating fully convolutional networks with spatial and channel "squeeze and excitation" blocks. IEEE Trans. Medical Imaging **38**(2), 540–549 (2019)

22. Geng, X., Li, Y., Wang, L., Zhang, L., Yang, Q., Ye, J., Liu, Y.: Spatiotemporal multi-graph convolution network for ride-hailing demand forecasting. In: The Thirty-Third AAAI Conference on Artificial Intelligence, AAAI 2019, The Thirty-First Innovative Applications of Artificial Intelligence Conference. IAAI 2019, The Ninth AAAI Symposium on Educational Advances in Artificial Intelligence. EAAI 2019, Honolulu, Hawaii, USA, 27 January–1 February 2019, pp. 3656–3663. AAAI Press (2019)

23. Church, K.W., Hanks, P.: Word association norms, mutual information, and lexicography. Comput. Linguist. **16**(1), 22–29 (1990)

Information Cascading in Social Networks

Liqun Gao[1], Bin Zhou[1(✉)], Yan Jia[2], Hongkui Tu[1], and Ye Wang[1]

[1] National University of Defense Technology, Changsha 410073, China
wycmglq@outlook.com, {binzhou,ye.wang}@nudt.edu.cn, tuhkjet@foxmail.com
[2] Harbin Institute of Technology, Shenzhen 518055, China
jiayanjy@vip.sina.com

Abstract. This chapter introduces the application of information cascading analysis in social networks. We present a deep learning based framework of social network information cascade analysis, and we show the challenges of applying the MDATA model. The phenomenon of information dissemination in social networks is widespread, and Social Network Information Cascade Analysis (SNICA) aims to acquire valuable knowledge in the process of information dissemination in social networks. As the number, volume, and resolution of social network data increase rapidly, traditional social network data analysis methods, especially the analysis method of social network graph (SNG) data have become overwhelmed in SNICA. At the same time, the MDATA model fuses data from multiple sources in a graph, which can be applied to the SNICA problems. Recently, deep learning models have changed this situation, and it has achieved success in SNICA with its powerful implicit feature extraction capabilities. This chapter provides a comprehensive survey of recent progress in applying deep learning techniques for SNICA.

Keywords: MDATA · Social network · Information cascading

1 Introduction

In recent years, with the rapid development of various social applications such as Twitter, Facebook, Weibo, WeChat, TikTok, etc., more and more network users share news, ideas, and interests in social networks. When the shared information flows from one person or community to another in such a way, a cascading effect of information is generated [1]. There are also other forms of information cascade of Internet services such as blog post forwarding [2,3], paper citation [4], email sending [5], etc. Research on information cascade will benefit the understanding of the process and results of information dissemination. It also facilitates many downstream tasks of social network analysis, such as online marketing [6–8], influence analysis [9,10], cascade prediction [10–12] and rumor detection [13].

Studying Social Network Information Cascade Analysis (SNICA) has become significant research in social network analysis. Recently, deep learning models, such as Convolutional Neural Networks (CNN) [14] and Recurrent Neural Networks (RNN) [15], have achieved considerable success in various machine learning tasks. With the advent of graph neural network (GNN) [16], deep learning

© Springer Nature Switzerland AG 2021
Y. Jia et al. (Eds.): MDATA: A New Knowledge Representation Model, LNCS 12647, pp. 234–254, 2021.
https://doi.org/10.1007/978-3-030-71590-8_14

handles relational data more easily and effectively. Meanwhile, the application of deep learning models in the field of SNICA are proved to be feasible [17], and a large number of deep learning models were successfully applied in SNICA, promoting the research works in this field.

The research on SNICA remained a high degree of popularity in the past decade, and some surveys have reviewed issues related to SNICA from different perspectives. In [18], it focuses on the traditional methods of information dissemination, and divides the application intos three directions: detection of hot topics, cascading diffusion of information, and maximizing influence. Similar to [18], it investigates the application of cascading propagation from the perspective of maximizing and minimizing the influence of cascading propagation in [19], and it introduces the traditional diffusion model method. In [20], it investigates information dissemination methods of social networks, from three perspectives: structural properties and evolving laws, social crowds and their interaction behaviors, and information and its diffusion. In [21], it introduces the characteristics required for communication analysis from two perspectives of user characteristics and networks in the dissemination of information on social networks. Among them, user characteristics include influence, social roles, and viewpoints, while networks include network relationship strength, isomorphism, temporal characteristics, and community structure.

However, most of these works review SNICA based on traditional methods rather than deep learning techniques. Because of the increasing usage of deep learning technology in this field in recent years, there is still a lack of extensive and comprehensive investigation into the application of deep learning methods in SNICA and the classification of SNICA applications. Compared with existing works, the main contributions of this chapter can be summarized as follows:

- To the best of our knowledge, this chapter is a systematic survey of investigating the application of deep learning methods in SNICA. Since SNICA uses more and more deep learning models, a comprehensive survey of deep learning applications in SNICA becomes necessary;
- This chapter propose a general model framework based on deep learning, which covers the process of the entire task model with the idea of MDATA. Under the guidance of this framework, data and methods can be better selected to design a more suitable deep learning model for the SNICA tasks;
- This chapter provide a comprehensive SNICA application classification, which explains the application models of deep learning technology in the field of SNICA from four aspects: user behavior analysis, cascade prediction, rumor detection, and social network event analysis.

In the next section, we introduce related concepts and summarizes the advantages of deep learning technology in SNICA. Then, we propose a general framework for deep learning technology, which applies to SNICA in Sect. 3. Different SNICA application scenarios in the framework are classified and discussed according to user behavior analysis, information cascade analysis, rumor detection, and social network event prediction in Sect. 4. Finally, we discuss the limitations of the current work and suggest future directions in Sect. 5; this chapter is summarized in Sect. 6.

2   Background

The traditional SNICA methods model the information dissemination process via social network relational data, and explain the phenomenon of an information cascade or predict the future state of information cascade.

2.1   Social Network Graph Data

Before introducing the concept of SNICA, we introduce some characteristics of social network data briefly. Social network data is usually represented as graph data, called Social Network Graph (SNG), which is composed of nodes and edges. Nodes can be users who participate in social network activities or virtual individuals such as organizations; edges correspond to the relationship of nodes and can be different relationships such as interaction, follow, sending, or receiving behaviors. The behavior of nodes in the social network causes the relationship in the SNG to change regularly [20].

2.2   Traditional SNICA Methods

Some researchers have divided traditional information cascading methods into three categories: diffusion model-based method, generation process-based method, and feature-based method.

Early research on information cascade are base on the diffusion model [11, 22–24], but the disadvantage is that these methods need a strong hypothesis basis. Generally, the method based on diffusion model uses the dynamic equation of propagation to analyze the propagation phenomenon, such as Independent Cascade model (IC) [25].

Then methods based on generation process [4, 8, 26, 27] mainly use the probabilistic method to characterize and model the process of information propagation; these methods have good interpretability to the dynamic propagation mechanism of information, such as the point estimation-based generation model.

Unlike generation process-based methods, feature-based methods [28–31] treat information cascade analysis tasks as regression or classification problems; they extract manual features through social network data and adopt machine learning techniques to model and learn manual features for analysis and prediction.

2.3   Embedding Methods of Social Network Graph Data

The feature-based methods for analyzing social network information cascade could achieve good results, it is the key to solve the problem by using the social network data's topological structure and node attribute features. For example, the attributes of graph statistical information in the diffusion model (node degree or clustering coefficient [32]), or the cascading structural features in the feature method (kernel function [33]).

The challenge of solving the cascading information problem through the feature method is to reduce the non-Euclidean structured data [16] to the Euclidean vector space. The commonly adopted method is feature mapping of the implicit relationship information between nodes. The advantage of data reduction is that the distance between nodes can be calculated through spatial measurement to construct a downstream machine learning prediction model for specific analysis.

The methods of graph embedding can solve the above challenges better. Graph embedding can be regarded as a conversion function that maps nodes, subgraphs, and even the entire network as vectors to a low-dimensional feature space while retaining network topology and node attribute information. In this way, unstructured data, such as social network graph, can be converted into vectors, and the features are guaranteed to the maximum extent.

Existing graph embedding methods mainly focused on preserving the first-order proximity of nodes. For example, two nodes are linked in the graph with similar embedding vectors directly [34]. Word2Vec [35] learns the representation of distributed words from a sparse text corpus based on Skip-Gram [36], which can place semantically similar words close to each other in space. Furthermore, DeepWalk [37] is the first graph embedding method based on representation learning. Inspired by [35], DeepWalk is used to generate a sequence of nodes from the network to learn a language model, ensuring that similar nodes are close in the distance after embedding. LINE [38] attempts to retain both first-order and second-order approximations to obtain useful structural information. Node2Vec [39] generated a biased second-order random walk representation to capture the network structure's diversity.

However, these traditional methods have two disadvantages [40]. First, there is no shared parameter between the nodes of the encoder because the parameter increases linearly with the number of nodes, which will lead to low calculation efficiency. Second, direct embedding methods lack generalization capabilities, which means they cannot process dynamic graphs or generalize to new graphs.

2.4 Deep Learning Models in SNICA

In recent years, deep learning technologies have achieved significant performance in many tasks, such as image classification, audio recognition, and natural language processing [41]. These technologies accelerate the research of SNICA tasks. Deep learning technology has been applied in many cascade analysis application scenarios, such as influence prediction, cascade size prediction, and user behavior analysis, which obtained better performance. Many surveys introduce deep learning techniques [41–43]. In this section, we mainly introduces several deep learning techniques that are used in solving SNICA problems, including three mainstream deep learning frameworks (CNN, RNN, GNN).

CNN for SNICA. Convolutional Neural Network (CNN) [14] was used for visual image analysis. A typical CNN model usually includes an input layer, convolutional layers, pooling layers, fully connected layers, and an output layer. Different layers have different feature representation functions. The convolutional layer extracts local features and shares weights. The pooling layer mainly performs downsampling to prevent the model from overfitting. The fully connected layer and the output layer are the same as the traditional multi-layer perceptron (MLP) [44].

CNN has the powerful ability to capture the correlation of data and is mainly responsible for capturing the correlation of different features in tensor data of the information cascade work [45–47].

RNN for SNICA. Recurrent neural networks (RNN) [15] are mainly used for sequence data, which aim to identify sequential features and predict the next possible result. However, the standard RNN has the problem of gradient disappearance and only has a short-term memory. Long Short-Term Memory (LSTM) [48] solves the problem of short RNN memory, and learns the long-term dependence of data through the mechanism of input gate, output gate, and forget gate. The Gated Recurrent Unit (GRU) [49] is the most popular improvement of LSTM. The model only retains the reset gate and update gate. In general, the sequence of LSTM memory is longer than GRU, and the problem of sequence modeling can be more easily solved in the task of modeling long-distance relationships. GRU trains faster on models with fewer sequence data and performs better than LSTM. In addition to the three most typical RNN, there are related variants, such as Bi-GRU, Bi-LSTM [50], and other RNN variant networks.

The RNN model is widely used to process sequence and time data. This characteristic meets the needs of the cascading information problem. The information cascading process can be regarded as a continuous evolution of data in the time series. A large number of RNNs and the improved models have been applied to SNICA.

GNN for SNICA. Graph neural network (GNN) was first proposed in [51], which extends the existing neural network and becomes a representation method of graph data. Standard neural networks, such as CNN and RNN, cannot process graph data as input data directly, because the input must be structured ones, such as a tensor. However, GNN provides a neural network embedding method for unstructured data, which better integrates global and local features in graph data. Specifically, GNN updates the node's hidden state by calculating the weight of the neighbor's state. The goal is to embed the graph data. The nodes' structural features and attribute features are obtained through the embedding method and combined into the node representation.

At present, there are two most commonly used GNN methods in the information cascade model: the graph convolution network (GCN) [52] and the graph attention network (GAT) [53]. GCN calculates the Laplacian feature decomposition of graph data, establishes the relationship between spectral graph theory and deep neural network, and realizes the convolution operation on graph data. From the perspective of nodes, GAT introduces the attention mechanism [54] into the graph data. It uses the attention mechanism to learn the relative weight between two connected nodes, which could reduce the dependence on the graph structure and can improve the model's expressive ability. These two typical graph neural network models are widely used in the research of SNICA because they are beneficial to obtain the potential relationship of the graph structure.

In the application of deep learning in SNICA, it also uses the autoencoder (AE) [55] and some variants of neural network models, such as CNN-LSTM [56].

2.5   The Advantages of Deep Learning in SNICA

In general, the development of deep learning technology has promoted the research of information cascade analysis. Compared with traditional methods, the information cascade analysis based on deep learning has the following advantages:

- For the SNICA graph data, deep learning technologies have stronger ability to capture the relationship features of nodes in the information propagation cascade graph; which are superior to traditional methods. Especially after the emergence of GNN, it has more powerful graph data embedding and representation capabilities for different tasks to obtain more comprehensive implicit relationship features;
- For the dynamic time series process of SNICA, deep learning analysis methods are based on time series, such as RNN has many advantages in representing such data. Because the existing deep learning models have strong abilities to express the spatial proximity and temporal correlation of graph data, especially the recurrent neural network and various variants have significant advantages for the analysis of time-series data;
- For the modeling process of SNICA, deep learning methods are more flexible than traditional methods. For different modeling steps, different deep learning frameworks are designed according to tasks, and the network structures can be adjusted according to different tasks to meet the needs. We can find the hidden relationship in the objective equation and get better performance through the flexible combination of models.

3   A General Framework for Deep Learning Methods in SNICA

In order to better fuse the features of social network information dissemination, the MDATA model proposes a general data integration and association framework, which also solve the same problem that SNICA faces. In this section, we propose a general deep learning based framework for handling the SNICA problems, which can also be used in the MDATA model. The SNICA modeling process using the deep learning methods is illustrated in Fig. 1, which includes six steps.

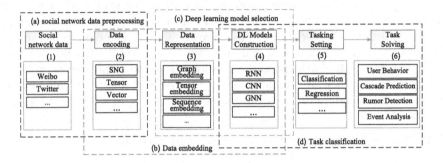

Fig. 1. A general framework for using deep learning models in SNICA

1) Data Collection: Obtain original social network data from different social network media, such as Weibo and Twitter;
2) Data Encoding: Construct SNG data based on the information propagation relationship from the original data of the social network, and encode data such as node attributes into a specific vector format, such as word2vec;
3) Data Representation: Obtain a suitable input format for deep learning models, for example, mapping graph data into tensor data, or embedding text data into vector data;
4) Deep learning Models Construction: Construct different deep learning frameworks for different task requirements;
5) Tasking Setting: Use the selected deep learning model to process the corresponding task, such as classification, regression;
6) Task Solving: These tasks are linked to SNICA specific problems, such as influence prediction, cascade prediction, popularity prediction, rumor detection, event analysis.

Figure 1 also shows the following four processes. (a) represents the process of data preprocessing; (b) is the process of data representation; (c) constructs the deep learning framework, and we can regard the feature extraction process of deep learning as a data representation method; and (d) is the process of task classification, different deep learning tasks solve different tasks of SNICA. We introduce these processes in the following sections.

3.1   Preprocessing of Social Network Data

The preprocessing of social network data aims to transform the social network raw data into the deep learning framework's input data.

As shown in Fig. 1(a), the SNG data introduced in Sect. 2 needs to be constructed during the data preprocessing step. For example, the cascading data can be constructed as the directed graph structure, and the temporal relationship structure can be constructed as a subgraph representation in different time windows. Naturally, the process of data preprocessing is not limited to the construction of SNG data. For example, in the processing of node data, the relevant attributes of the node need to be preprocessed, such as data encoding of nodes' fans or the users' semantic context. The specific data processing needs to be organized according to the task requirements.

3.2   Data Embedding

Generally speaking, for different models, the input data format of the deep learning model can be a graph (e.g., represented by the adjacency matrix), vector, matrix, or tensor. After preprocessing of the social network data, the preprocessed data usually needs to be represented in the data format, which is available for deep learning algorithms. This process is consistent with the embedding process introduced in Sect. 2.3, and the social network data needs to be mapped to the tensor space, serving as the input of the deep learning framework.

Naturally, deep learning can also be viewed as an embedded learning process that maps features to a low-dimensional vector space, as shown in Fig. 1(b). For SNICA, the main problem is how to map SNG data to a tensor space, while retaining information about the relationship structure as much as possible. The next step is to choose an appropriate method of graph data embedding, the random walk method is usually adopted to simulate the path of information propagation. Similar to the word relationship in natural language processing, using a random walk path is to learn the "context" of network nodes. Following this idea, different sequences of information propagation can be sampled, and these sequences are represented as vectors of information cascade.

Specifically, the DeepWalk method is utilized as a graph representation method in [51,56,57]. The GNN methods, such as GCN and GAT, are adopted in [45,58,59] to embed SNG data, and to map node relationships and features to a vector space as input of downstream tasks. There are also some other methods for embedding and representing social network data. For example, in [60], it uses the mapping matrix method for embedding, the meta-paths methods are used in [55,61], and a fully connected layer (MLP) for embedding the data is introduced in [62]. For vectors or scalars with node features, such as node semantic text, node degree, they are usually formalized as tensors to be used as input for deep learning models. For example, the word2vec method is used in [63,64] to encode text semantic information, the traditional TF-IDF method is adopted in [65] to embed phrases, and the one-hot method is applied in [27,66] to represent scalar data.

3.3   Selection of Deep Learning Models

For the embedding social network data, the next step is to input it into different SNICA tasks or different deep learning models. Different deep models are available for different applications. RNN model is mainly used to process sequence data and can be regarded as a time series model. The information cascade process meets the requirements of this model.

There are various kinds of RNN models that could be used for information cascade prediction. For example, the GRU (or Bi-GRU) method is adopted in [48,56,67,68] to learn the dependent features of node relationships in the process of information cascading; meanwhile, it can obtain the connection between the cascade sequences through the attention mechanism. The LSTM model is also utilized in [66,69–72] to learn users' cascading temporal relationships.

GNN can also be viewed as a part of the data embedding process for SNG to obtain a joint representation of the structural and attribute characteristics of nodes. Among them, GCN is a commonly adopted deep learning model to deal with the relationship between graph data structures and attributes. In [73], it uses the GCN model to learn the cascading subgraphs at different moments in the cascade graph, to achieve the representation of cascaded feature in the time window, and then uses LSTM to learn the timing features, finally predicts the results by MLP.

GAT is a kind of deep learning model which could obtain the importance of the relationship between nodes. In [59], it uses GAT to realize embedding and learning of the nodes in the cascade graph and combines the Bi-LSTM and gate mechanism to capture the timing features of the nodes in the propagation process. Separately embedding GCN in the user relationship graph and user state graph is proposed in [58], which establishes the weight relationship between the two graphs through the gate sharing mechanism.

CNN models usually use tensors in input layer, which have some certain advantages in the feature extraction of tensor data [74]. In the task of SNICA, CNN is usually used as an embedding method of node tensor attributes [47]. Some works use CNN as the end model of the classification task [46]. In addition, CNN could be used to perform low-dimensional representation learning on the images and text of social network user nodes [47], and it is used to complete the prediction task in [46], which is cascade outbreaking. MLP is similar to CNN in terms of network structure and it is usually used at the end of network related to classification tasks [57,59,73,75].

3.4   Task Classification

Finally, the selected or designed deep learning model is used to handle different SNICA tasks, such as classification or regression. However, In the SNICA problem, most of these tasks need to be used to analyze cascading data, such as using classification to predict user status. Alternatively, using regression to predict the magnitude of the spread in the future to assess the degree of information spread. Two kind of tasks can be distinguished by defining different loss functions in

Table 1. Different methods for frame-based views

Method	Representation	DL model	Task	Application
Cas2vec [46]	CNN	CNN	C	CP
DeepCas [67]	DeepWalk	GRU+AM	R	CP
CasCN [73]	GCN	GCN+LSTM	R	CP
[76]	GCN	GCN+GRU	R	CP
DeepStr [75]	word2vec	MLP	R	CP
DCGT [56]	DeepWalk	RNN+AM	R	CP
DMT-LIC [59]	GAT	Bi-LSTM+SG	C	CP
NDM [45]	AM	CNN+AM	C	UB
CYAN-RNN [77]	GRU	GRU+AM	C	UB
Topo-LSTM [66]	LSTM	LSTM	C	UB
DeepInf [57]	DeepWalk	GAT/GCN	C	UB
DAN [78]	MLP	AM	C	UB
HUCE [61]	Meta-paths	MLP	C	UB
DCE [79]	AE	AE+MLP	C	UB
DeepDiffuse [72]	LSTM	LSTM+AM	C	UB
DeepHawkes [27]	One-hot	GRU	R	PP
UMAN [69]	CNN	LSTM	R	PP
UHAN [47]	CNN	LSTM +AM	R	PP
DFTC [62]	MLP	GRU+CNN+AM	R	PP
C-GNNs [58]	GCN/CAT	GCN/CAT	R	PP
HDD [55]	Meta-paths	CNN-LSTM	R	PP
RNN-MAS [70]	LSTM	LSTM	R	PP
CallAtRumors [65]	Tf*idf	LSTM+AM	C	RD
[80]	Tf*idf	GRU	C	RD
HSA-BLSTM [64]	Word2vec	Bi-LSTM	C	RD
CSI [81]	Doc2vec	RNN	C	RD
[82]	CNN	CNN+LSTM	C	RD
PPC [65]	CNN	CNN+GRU	C	RD
DGCN [83]	Word2vec	GCN	C	EA
[63]	Word2vec	CNN	C	EA
LANTERN [84]	DeepWalk	RNN+AM	C	EA
GBTPP [85]	GCN	GCN	C	EA

[a] In the "task" column, "C" means Classification task, and "R" means Regression task. [b] In the "application" column, "CP" means Cascade Prediction, "UB" means user Behavior Prediction analysis, "PP" means Popularity prediction, "RD" means Rumor Detection, and "EA" means social network Event Analysis.

the deep learning model. These tasks can correspond to actual problems in the SNICA problems, such as influence prediction, cascade prediction, popularity prediction, rumor detection, event analysis prediction, etc. We will introduce these in the next section in detail.

Table 1 summarizes the adaptation process with different methods in the general framework. The data flow of different methods is summarized from the four steps of data representation method, deep learning model, task, and application.

4   Application Classification in SNICA

With the continuous growth of social network users, the magnitude of social application data also increases sharply. As we all know, deep learning can be used as representative learning, and large amounts of data in social network could provide data for it. Furthermore, the SNICA modeling approach based on deep learning will provide strong technical support for typical tasks in machine learning.

For example, the categorization task can be used to predict user behavior during cascade propagation, and the regression task can be used as the solution to the cascade predicting. In this section, we will introduce specific applications of SNICA based on deep learning technology in some tasks.

4.1   User Behavior Analysis

As an essential application of SNICA, user behavior analysis can analyze and predict users' social behavior, such as paper citations, blog post forwarding, event participation, user recommendations, etc.

User behavior analysis can be viewed as an analysis process of information cascading from a micro perspective [66]. User behavior analysis in SNICA usually focuses on two characteristics: user interaction and propagation time series. Furthermore, cascading data is used to judge whether users will be activated (infected) at a certain time window in the feature. The main idea behind is to take the characteristics of historical interaction and user interests as the input of deep learning in the process of information cascading, and to learn from historical data to predict user behavior.

In [57], it predicts the user behavior based on the behavior of the user's neighbors with local structural information through the local behavior of micro-user influence. Deep learning technologies are adopted in [66,77,78] to establish dependencies between different features. Especially, it establishes dependency relationship between different diffusion trees in [77] and it predicts whether users are infected or not by introducing a coverage strategy. In [78], it obtains the user dependency of non-sequential activation in the process of information cascading by using the attention mechanism. Similar to [78], different network structures are designed in [66]. Improving the hypothesis is proposed by [66], while it is introduced in [60] that the source of infection is not the only reason for user infection; hence, a loose assumption method is needed. In [79], it shows that the closer nodes in the feature space are more susceptible to co-infection, learning the node representation by using auto-encoding, and predicting node behavior using the spatial distance of nodes.

4.2   Information Cascade Prediction

As an important application of predicting the quantity of information dissemination in the future, cascade forecasting has specific practical significance for the analysis from a macro perspective of information dissemination.

The modeling process mainly extracts the propagation relationship of the historical information propagation nodes in the time window, and the cascade increment is predicted by performing the regression task. In [67], it successfully introduces deep learning technology into the information cascade prediction, which applies RNN to predict the future cascade increment, and obtains better results compared to some traditional methods.

In [56], it introduces the specific content and preferences of cascading nodes, and incorporates the semantic information into the deep learning model using the gated unit mechanism. The method has some good properties. On the one hand, it can obtain a cascading structure's features. On the other hand, it can acquire semantic information in the dissemination process. Different from [67], the proposed method in [75] pays more attention to the embedding of subgraphs, particularly in the embedding of content information and structural information in social networks. The proposed method could predict the cascading scale using MLP model.

According to the infrastructure that controls the dissemination of information and the inherent dependence of users' transfer, it predicts cascade by learning potential representations in [73], which uses social structures and cascading temporal information. Some works also integrate multiple tasks, such as both cascade prediction and user behavior prediction are integrated in [59], which realizes a multitask learning model of cascading scale prediction and user behavior prediction on a cascading path.

Information cascade prediction is usually migrated to social networks for topic popularity prediction. In [69], it defines popularity as the total amount of content interactions, indicating how popular the content is. This quantitative indicator can be expressed with the help of some social network indicators, such as the future cascade increment of new tweets or the total amount of communication. Popularity prediction not only helps users discover popular content in advance, but also supports marketing strategies and content distribution mechanisms [86]. It is widely used in various fields recommended by the business. The specific modeling method is similar to information cascade prediction, but there may be differences in prediction metrics (the popularity metrics are not only limited to the forwarding magnitude).

In [69], it mainly models the correlation between sequential content and sequential popularity, using the LTSM to obtain future retweets magnitude by capturing the user's popularity status as well as user text information simultaneously. LSTM is also adopted in [71] to predict the prevalence dynamics of online data, by linking the online data to existing knowledge based entities and embedding the data through potential vectors.

Some works pay more attention to the social content, user and time-series; it uses three encoders to get the combination of time embedding and user and text embedding[68], which can predict the prevalence of user retweets using attention mechanisms. In [47], it proposes a user-oriented hierarchical attention network that participates in user pictures and text data hierarchically. The proposed method could predict the popularity of images in social networks through a hierarchical attention network formed by two attention layers.

Some works model the temporal features and content features of information dissemination; RNN is utilized in [62] to capture the long-term popularity features, and it uses hierarchical attention network to capture the dependence of text content. The neural network model is also combined with user activation state graph and user relationship graph in [58]. The method could use the gated unit mechanism to fuse the features of the two graphs to predict the future popularity of the globally diffuse graph.

The functional heterostructure of the network is learned in [79] by using meta-paths as the main entities in the network; it can also predict the prevalence of the content through a continuous representation of potential. In [70], it mainly focuses on the impact of multi-source data on information dissemination. Through sequence modeling of multi-source asynchronous stream data, RNN is also used to predict the popularity of different twitter video content.

4.3   Rumor Detection

The unrestricted sharing mechanism of social networks can easily lead to the spread of rumors and can even cause social panic and turmoil. Therefore, the analysis and prediction of rumor spread is very important in SNICA.

The modeling process is mainly conducted on a time-series model by building a time loop through a deep learning approach, which can capture dynamic signals with rumor diffusion properties through a network approach. In [80], it defines the spreading process of rumors as a continuous stream of content, the proposed method slices and embeds the spreading time of rumor posts, models the text of rumors in the time series as well as the propagation relationship, and then detects rumors using the RNN (GRU/LSTM) models. Based on the method in [80], the attention mechanism is designed in [87] to model the importance of the rumor text.

In addition, the social situation is integrated into the network through the attention mechanism in [64]; the method uses the Bi-LSTM to represent the heterogeneous communication network and predicts whether the information is a rumor or not. In [88], it focuses on the trend of changes in emotion during rumor propagation, and it uses the RNN and attention mechanism to model emotion changes with time, and analyzes the propagation changes from the perspective of emotion to detect rumors. In [81], it models three main characteristics of rumors: semantics, user replies, and users of the rumors. The hybrid model is used to analyze the characteristics of the above three modules; then the method could detect rumors.

Some works focus on the detection in the early stages of rumors propagation [65,82], they adopt the CNN method to model the representation of blog posts and apply the RNN method to discover the early rumors propagation process.

4.4 Analysis of Social Network Event

Event analysis in social network has been a hot research direction for a long time [89]. Social networks allow users to post "ongoing events"; while real-life events are posted to social networks, they can be useful for detecting real events in the information dissemination process, or predicting upcoming events [90].

The modeling idea behind this application is to establish the relationship between the relevant features of the event on the time sliding window, such as the event semantic feature [83] and the event temporal feature [84]. These methods could extract the features that meet the needs of the task through deep learning approaches for clustering or classification; then they can be adopted to detect or predict the event.

Specifically, the CNN method is applied in [63] to perform representation learning on historical Twitter text data. The method also uses deep learning techniques to predict the probability of crisis events. In [83], it uses text semantic embedding on social network data, which establishes a semantic relationship network based on time series through semantic relations. In addition, it uses GCN to embed semantic representations to extract event features for predicting whether future events will occur. The process of cascading social network information is defined as the transmission process of high-dimensional events [84]. The proposed method constructs the samples into a cascade sequence, simulates the generation mode of events through the reinforcement learning process, and finally predicts the occurrence of events on the sequence. A novel method proposed in [85] is similar to [84], which regard the social network propagation process as the transfer process of events. A graph-biased time point process (GBTPP) is proposed, which uses graphs to represent learned structural information. The direct effects between nodes and the indirect effects of event histories are also simulated to predict the occurrence of propagation events respectively.

5   Future Direction

In recent years, many deep learning methods are applied to SNICA, which has promoted technological innovation in this field. However, due to the highly complex, massive and rapid growth of social network data, there are still many challenges. In this section, we mainly introduce some problems that have not been solved from the data perspective and the method perspective. Further research could move forward on these directions in the future.

5.1   SNICA Data Perspective

In the era of big data, the rapid growth of social network data has affected SNICA, which plays the role as a double-edged sword. Big data requires more resources and more suitable algorithms, but it can also solve problems with better performance. SNICA analysis becomes more meaningful as data sources (such as social media, news, public accounts, etc.) expand and data modalities (such as text, images, voice, etc.) increase. But the difficulty is how to fuse these data to obtain more targeted features.

Multi-modal Data. The multi-modal characteristics of social network data will affect the process of information dissemination. For example, pictures in social networks are more likely to cause resonance in the transmission than texts [91]. Audio and video can effectively infect other people, and arguments that use video as a point of view are more comfortable to accept [92]. Although recent studies have tried to fuse multi-modal features to predict the popularity of topics [47], multi-modal data fusion has not yet been fully effectively mined in the field of SNICA and needs more attention.

Multi-source Data. There are specific correlations among multiple data sources in the network. For example, some hot social networking events will spread through different data sources and affect each other. Such spreading would range from self-media to news clients, and even social media; the integration of multi-source data can be more comprehensive if we can obtain the path and characteristics of information dissemination. However, the current process of cascading information from different data sources lacks specific and solid research. A large part of existing research analyzed only homologous data, while the impact of multiple data sources is not fully considered. Even in recent years, research has applied to news and social media data analysis [70,83], there still lacks research on the fusion of multi-source data. This could be an important future direction.

5.2   SNICA Deep Learning Model Perspective

The innovation of deep learning models continues to advance the application field. SNICA applications that incorporate new technologies can solve specific problems more accurately and efficiently. However, the selection errors of deep learning models and the weak interpretability of the algorithms have become the limitations of SNICA research from the model level.

Selection of Deep Learning Models. At present, the magnitude of social network data continues to expand, and a large number of task-related social network data can be collected. However, as deep learning technology continues to innovate, for a given SNICA task, it is still a challenging problem to choose appropriate models. The representation of social network data and deep learning models require further in-depth understanding. For example, the information cascade process has dynamic, time-series, heterogeneous, and other features. How to select or create a more suitable deep learning model to mine these latent features would become an important and necessary problem. However, existing work has not solved this problem well.

Interpretability of Deep Models. Deep learning models are usually considered as black boxes and there still lacks theoretical analysis of these models. Currently, many works intend to explain the deep learning models such that they have good interpretability. Explaining and understanding deep learning models also have a positive impact on the analysis of information dissemination in the SNICA issues. This is because, there is a lack of arguments to support the diffusion of prediction results. Therefore, interpretability enables deep learning models to explain or present model behaviors to humans in an easy-to-understand manner. It is an essential part of machine learning models to serve people better and bring benefits to society [93]. Although there exist some works, working on the attention mechanism [56,83], try to explain the relationship mechanism of SNG data, constructing an interpretable communication process design for prediction results has not yet achieved effective results. Interpretable (explainable) deep learning models are still challenging in the future.

6   Chapter Summary

In recent years, we have witnessed a surge in leveraging deep learning techniques for various fields. In this chapter, we present a comprehensive survey of the latest applications of deep learning in SNICA within the MDATA framework. In addition to provide a comprehensive investigation, comparison, and review of the traditional SNICA methods, we also summarize the advantages of deep learning in the application of SNICA, and introduce some existing deep learning methods that are commonly adopted in SNICA. We believe that this chapter will be beneficial to researchers who would like to learn about deep learning models in the SNICA field. We also classify the applications of SNICA based on the deep learning methods and introduce some typical methods in detail. Finally, we suggest some interesting and important future directions for SNICA based on deep learning methods from both data perspective and model perspective.

References

1. Osho, A., Goodman, C., Amariucai, G.: MIDMod-OSN: a microscopic-level information diffusion model for online social networks. In: Chellappan, S., Choo, K.-K.R., Phan, N.H. (eds.) CSoNet 2020. LNCS, vol. 12575, pp. 437–450. Springer, Cham (2020). https://doi.org/10.1007/978-3-030-66046-8_36
2. Gruhl, D., Guha, R., Liben-Nowell, D., Tomkins, A.: Information diffusion through blogspace. In: Proceedings of the 13th international conference on World Wide Web, pp. 491–501 (2004)

3. Leskovec, J., McGlohon, M., Faloutsos, C., Glance, N., Hurst, M.: Patterns of cascading behavior in large blog graphs. In: Proceedings of the 2007 SIAM International Conference on Data Mining, pp. 551–556. SIAM (2007)

4. Shen, H.-W., Wang, D., Song, C., Barabási, A.-L.: Modeling and predicting popularity dynamics via reinforced poisson processes. arXiv preprint arXiv:1401.0778 (2014)

5. Liben-Nowell, D., Kleinberg, J.: Tracing information flow on a global scale using internet chain-letter data. Proc. Natl. Acad. Sci. **105**(12), 4633–4638 (2008)

6. Domingos, P., Richardson, M.: Mining the network value of customers. In: Proceedings of the Seventh ACM SIGKDD International Conference on Knowledge Discovery and Data Mining, pp. 57–66 (2001)

7. Leskovec, J., Singh, A., Kleinberg, J.: Patterns of influence in a recommendation network. In: Ng, W.-K., Kitsuregawa, M., Li, J., Chang, K. (eds.) PAKDD 2006. LNCS (LNAI), vol. 3918, pp. 380–389. Springer, Heidelberg (2006). https://doi.org/10.1007/11731139_44

8. Leskovec, J., Adamic, L.A., Huberman, B.A.: The dynamics of viral marketing. ACM Trans. Web (TWEB) **1**(1), 5-es (2007)

9. Watts, D.J., Dodds, P.S.: Influentials, networks, and public opinion formation. J. Consum. Res. **34**(4), 441–458 (2007)

10. Kempe, D., Kleinberg, J., Tardos, É.: Maximizing the spread of influence through a social network. In: Proceedings of the Ninth ACM SIGKDD International Conference on Knowledge Discovery and Data Mining, pp. 137–146 (2003)

11. Lappas, T., Terzi, E., Gunopulos, D., Mannila, H.: Finding effectors in social networks. In: Proceedings of the 16th ACM SIGKDD International Conference on Knowledge Discovery and Data Mining, pp. 1059–1068 (2010)

12. Dow, P.A., Adamic, L.A., Friggeri, A.: The anatomy of large Facebook cascades. In: Seventh International AAAI Conference on Weblogs and Social Media (2013)

13. Leskovec, J., Backstrom, L., Kleinberg, J.: Meme-tracking and the dynamics of the news cycle. In: Proceedings of the 15th ACM SIGKDD International Conference on Knowledge Discovery and Data Mining, pp. 497–506 (2009)

14. Kalchbrenner, N., Grefenstette, E., Blunsom, P.: A convolutional neural network for modelling sentences. arXiv preprint arXiv:1404.2188 (2014)

15. Mikolov, T., Kombrink, S., Burget, L., Černocký, J., Khudanpur, S.: Extensions of recurrent neural network language model. In: 2011 IEEE International Conference on Acoustics, Speech and Signal Processing (ICASSP), pp. 5528–5531. IEEE (2011)

16. Zhou, J., et al.: Graph neural networks: a review of methods and applications. arXiv preprint arXiv:1812.08434 (2018)

17. Cheng, J., Adamic, L., Dow, P.A., Kleinberg, J.M., Leskovec, J.: Can cascades be predicted? In: Proceedings of the 23rd International Conference on World Wide Web, pp. 925–936 (2014)

18. Guille, A., Hacid, H., Favre, C., Zighed, D.A.: Information diffusion in online social networks: a survey. ACM Sigmod Rec. **42**(2), 17–28 (2013)

19. Ibrahim, R.A., Hefny, H.A., Hassanien, A.E.: Controlling social information cascade: a survey. In: Big Data Analytics, pp. 196–212. CRC Press (2018)

20. Fang, B., Jia, Y., Han, Y., Li, S., Zhou, B.: A survey of social network and information dissemination analysis. Chin. Sci. Bull. **59**(32), 4163–4172 (2014)

21. Wani, M., Ahmad, M.: Information diffusion modelling and social network parameters (a survey). In: Proceedings of the International Conference on Advances in Computers, Communication and Electronic Engineering, Kashmir, India, pp. 16–18 (2015)

22. Gomez-Rodriguez, M., Leskovec, J., Schölkopf, B.: Modeling information propagation with survival theory. In: International Conference on Machine Learning, pp. 666–674 (2013)

23. Wang, Y., Shen, H.-W., Liu, S., Cheng, X.-Q.: Learning user-specific latent influence and susceptibility from information cascades. arXiv preprint arXiv:1310.3911 (2013)

24. Ohsaka, N., Sonobe, T., Fujita, S., Kawarabayashi, K.-I.: Coarsening massive influence networks for scalable diffusion analysis. In: Proceedings of the 2017 ACM International Conference on Management of Data, pp. 635–650 (2017)

25. Saito, K., Nakano, R., Kimura, M.: Prediction of information diffusion probabilities for independent cascade model. In: Lovrek, I., Howlett, R.J., Jain, L.C. (eds.) KES 2008. LNCS (LNAI), vol. 5179, pp. 67–75. Springer, Heidelberg (2008). https://doi.org/10.1007/978-3-540-85567-5_9

26. Gao, S., Ma, J., Chen, Z.: Modeling and predicting retweeting dynamics on microblogging platforms. In: Proceedings of the Eighth ACM International Conference on Web Search and Data Mining, pp. 107–116 (2015)

27. Cao, Q., Shen, H., Cen, K., Ouyang, W., Cheng, X.: DeepHawkes: bridging the gap between prediction and understanding of information cascades. In: Proceedings of the 2017 ACM on Conference on Information and Knowledge Management, pp. 1149–1158 (2017)

28. Hong, L., Dan, O., Davison, B.D.: Predicting popular messages in Twitter. In: Proceedings of the 20th International Conference Companion on World Wide Web, pp. 57–58 (2011)

29. Tsur, O., Rappoport, A.: What's in a hashtag? Content based prediction of the spread of ideas in microblogging communities. In: Proceedings of the Fifth ACM International Conference on Web Search and Data Mining, pp. 643–652 (2012)

30. Petrovic, S., Osborne, M., Lavrenko, V.: RT to win! Predicting message propagation in Twitter. Icwsm **11**, 586–589 (2011)

31. Berger, J., Milkman, K.L.: What makes online content viral? J. Mark. Res. **49**(2), 192–205 (2012)

32. Bhagat, S., Cormode, G., Muthukrishnan, S.: Node classification in social networks. In: Aggarwal, C. (ed.) Social Network Data Analytics, pp. 115–148. Springer, Boston (2011). https://doi.org/10.1007/978-1-4419-8462-3_5

33. Vishwanathan, S.V.N., Schraudolph, N.N., Kondor, R., Borgwardt, K.M.: Graph kernels. J. Mach. Learn. Res. **11**, 1201–1242 (2010)

34. Roweis, S.T., Saul, L.K.: Nonlinear dimensionality reduction by locally linear embedding. Science **290**(5500), 2323–2326 (2000)

35. Rong, X.: Word2vec parameter learning explained. arXiv preprint arXiv:1411.2738 (2014)

36. Guthrie, D., Allison, B., Liu, W., Guthrie, L., Wilks, Y.: A closer look at skip-gram modelling. In: LREC, vol. 6, pp. 1222–1225 (2006)

37. Perozzi, B., Al-Rfou, R., Skiena, S.: DeepWalk: online learning of social representations. In: Proceedings of the 20th ACM SIGKDD International Conference on Knowledge Discovery and Data Mining, pp. 701–710 (2014)

38. Tang, J., Qu, M., Wang, M., Zhang, M., Yan, J., Mei, Q.: LINE: large-scale information network embedding. In: Proceedings of the 24th International Conference on World Wide Web, pp. 1067–1077 (2015)

39. Grover, A., Leskovec, J.: node2vec: scalable feature learning for networks. In: Proceedings of the 22nd ACM SIGKDD International Conference on Knowledge Discovery and Data Mining, pp. 855–864 (2016)

40. Hamilton, W.L., Ying, R., Leskovec, J.: Representation learning on graphs: methods and applications. arXiv preprint arXiv:1709.05584 (2017)
41. Bengio, Y.: Learning Deep Architectures for AI. Now Publishers Inc. (2009)
42. Wu, Z., Pan, S., Chen, F., Long, G., Zhang, C., Philip, S.Y.: A comprehensive survey on graph neural networks. IEEE Trans. Neural Netw. Learn. Syst. (2020)
43. Liu, Y., Safavi, T., Dighe, A., Koutra, D.: Graph summarization methods and applications: a survey. ACM Comput. Surv. (CSUR) **51**(3), 1–34 (2018)
44. Gardner, M.W., Dorling, S.: Artificial neural networks (the multilayer perceptron)—a review of applications in the atmospheric sciences. Atmos. Environ. **32**(14–15), 2627–2636 (1998)
45. Yang, C., Sun, M., Liu, H., Han, S., Liu, Z., Luan, H.: Neural diffusion model for microscopic cascade prediction. arXiv preprint arXiv:1812.08933 (2018)
46. Kefato, Z.T., Sheikh, N., Bahri, L., Soliman, A., Montresor, A., Girdzijauskas, S.: Cas2vec: network-agnostic cascade prediction in online social networks. In: 2018 Fifth International Conference on Social Networks Analysis, Management and Security (SNAMS), pp. 72–79. IEEE (2018)
47. Zhang, W., Wang, W., Wang, J., Zha, H.: User-guided hierarchical attention network for multi-modal social image popularity prediction. In: Proceedings of the 2018 World Wide Web Conference, pp. 1277–1286 (2018)
48. Gers, F.A., Schmidhuber, J., Cummins, F.: Learning to forget: continual prediction with LSTM (1999)
49. Chung, J., Gulcehre, C., Cho, K., Bengio, Y.: Empirical evaluation of gated recurrent neural networks on sequence modeling. arXiv preprint arXiv:1412.3555 (2014)
50. Huang, Z., Xu, W., Yu, K.: Bidirectional LSTM-CRF models for sequence tagging. arXiv preprint arXiv:1508.01991 (2015)
51. Scarselli, F., Gori, M., Tsoi, A.C., Hagenbuchner, M., Monfardini, G.: The graph neural network model. IEEE Trans. Neural Netw. **20**(1), 61–80 (2008)
52. Kipf, T.N., Welling, M.: Semi-supervised classification with graph convolutional networks. arXiv preprint arXiv:1609.02907 (2016)
53. Veličković, P., Cucurull, G., Casanova, A., Romero, A., Lio, P., Bengio, Y.: Graph attention networks. arXiv preprint arXiv:1710.10903 (2017)
54. Vaswani, A., et al.: Attention is all you need. In: Advances in Neural Information Processing Systems, pp. 5998–6008 (2017)
55. Molaei, S., Zare, H., Veisi, H.: Deep learning approach on information diffusion in heterogeneous networks. Knowl.-Based Syst. **189**, 105153 (2020)
56. Li, C., Guo, X., Mei, Q.: Joint modeling of text and networks for cascade prediction. In: Twelfth International AAAI Conference on Web and Social Media (2018)
57. Qiu, J., Tang, J., Ma, H., Dong, Y., Wang, K., Tang, J.: DeepInf: social influence prediction with deep learning. In: Proceedings of the 24th ACM SIGKDD International Conference on Knowledge Discovery & Data Mining, pp. 2110–2119 (2018)
58. Cao, Q. Shen, H., Gao, J., Wei, B., Cheng, X.: Coupled graph neural networks for predicting the popularity of online content. arXiv preprint arXiv:1906.09032 (2019)
59. Chen, X., Zhang, K., Zhou, F., Trajcevski, G., Zhong, T., Zhang, F.: Information cascades modeling via deep multi-task learning. In: Proceedings of the 42nd International ACM SIGIR Conference on Research and Development in Information Retrieval, pp. 885–888 (2019)
60. Wang, Z., Chen, C., Li, W.: A sequential neural information diffusion model with structure attention. In: Proceedings of the 27th ACM International Conference on Information and Knowledge Management, pp. 1795–1798 (2018)

61. Su, Y., Zhang, X., Wang, S., Fang, B., Zhang, T., Yu, P.S.: Understanding information diffusion via heterogeneous information network embeddings. In: Li, G., Yang, J., Gama, J., Natwichai, J., Tong, Y. (eds.) DASFAA 2019. LNCS, vol. 11446, pp. 501–516. Springer, Cham (2019). https://doi.org/10.1007/978-3-030-18576-3_30

62. Liao, D., Xu, J., Li, G., Huang, W., Liu, W., Li, J.: Popularity prediction on online articles with deep fusion of temporal process and content features. In: Proceedings of the AAAI Conference on Artificial Intelligence, vol. 33, pp. 200–207 (2019)

63. Nguyen, D.T., Al-Mannai, K., Joty, S.R., Sajjad, H., Imran, M., Mitra, P.: Robust classification of crisis-related data on social networks using convolutional neural networks. ICWSM **31**(3), 632–635 (2017)

64. Guo, H., Cao, J., Zhang, Y., Guo, J., Li, J.: Rumor detection with hierarchical social attention network. In: Proceedings of the 27th ACM International Conference on Information and Knowledge Management, pp. 943–951 (2018)

65. Liu, Y., Wu, Y.-F.B.: Early detection of fake news on social media through propagation path classification with recurrent and convolutional networks. In: Thirty-Second AAAI Conference on Artificial Intelligence (2018)

66. Wang, J. Zheng, V.W., Liu, Z., Chang, K.C.-C.: Topological recurrent neural network for diffusion prediction. In: 2017 IEEE International Conference on Data Mining (ICDM), pp. 475–484. IEEE (2017)

67. Li, C., Ma, J., Guo, X., Mei, Q.: DeepCas: an end-to-end predictor of information cascades. In: Proceedings of the 26th International Conference on World Wide Web, pp. 577–586 (2017)

68. Chen, G., Kong, Q., Xu, N., Mao, W.: NPP: a neural popularity prediction model for social media content. Neurocomputing **333**, 221–230 (2019)

69. Wang, W., Zhang, W., Wang, J., Yan, J., Zha, H.: Learning sequential correlation for user generated textual content popularity prediction. In: IJCAI, pp. 1625–1631 (2018)

70. Mishra, S., Rizoiu, M.-A., Xie, L.: Modeling popularity in asynchronous social media streams with recurrent neural networks. arXiv preprint arXiv:1804.02101 (2018)

71. Dou, H., Zhao, W.X., Zhao, Y., Dong, D., Wen, J.-R., Chang, E.Y.: Predicting the popularity of online content with knowledge-enhanced neural networks. In: ACM KDD (2018)

72. Islam, M.R., Muthiah, S., Adhikari, B., Prakash, B.A., Ramakrishnan, N.: DeepDiffuse: predicting the 'who' and 'when' in cascades. In: 2018 IEEE International Conference on Data Mining (ICDM), pp. 1055–1060. IEEE (2018)

73. Chen, X., Zhou, F., Zhang, K., Trajcevski, G., Zhong, T., Zhang, F.: Information diffusion prediction via recurrent cascades convolution. In: 2019 IEEE 35th International Conference on Data Engineering (ICDE), pp. 770–781. IEEE (2019)

74. Qiu, X., Huang, X.: Convolutional neural tensor network architecture for community-based question answering. In: Twenty-Fourth International Joint Conference on Artificial Intelligence (2015)

75. Feng, X., Zhao, Q., Liu, Z.: Prediction of information cascades via content and structure integrated whole graph embedding. In: IJCAI (2019)

76. Yang, C., Tang, J., Sun, M., Cui, G., Liu, Z.: Multi-scale information diffusion prediction with reinforced recurrent networks. In: IJCAI, pp. 4033–4039 (2019)

77. Wang, Y., Shen, H., Liu, S., Gao, J., Cheng, X.: Cascade dynamics modeling with attention-based recurrent neural network. In: IJCAI, pp. 2985–2991 (2017)

78. Wang, Z., Chen, C., Li, W.: Attention network for information diffusion prediction. In: Companion Proceedings of the The Web Conference 2018, pp. 65–66 (2018)

79. Zhao, Y., Yang, N., Lin, T., Philip, S.Y.: Deep collaborative embedding for information cascade prediction. Knowl.-Based Syst. **193**, 105502 (2020)

80. Ma, J., et al.: Detecting rumors from microblogs with recurrent neural networks (2016)

81. Ruchansky, N., Seo, S., Liu, Y.: CSI: a hybrid deep model for fake news detection. In: Proceedings of the 2017 ACM on Conference on Information and Knowledge Management, pp. 797–806 (2017)

82. Nguyen, T.N., Li, C., Niederée, C.: On early-stage debunking rumors on Twitter: leveraging the wisdom of weak learners. In: Ciampaglia, G.L., Mashhadi, A., Yasseri, T. (eds.) SocInfo 2017. LNCS, vol. 10540, pp. 141–158. Springer, Cham (2017). https://doi.org/10.1007/978-3-319-67256-4_13

83. Deng, S., Rangwala, H., Ning, Y.: Learning dynamic context graphs for predicting social events. In: Proceedings of the 25th ACM SIGKDD International Conference on Knowledge Discovery & Data Mining, pp. 1007–1016 (2019)

84. Wu, Q., Zhang, Z., Gao, X., Yan, J., Chen, G.: Learning latent process from high-dimensional event sequences via efficient sampling. In: Advances in Neural Information Processing Systems, pp. 3847–3856 (2019)

85. Wu, W., Liu, H., Zhang, X., Liu, Y., Zha, H.: Modeling event propagation via graph biased temporal point process. IEEE Trans. Neural Netw. Learn. Syst. (2020)

86. Figueiredo, F., Benevenuto, F., Almeida, J.M.: The tube over time: characterizing popularity growth of YouTube videos. In: Proceedings of the fourth ACM International Conference on Web Search and Data Mining, pp. 745–754 (2011)

87. Chen, T., Li, X., Yin, H., Zhang, J.: Call attention to rumors: deep attention based recurrent neural networks for early rumor detection. In: Ganji, M., Rashidi, L., Fung, B.C.M., Wang, C. (eds.) PAKDD 2018. LNCS (LNAI), vol. 11154, pp. 40–52. Springer, Cham (2018). https://doi.org/10.1007/978-3-030-04503-6_4

88. Wang, Z., Guo, Y.: Rumor events detection enhanced by encoding sentimental information into time series division and word representations. Neurocomputing **397**, 224–243 (2020)

89. Kleinberg, J.: Bursty and hierarchical structure in streams. Data Min. Knowl. Disc. **7**(4), 373–397 (2003)

90. Weng, J., Lee, B.-S.: Event detection in Twitter. Icwsm **11**(2011), 401–408 (2011)

91. Hussain, A., Keshavamurthy, B.N., Wazarkar, S.: An efficient approach for classifying social network events using convolution neural networks. In: Kolhe, M.L., Trivedi, M.C., Tiwari, S., Singh, V.K. (eds.) Advances in Data and Information Sciences. LNNS, vol. 39, pp. 177–184. Springer, Singapore (2019). https://doi.org/10.1007/978-981-13-0277-0_15

92. Karahalios, K.G., Viégas, F.B.: Social visualization: exploring text, audio, and video interaction. In: CHI 2006 Extended Abstracts on Human Factors in Computing Systems, pp. 1667–1670 (2006)

93. Du, M., Liu, N., Hu, X.: Techniques for interpretable machine learning. Commun. ACM **63**(1), 68–77 (2019)

Author Index

Printed in the United States
By Bookmasters